SAILORS' TALES

Thanks mainly to the novels of C S Forester, Patrick O'Brian and Dudley Pope, there has been an upsurge of interest in the navy and sea life in the age of sail. This new series of contemporary memoirs and autobiographies fully supports the old notion that truth is stranger than fiction, since the best of the sailors' own tales are just as entertaining, informative and amusing, while they shed faithful light on the curious and outlandish world of the seaman. Avoiding the oft-reprinted or anthologised pieces, 'Sailors' Tales' offers only the rarest and most authentic accounts; but just as importantly they have been selected for their entertainment value, much enhanced in these newly designed editions.

A SAILOR OF KING GEORGE

The Journals of Captain Frederick Hoffman RN 1793–1814

Captain Frederick Hoffman

Edited by A Beckford Bevan
and
H B Wolryche-Whitmore

Introduction by Colin White

CHATHAM PUBLISHING

LONDON

Publisher's Note

This edition was typeset from the edition of 1901 edited by
A Beckford Bevan and H B Wolryche-Whitmore.
Apart from some minor stylistic changes, and the deletion of chapter
contents, the text is reproduced as originally published.

Published in 1999 by
Chatham Publishing
61 Frith Street, London W1V 5TA

Chatham Publishing is an imprint of Gerald Duckworth & Co Ltd

First published in 1901 by John Murray, London.

British Library Cataloguing in Publication Data
A catalogue record for this book is available from the British Library

ISBN 1 86176 107 4

Introduction © Colin White 1999

Type format of this edition © Chatham Publishing 1999

Printed and bound in Great Britain by
The Cromwell Press, Trowbridge, Wilts

CONTENTS

INTRODUCTION
by *Colin White*

When Frederick Hoffman started writing this memoir in 1838, he was a bewildered and, to some extent, a bitter man. A veteran of numerous actions during the Great War against France (1793–1815), he had been three times wounded and twice captured and imprisoned. Although he had lost his ship, HMS *Apelles*, to the French in May 1812, a court martial two years later had honourably acquitted him and, at the end of the trial, the President, Sir George Martin (one of Nelson's captains) had handed back his sword, 'which by your conduct you so well merit'.

Yet, despite such a distinguished war record, his naval career had run into the doldrums. After 1814, no further offers of employment had come his way and he had been forced to support his family on his half-pay as a commander. In 1835, he wrote a despairing memorial to the Admiralty detailing his many services and, when this produced no result, decided to turn his memorial into a memoir and publish a full account of his deeds.

The result is a straightforward, and often vivid, picture of everyday life in the Royal Navy during one of the key periods in its history. There are great events, such as Jervis's capture of Martinique in 1794 and Trafalgar, viewed from the lower gun deck of one of the ships of Collingwood's division. There is humour: an alligator hunt, for example or some runaway sailors who dressed themselves as rather unconvincing women to escape the press gang in Kingston, Jamaica. And there are polemics: on the inequities of prize money and the half-pay system. Yet, despite his own personal disappointment, Hoffman emerges as an engaging and usually sympathetic character: although he is often embarrassingly un-'PC' and chauvinistic, and occasionally somewhat mawkish in a Dickensian sort of way, he is seldom boring.

He joined the Royal Navy in 1793 as a midshipman in the frigate HMS *Blonde*. In her he sailed to the West Indies, where he almost immediately saw active service during the capture of Martinique in 1794. After returning briefly to England in the ship bringing home the dispatches, he was sent out again to the West Indies, where he was promoted to lieutenant on 17 October 1799. He saw much fighting, mostly in the form of minor boat actions, during one of which he was wounded in the head and lost the hearing in his left ear. He also suffered his first experience as a prisoner of war, when he was captured by Spanish privateers.

After the Peace of Amiens he again went to sea but his service was interrupted by a severe attack of rheumatic fever. He recovered in time to take part in Trafalgar, as third lieutenant of HMS *Tonnant*, and was wounded in the left hand, for which he received a grant from the Lloyd's Patriotic Fund. After a brief spell on the coast of West Africa, he returned to the West Indies in 1808, in his first command, the sloop HMS *Favourite*. But he was struck down with yellow fever which nearly destroyed his sight and was forced to return to England to recover.

In 1810, he was appointed to the sloop *Apelles*, and saw much service in her in the Channel. However, on 2 May 1812, she ran aground between Boulogne and Etaples, while patrolling close inshore with HMS *Skylark* in an attempt to prevent a French flotilla from escaping to Cherbourg. When dawn broke, the two sloops found they were under the guns of a large shore battery which opened fire with devastating effect. Desperate attempts to lighten the vessels were of no avail: both vessels stuck fast and, as the tide receded, the *Apelles* fell over onto her starboard side. Captain James Boxer of the *Skylark* set fire to his sloop and abandoned her, taking his entire ship's company with him in their boats. But some of the *Apelles*'s boats had been destroyed by gunfire and so only part of Hoffman's company could escape. Realising that he would have to leave some of his men behind to be captured, he honourably decided to stay with them.

He was a prisoner of war for some two years, including a long spell in Verdun, where he organised a school for the midshipmen. Released following Napoleon's first abdication in 1814, he witnessed the arrival of Louis XVIII in Paris before returning to England, where, as we have seen, he was honourably acquitted for the loss of his ship.

Why then, did his career peter out so suddenly? Hoffman himself offers us no clues. But the answer may lie in the sequel to the story of the *Apelles*. Reading Hoffman's vivid account, the reader could be forgiven for supposing that the sloop was a complete wreck, of little use to the French. However, research in the contemporary accounts reveals a rather different story. News of the bloody little battle reached other English ships at Dungeness on the afternoon of 3 May and Captain Alexander Cunningham of the 10-gun brig sloop *Bermuda* immediately decided to go to the rescue of his beleaguered comrades, accompanied by the brig sloop *Rinaldo*. By the time they arrived on the scene, the *Skylark* had blown up – but the supposedly wrecked *Apelles* had been refloated by the French and jury sails hoisted. The English sloops first drove her onshore again and then, assisted by another brig sloop *Phipps*, attacked in line of battle, pouring well-aimed broadsides into her. Under the cover of this hail of fire, a party under the *Bermuda*'s first lieutenant Thomas Saunders attacked in the squadron's boats, boarded her, got her afloat again and brought her out triumphantly from right underneath the French shore guns. It was a classic, well-planned cutting out operation and, remarkably, not a single man on the English side was killed or wounded.[1]

As we have seen, Hoffman was honourably acquitted by his court martial for the loss of the *Apelles*. And if she had been left a useless wreck on the French shoals, it is possible that Hoffman's career would have prospered. Unfortunately for him, she had been recovered in a very striking and well-planned operation which must have raised some doubts, at least unofficially, as to whether Hoffman had really done everything possible to save his ship. Moreover, he arrived home just as the war were ending and the Royal Navy was contracting sharply. In such a climate, when competition for the few available active postings was so keen, a man with a question mark against his name, however faint, was unlikely to find himself high on the Admiralty's list of eligible commanders.

So, he was dooned to a long and increasingly embittered spell of unemployment, spent mostly in Dover. And so it was that, eventually, he wrote this memoir ending with the sad warning to parents not to send one of their sons to sea for fear that he might die 'with scarcely an income to support himself, and if he should have the misfortune to have married and have children, God, I hope, will help him, for I very much fear no one else will!'

Which brings us to the final mystery. Having written his lament, Hoffman never published it. It remained unknown until 1901, when it was printed in a handsome edition by John Murray.

Why did Hoffman decide to leave his story untold? It may have been that the publication costs were prohibitive. But there is another possibility, perhaps more in keeping with the essentially honest and decent character of the man. In 1840, the Admiralty, in an attempt to clear the large 'backlog' of half-pay officers, offered special retirement with the rank of captain to the fifty most senior commanders, Hoffman among them. He duly accepted the promotion[2] – and the increase in his half-pay that came with it. And, having done so, he may well have thought it would not be right to publish his very forthright criticisms of the half-pay system.

1. Captain Cunningham's dispatch, *Naval Chronicle* Vol XXVII pp505–6.
2. *A Naval Biography*, W O'Byrne, p526.

He was able to enjoy his increased pay for a further nine years and, shortly before his death in 1849, received one last official recognition of his services in the shape of a Naval General Service Medal with a single clasp for Trafalgar.[3] He had, in theory, won it many times – but, in hard practice, none of the many other actions in which he had been involved qualified for a clasp.

Colin White
Royal Naval Museum

---

3. *The Naval General Service Medal Roll*, K J Douglas-Morris.

CHAPTER 1

EARLY EXPERIENCES

One morning sitting with my mother in the drawing-room and entreating her to comply with my wish to enter the Navy, she was so intent on listening to my importunities and her patchwork that she did not observe that the cat was running away with her favourite goldfinch; the cat, with the poor bird in its mouth, was near the door, waiting to escape. Seeing what had happened, I immediately ran to the poor little bird's assistance, but, alas! too late, as the cruel animal had torn off one of its wings.

Whilst my mother was feelingly lamenting her favourite's untimely death, and deliberating whether the cat should be given away, the door opened, the culprit escaped, and Captain Elphinstone entered. On his observing my mother's paleness, he requested to know if anything of a serious nature had occurred in the family. 'No,' replied she, 'except the loss of a favourite bird, which I certainly regret, as it was killed by the cat in a most distressing manner, and,' added she, 'my spirits are not at this moment very good in consequence of my son's wishing to enter the Navy.' 'The first,' said he, 'I lament, as it has deprived you of a pet; the latter may in the end be a matter of rejoicing. Who knows but that your son, if he enters that noble service, may turn out a second Hawke.' My ears thrilled at his remark.

'Do you really think, Captain Elphinstone,' said my mother, with a half-sorrowful countenance, 'that it would be to his advantage?' 'Most assuredly,' replied he, 'as I think it very likely war will shortly be declared against that unhappy and distracted France, and he will have a very fair chance of making prize money, and in time will gain his promotion.'

'Quit the room a short time, my love,' said my mother to me. In about a quarter of an hour, which I thought an hour, I was sent for. Captain Elphinstone had taken his leave. I found my mother still very pale. 'I am afraid, dear boy,' she began, 'that Captain Elphinstone has almost persuaded me against my will. He has spoken of the prospects of the Naval Service in so favourable a manner that I am nearly tempted to let you enter it, and should war unhappily be declared against our unfortunate neighbours, the French, and my friend Captain Markham be appointed to a ship, I believe I must make up my mind to be quite persuaded and let you have your wish.' 'Thank you, my dear mother,' replied I, overjoyed at what I knew nothing about. A short time after this conversation, war was declared against France, or rather France provoked it, and Captain Markham was appointed to the *Blonde* frigate. My mother instantly wrote to him; his answer was favourable, and he requested her to let me join him as soon as possible. All now was bustle and preparation. My brothers were sent for home, and begged to be allowed to go with me. Poor fellows! they little knew what they asked. In a few days I was fully equipped. I mounted my uniform, and I thought my brothers and the young friends who came to take leave of me appeared to envy me my finery, particularly my dirk, which they examined so often that I began to think they would wear it out. At length the evening arrived for me to quit my dear, happy home. My mother was sensibly affected, my sister looked serious, but my brothers, who were younger than myself – little rogues! – only looked disappointed that they could not go with me. I am sorry to say that my spirits were so buoyant that sorrow did not enter my head.

Captain Elphinstone was kind enough to accompany me to the coach, and on the 12th day of October, 1793, – oh! happy day, at least I thought so – we repaired to the sign of that nondescript bird, the 'Swan with Two Necks' in Lad Lane, Cheapside. After taking an affectionate farewell of those who came with me, I stepped into the vehicle of transport with a light foot, a light heart, and, I fear, a light head, as I fancied by the people staring at me that I was the lion of the occasion. When we stopped for supper a gentlemanly person, who sat opposite, asked me what ship I belonged to. I informed him, and he told me he was Captain W, of the 31st Regiment, going to join his division at Portsea, destined for Gibraltar. 'It is probable you will not join the frigate for a few days after your arrival,' said he, 'and if you do not, we have a mess at Portsmouth where I shall be happy to see you.' I thanked him warmly for his considerate and kind invitation. I had only one opportunity of dining with him, as he embarked three days after his arrival. About six o'clock in the evening I reached the 'Blue Postesses' where the midshipmen put their chestesses and eat their breakfastesses. Next morning, and whilst I was prosing over my breakfast, in walked a midshipman, about twenty years of age, with a face which appeared to have been rolled down Deal beach a dozen times. 'Waiter,' said he, 'have you in the house a young officer lately arrived from Lunnen?' 'Ho, ho!' thinks I, 'my boy, you are from my country the West, and probably from where it rains upon Dock* nine

* Plymouth Dock.

months in the twelve.' 'Yes, sir,' said the waiter, 'the young officer is eating his breakfastesses'; saying this he brought him to my box. 'Good morning, sir,' said he, 'I have come on shore to take you on board. Have you all your things ready?' 'Yes,' said I, 'I shall be ready in twenty minutes. Can you spare me that time? But,' continued I, 'have you breakfasted? – you look rather cold,' – I was afraid to say hungry – 'I think a cup of tea will warm you.' I then gave him one. 'If you will allow me,' said he, 'I'll put a poker in it.' I wondered what he meant. It was soon explained. He called the waiter and told him to bring a glass of rum, which he put into the tea, and, as he thought I should feel the cold going off, he said I had better do the same. As I considered him my superior officer I complied, although the fiery taste of the spirit almost burnt my mouth, which he perceiving smiled, and told me I should soon be used to it. 'You will oblige me,' said I, 'if you will give me a little insight into the characters of the officers of the ship.' 'Why,' said he, 'the captain is a tight one, and sometimes in a hurricane I never heard any officer pray so well or so heartily as he does: his prayers, if not heard elsewhere, are certainly heard by all on board, and are generally effective. However,' added he, 'you will soon be able to judge for yourself. The first lieutenant is one of the old woman's school, an easy and good kind of person, but not fit to be first of an active frigate. The second lieutenant is a regular-built sailor, and knows his duty well, but he is fond of mast-heading the youngsters when they think they do not deserve it. The third lieutenant would be a sailor if he knew how to set about it; he generally begins at the wrong end, and is always making stern way, but,' said he, 'he almost prays as good a stick as the skipper. As for the other officers, we have not so much to do with them as with those I have described. However,' added he, 'there is one more – I mean the purser: he is a complete nip-cheese, and as for his steward, he ought to have swung at the fore-yard arm long ago.' 'There is one more question I have to ask,' said I, 'which is, what sort of young gentlemen are the midshipmen?' 'Why,' replied he, 'two of what you term young gentlemen are old enough to be your father, but take them in a lump they are not so bad; four of them are about your age, and full of fun and frolic. Now,' said he, 'it's time to be off.' He beckoned to a seaman near the door, who, I found, was the coxswain of the cutter. 'Take this officer's chest to the boat.' Here the waiter interposed, and said it was customary for the waterman of the 'Blue Postesses' to take packages down to the water side. To this I consented, and away we trotted to sally port where the boat was lying. On our arrival at the stairs, I found another midshipman about my own age, who had been left in charge of the boat's crew during the other's absence. He eyed me obliquely; then turning to the elder, 'I thought,' said he, 'you would never come. I have been so bothered during the time you were away by three of the men's confounded trulls, who wanted me to give them a passage off, that every five minutes appeared an hour, and I have only this moment got rid of them.' 'Never mind, my boy,' said the other, 'let's shove off.'

Passing round a point, going out of the harbour, I observed a gibbet with part of a human skeleton hanging on it. 'You are looking at the remains of Jack the painter,' said the elder midshipman to me. 'Do you know his history?' I answered in the negative. 'Why,' said he, 'that burning rascal set fire to the rope-house in the dockyard about the time you were born, and there the gentleman's bones are rattling to the breeze as a warning to others.' The wind was blowing strong, and we were more than an hour before we reached the frigate, which was lying at Spithead. My eyes during that time were fixed on twelve sail of the line ready for sea. As I had never seen a line of battleship, I was much struck with their noble and imposing appearance, and I imagined everybody who served on board them must feel pride in belonging to them. After a severe pull we got alongside as the boatswain and his mates were piping to dinner. I followed the elder midshipman up the side, the other came up after me. On reaching the quarter-deck we made our bows, when I was introduced to the second lieutenant, who had the watch on deck. He asked me some indifferent questions, and sent for one of the master's mates to give orders respecting my hammock. The first lieutenant, an elderly, weather-beaten, gentlemanly looking person, now came on deck. I had a letter for him from my sister's husband-elect, which I gave him. After reading it he asked me how I had left my friends, and before I could answer the question I heard him say to the second lieutenant, 'What the devil do they send such delicate boys into the Service to be knocked on the head for? – much better make civilians of them.' Then turning to me, 'Well, youngster,' said he, with a good-humoured smile, 'you'll dine in the gun room with us at three o'clock.' He then sent for the gunner, and requested him to take me into his mess, who grinned assent. This last was a square, broad-shouldered Welshman, with an open countenance, and of no little consequence. I descended to his cabin, which was under water, and I could, when in it, distinctly hear that element bubbling like a kettle boiling as it ran by the ship's side above our heads. I found this said cabin not too large for three of us, as the surgeon's mate was an inmate as well as myself. Its dimensions were about eight feet by six, and when we were at table the boy who attended us handed everything in we wanted by the door. In a few days I was quite at home with the mids; some of them began spinning tough yarns respecting the hardships of a sea life – what a horrible bore it was to keep night watches, or any watch at all, and you are sure, said one of them, to catch the fever and ague after you have been four hours walking under the draught of the mizzen stay-sail; and, added another, to be mast-headed for three hours with your face to windward by those tyrants, the second and third lieutenants. They both ought to be turned out of the Service for tyranny and oppression, and as to the last he does not know how to put the ship about without the assistance of Hamilton Moore or the old quartermaster. I thought this all very encouraging. I, however, kept my own counsel, and as I did not appear much discomposed by the recital of so many miseries, they considered me a complete Johnny Newcome just caught.

We were now ready for sailing, and only waiting the arrival of a general officer and his suite. The second morning after I joined the frigate a most serious accident occurred which might easily have proved fatal to all on board. In a part called the after cockpit, where, after breakfast, the surgeon examines the sick, a large piece of iron called a loggerhead, well heated, is put into a bucket of tar in order to fumigate it after the sick have left it. On this occasion the tar caught fire. It soon reached the spirit-room hatches, which were underneath, and the powder magazine bulkhead. Unfortunately, without considering the consequences, a few buckets of water were thrown on the flaming tar, which made it spread more. At length the engine was set to work, and beds and blankets from the purser's store-room surcharged with water soon got it under. These last were of the greatest service in smothering the flame, and were more effectual in saving the ship than the engine. The captain and officers behaved nobly on this occasion. I had the honour of conducting the hose of the engine down the hatchway, and was almost stifled by the smoke for my pains. On looking through one of the gunports after the danger was over, I could not help laughing to see two of the women with a rope fastened under their arms and held by their husbands, paddling close to the ship's side, with their clothes rising like large bladders around them. A number of boats on seeing our danger came to our assistance, but they were ordered to lay on their oars at a distance. Providentially we did not require their aid.

On the 2nd of November we received on board General Prescott and his suite, and immediately afterwards got under weigh and made sail with a favourable wind down Channel. We had taken our departure from the Lizard, when, on the same night the wind, which had continued some time from the eastward, changed to the westward, and came on to blow fresh with very hazy weather. A number of West Indiamen passed us; they had been beating about in the chops of the Channel for more than a week. Some of them were in great distress for provisions. We relieved three of them by sending some bags of biscuit and casks of salt beef, and as we were feelingly alive to their situation, we took from their crews six of their seamen. I was much interested in two of these men. They had been absent nearly eighteen months from their wives and families, and were fondly looking forward to a meeting with those for whom they lived and toiled, but, alas! they were doomed to return to that foreign climate they had a few months before left, and from whence it was impossible to know when they would come back.

We kept the sea for two days longer notwithstanding the violence of the westerly gale, in the hope it would not long continue; but finding we were losing ground, we on the third day bore up for Falmouth, where we anchored in the evening and remained windbound four days, during which period we exercised the guns and sails.

On one of these days I went with a party of my shipmates on shore at St Maw's. Before coming off I bethought me of a pair of shoes, which I had forgotten to procure at Falmouth. I inquired of a boy who passed me where I could find a shop to supply my wants; he informed me the mayor was the best shoemaker in the town. To this worthy magistrate I repaired, who I found very busily employed on a pair of boots. He had spectacles on nose, which feature was not very prominent and of a reddish-blue. I acquainted him with my wish to have a pair of solid, good understanders. Pointing to some shoes, 'Good,' said he, 'young officer, here's a pair will fit you to a T. They were made for Captain H's son, but the ship sailed before he could send for them.' As they fitted me I bought them. 'So I understand,' said he, 'gentlemen,' – for two of the mids were with me – 'you are going to the Indies to make your fortunes.' 'Are we?' said I, 'that is more than we know.' 'Yes,' continued he, 'I am sure of it, and in a year's time you will return with your pockets well filled with French money; and I hope,' added he, 'that if you return to Falmouth you will pay my shop a second visit.' I need not inform my reader that the worshipful shoemaking magistrate proved a false prophet. We did return within a twelve-month, and to Falmouth, 'tis true, but nearly as poor as when he told us our fortunes; consequently we did not visit his shop a second time.

As we were the senior officer, and there being several sloops of war and cutters in the harbour, we fired the evening and morning guns. The first evening we fired proved fatal to a pilot and four boatmen, who imagined the firing proceeded from a ship seen standing for the harbour with the loss of her fore top-mast. The night was very dark and tempestuous, and a short time after leaving St Maw's the boat upset and they were all lost. This was the more distressing as they all left wives and families. The officers among the squadron made a subscription for them, and the mids, although not rich, were not backward. The wind becoming favourable, we on the fifth morning made sail out of the roads and stood down Channel. The same night, which was very dark and squally, we fell in with the *Venus* frigate, who, before we could answer the private signal, favoured us with a discharge of musketry. Fortunately, it did no other damage than cutting some of the ropes.

On the morning of the second day after leaving Falmouth we saw four ships about five miles distant to the S.W. At first we took them for Indiamen homeward bound. In the expectation of procuring some good seamen we stood towards them. After a short time we discovered them to be French frigates. We immediately altered our course, and made all possible sail to avoid them. On perceiving this they signalled each other and stood after us under a press of sail. The wind was moderate, and had again changed to the westward. The enemy was drawing fast on us. After a chase of five hours the nearest frigate fired her foremost guns at us, which cut away the maintop bowline. We returned their fire with our stern chasers. As they had neared us so rapidly, we thought it prudent to throw overboard the foreign stores in order to improve our sailing. Two of the enemy's frigates were now within gunshot and the two others nearing us fast. We had almost despaired of escaping, when fortunately one of our shot brought down the advanced frigate's fore topsail yard, and we soon found we were leaving her. The second yawed, and gave us a broadside; only two of her shot took effect by striking near the fore channels. Her yaw saved us, as we gained on her considerably. The wind had become light, which still further favoured us. We were now nearing our own coast, and towards sunset the enemy had given up the chase and hauled off to the S.W. The wind veering to the northward, we altered our course to the westward; but, singular to say, at daylight next morning we found ourselves about six miles from the same vessels, who, directly they perceived us, made all sail towards us. We tacked and stood again for Falmouth, where we anchored that evening and remained three days to complete our stores. We once more made sail for our destination, which I now found was the West Indies, without meeting further obstacle. As we neared the tropic those who had crossed it were anticipating the fun; others were kept in ignorance until Neptune came on board, which he did with one of his wives. It was my morning watch, when the frigate was hailed and desired to heave to, which was done. The cooper, a black man, personated the sea-god. His head was graced with a large wig and beard made of tarred oakum. His shoulders and waist were adorned by thumbed mats; on his feet were a pair of Greenland snow-shoes. In his right hand he held the grains (an instrument something resembling a trident, and used for striking fish). He was seated on a match tub placed on a grating, with his wife, a young topman, alongside of him. Her head-dress consisted of a white flowing wig made of oakum, with a green tur-ban; on her shoulders was an ample yellow shawl; her petticoat was red bunting; on her feet were sandals made from the green hide of a bullock. In her right hand she held a harpoon; her cheeks were thickly smeared with red ochre.

After being drawn round the decks three times in order to astonish those confined below by the noise and bustle it made, Neptune introduced his young bride to the captain, and informed him he was in mourning for his last wife, pointing to his skin. 'What occasioned her death?' inquired the captain. 'She,' replied the sea-god, 'died of a violent influenza she caught on the banks of Newfoundland nursing her last child in a thick fog, and,' added he, 'I intend next month blockading the coast of Shetland in order to compel the mermaids to give up one of their young women whom I hired three months ago to suckle my last infant, since the death of its mother.' He then requested to know if there were any new arrivals from his favourite island, England. The captain informed him there were several, and as some of them were rather delicate, with very little beard, he hoped his barber would not shave them too close. One of the midship-men was then brought up blindfolded. Neptune asked him how he had left his mamma, that he must refuse biscuit when he could have soft tommy (white bread), that he should lower his main-top gallant sail to a pretty girl, and make a stern board from an ugly one. After being taken to the sea-god's wife, who embraced him most cordially, leaving no small proportion of the ochre on his cheeks, he was desired to be seated, and was led to the narrow plank placed over a very large tub of water. The barber then began his operations with grease and tar, and as the mid did not admire the roughness of the razor, he began to be a little restive, when over he went into the tub, where he floundered for some short time. He was drawn out, the bandage removed from his eyes, and he appeared not a little surprised to see so many grotesque figures around him. He soon recovered himself and entered into the fun which followed.

All the others came up one at a time and went through the same cere-mony. Some were inclined not to submit to Neptune's directions. This only made matters worse for them, as the more they struggled the oftener they were plunged into the tub of water. After about two hours' amuse-ment the decks were dried, everything in order, and all hands at break-fast. I could not help laughing at one of the lieutenants of Marines who, to avoid getting wet, had placed himself on the forecastle to enjoy the pastime without partaking in it. One of the mids who had been ducked determined he should not escape, and had a couple of buckets filled with water on the gangway, ready to throw on him when he quitted his post, which he did when he saw the tub removed from the quarter-deck. As the youngster wished, he went along the main-deck, when, as he passed, over his shoulders went the first bucket of water; he unfortunately lifted his head to see who threw it, when over went the other right in his face and breast, so that he was as completely drenched as if he had been ducked. Unluckily, he had on his red coat, which was completely spoiled; salt water is a bitter enemy to red cloth, as it turns it black. A few days afterwards we caught several dolphins and a shark seventeen feet in length. We were obliged to fire seven pistol balls into its head to kill it before we could get it on board. It was cut up and put into pickle for those who chose to eat it. There was a beautiful fish, striped alternately black and yellow, swimming under it. The sailors called it a pilot-fish, and they informed me that sharks are very seldom without one or two, and that they appear to direct them where to go; this last must be mere conjecture. The pilot-fish is generally about a foot long, and in shape like a mullet.

CHAPTER 2

WEST INDIES

After a pleasant passage of thirty-four days we anchored in Carlisle Bay, Barbadoes. Two days after our arrival I had permission to go on shore with the gunner, who had been here before. I found the town not very extensive. The houses are built much in the same style as those at Kingston, in Jamaica, except that they have more garden ground. The streets are very sandy, but they are ornamented with a profusion of cocoa, plantain and banana trees, which afford a partial shade. It appeared to me that most of the people who inhabited Bridge Town maintained themselves by washing clothes. The women are well made and very indolent. The men are sufficiently conceited but active. I procured here a quantity of very pretty small sea-shells. They assort them very tastefully in cases, and for about two dollars you may purchase a tolerable collection. The natives of this island pride themselves on not being creoles, that is not being of the Caribbean race, although it assuredly is one of the Caribbean Islands. If you are unfortunate enough to speak in favour of any of the other West Indian Islands in their presence, they immediately exclaim, 'Me tankey my God dat I needer Crab nor Creole, but true Barbadeen born.' They drawl out their words most horribly. I happened one day to hear two of the dignity ladies of Bridge Town, as black as ink, returning the salutations of the morning. The first began by drawling out, 'How you do dis maurning. I hope you berry well, m-a-a-m, but I tink you look a little p-a-a-le.' The other answered, 'I tank you body, I hab berry b-a-a-d niete (night), but I better dis mording, I tank you, m-a-a-m.' This island is famed for its noyeau, guava jelly, candied fruits – particularly the pineapple, which is put on table in glass cases – and its potted flying-fish, which I thought equal in flavour to potted pilchards. Were I to make this assertion at Mevagissey I fear I should stand but little chance of being invited to dine off star gazy pie;* but for fear my reader should be from that neighbourhood, I beg him to understand that I do not think them

---

* A pie made of pilchards with their heads peeping through the crust, hence the name 'Star gazing'.

better, but, in my individual opinion, as good. After remaining among these true Barbadian-born drawlers about ten days, we left them, and made sail for St Pierre Dominique, where we anchored two days after. The manners and customs of the people at this island were totally different to those in vogue in Barbadoes; all, with the exception of a few, spoke creole French.

This island is mountainous, but not very picturesque. It produces sugar which undergoes the process of being clayed – that is, after a great part of the molasses has been drained from it, it is put into forms made of clay, which extract the remaining moisture; it then becomes a beautiful straw colour; it is exported in cases. Coffee also grows here, but not of the finest quality. We also saw abundance of different fruits. The purser purchased several tons of yams for the use of the ship's crew, some of which weighed upwards of twenty pounds each. We bought for our mess some sweet potatoes, plantains, bananas, shaddocks, forbidden fruit, and limes. There were groves of oranges, but we had not time to visit them. We saw in the market melons, guavas, sour-sops, alligator-pears, love-apples and mangoes. I remarked that oxen were the only animals used for burthen. I did not see a single horse. The streets of the town of St Pierre are not laid out with much regularity, nor are the houses well built. I thought it an ugly town; it is, however, ornamented with a number of cocoanut-trees, some of which are forty and fifty feet high.

The general officer we brought from England and his suite left us at this place. The object of his visit was to raise a mongrel regiment for the purpose of acting against the French islands, as a fleet with troops from England was daily expected to effect their capture. We remained here a few days, and afterwards amused ourselves by cruising off the islands of Martinique, Guadaloupe, St Lucie and Marie Galante, but were not fortunate enough to effect any captures. We repaired a second time to St Pierre roads and received on board two companies of mongrels to transport to Barbadoes. We wished them, and sometimes ourselves, in heaven. All the mids thought it a great pity that we had not fallen in with a first-class French frigate. We might have walked on board of her, said they, in such fine style. There were several women with the troops, some of whom had children at the breast. I pitied them, and endeavoured to assist them all in my power. For them to stay below was impossible, as we had almost as many soldiers on board as our ship's company, and to keep their children quiet was equally difficult. To effect this they frequently gave them strong rum and water, which threw them into a state of stupor – poor, miserable little beings! After having these suffering people on board for five days we at length, to their relief and our great joy, arrived amongst our drawling – no, creole friends, and the following morning all the redcoats were disembarked. On the second day after our anchoring the expected fleet made its appearance. It consisted of the *Boyne*, Vice-Admiral Sir J Jervis, one 70 and two 64-gun ships, several frigates, sloops of war, bomb-ships, and transports with troops. We saluted the admiral, which he returned. All now was life and bustle, and in a short time the gun-boats were ready; each man-of-war received two flat boats to tow astern. In the latter end of February, 1794, we finally bid an affecting adieu to our yellow and black legged female friends at Bridge Town, who remained on the shore waving handkerchiefs much whiter than themselves until the fleet cleared the harbour. On making sail, Needham's Fort, which commands the harbour, saluted the admiral, which he returned. The fleet and transports soon cleared the bay, when each ship took her station. It was a majestic sight to see so many vessels with all their canvas spread and swelling to a strong sea-breeze.

The second day we reached Fort Royale Bay, Martinique, in admirable order, and took French leave to let go our anchors out of range of the enemy's shells. The nearest vessels of the fleet had been warmly saluted by Pigeon Island, as they were going in, which, however, we treated with contempt. On the third day after our arrival a frigate with a bomb-ship and three gun-boats engaged it, and three hours afterwards it capitulated. One of the sixty-four-gun ships, some frigates, and a bomb with transports, had gone round to subdue the northern part of the island. We were now all actively employed getting ready the gun and flat-bottomed boats for landing the troops, who were commanded by Lieut-Gen Sir C Gray. The Duke of Kent shortly after arrived with some troops from Halifax. As it was thought advisable to reduce some of the smaller towns before the attack on Fort Royale, we were ordered with one of the sixty-fours, two frigates, the bomb-ship and some gun-boats to assault the town of St Pierre. We gave three cheers in the cockpit on hearing this news. At daylight we weighed, and in the evening entered the bay of St Pierre; we were ordered to take off the hard knocks from the bomb by anchoring between her and the enemy. About 9pm we all opened our fire as nearly as possible at the same time. It was a most brilliant sight; the bay was literally illuminated. The enemy's batteries began to play with some trifling effect; this added to the splendour of the scene. The night, fortunately for us, was very dark, which made it difficult for them to strike us, as they could but imperfectly discern the object they fired at; this was evident, as they fired immediately after we did. Our shot and shell could not fail every time we fired them, as we had taken the bearings of the principal places when we anchored. The cannonading ceased about 3am, when all the enemy's batteries, except one, struck their colours. This was in a great measure owing to our troops investing the back of the town. At four o'clock the remaining fort, finding the town had surrendered, hauled down the tricoloured flag. The losses on our part were twelve killed and twenty wounded. Those of the enemy must have been considerable. All the flat-bottomed boats and those belonging to the squadron were ordered to land a number of marines. I was in the first division. We landed about 7am, and were astonished at the mischief our shot and shell had done. The roof of the municipality, or town house, was nearly knocked in. At the time some of the shells fell through it, all the wise men of the town were assembled under its, as they imagined, bomb-proof roof. Two of them were killed and several wounded. The principal church had also suffered, as two sacrilegious shells had penetrated it and fallen near the altar. On entering it we found the models of three frigates. As they had not struck their colours, we did them that favour, and made prizes of them. There were also some pictures of grim-looking saints, which one of the sailors was endeavouring to unhook until another called out, 'Let them alone, Jack, they'll only bring you bad luck,' on which he desisted. This church was very dirty, and the ceilings of it filled with cobwebs; the priests had taken everything from the altar, as well as from the recesses or small chapels. A party of marines, with some artillerymen, took possession of the forts, and sentinels were stationed over the public buildings, and picquets round the town. Terms of capitulation had been drawn out by the authorities, which, as the town was taken by assault, were not agreed to. All found in arms were considered prisoners of war; everything belonging to the Republic was given up. The citizens were not molested, and allowed to keep their private effects. I was much amused at the genuine *sang-froid*, or more properly speaking, the French philosophy, of the people who kept the coffee-houses. They moved about as gay as if nothing had happened, everything was regularly paid for, and the most perfect discipline observed.

Having taken on board some of the principal French officers and a party of our troops, we arrived at our former anchorage, Fort Royale Bay, the next morning. Fort Royale, which was of considerable strength, had been bombarded for several days, when it was decided to carry it by storm. On the third day after our anchoring, at 3am, the attack took place. The gun and flat-bottomed boats were covered by the bomb-ships and frigates. A landing was soon effected; the bamboo ladders for two men to mount abreast were placed against the outer bastion of the fort. The soldiers and sailors vied with each other who should mount first.

Unfortunately, some of the ladders gave way, and the men were precipitated to the ground; and, what was still more unfortunate, some few fell on the bayonets of those below and were shockingly wounded. In about ten minutes the outer works were carried, and a marine's jacket, for want of other colours, was hoisted on the flagstaff. The enemy retreated to the inner work, but it availed them little. In less than a quarter of an hour they were compelled to give way. Several of them were cut down by the sailors, who had thrown away their pistols after discharging them. Most of them had abandoned their half-pikes before mounting, as they declared they were only in their way, and that they preferred the honest cutlass to any other weapon. The sailors and soldiers behaved well on this occasion; those who did not form the escalade covered those who did by firing incessant volleys of musketry, which brought down those of the enemy who were unwise enough to show their unlucky heads above the parapet. In about twenty minutes the British flags were floating on the flagstaffs, the French officers surrendered their swords, and were sent on board the *Boyne*. I forgot to mention that an explosion had taken place in one of the magazines of the fort before we entered it, which killed and wounded more than fifty of the enemy. About ninety of the enemy were killed and more than twenty wounded. We had forty-six killed and wounded; among the number were eleven officers. We found in the harbour a frigate of thirty-six guns and a corvette fitted up as a receiving ship for the wounded. Several merchant ships, loading with sugar when we first entered the bay, had re-landed their cargoes. The warehouses were more than half filled with sugar, rum and coffee. A party of seamen were immediately employed to load the shipping.

The town had suffered considerably from the shells and shot. Some of the houses were in ruins and the public buildings much damaged, particularly those in the dockyard.

We now encamped before and laid siege to the principal Republican fort, commanded by the French General Rochambeau. It had before been called 'Fort Bourbon,' and had a garrison of 3,000 men.*

We had already taken one of its principal redoubts within gunshot of it and Fort Royale. A party of sailors who had the management of it under a lieutenant and three midshipmen, christened it by a name that would shock ladies' ears. When the enemy's shot fired at them were not too deeply entrenched in the ground, they dug them up and returned them, the middies first writing on them in chalk the names of those quack doctors who sold pills as a remedy for all complaints.

For the first fourteen days we all appeared to enjoy the novelty of our

* See Appendix note (*a*).

situation, although it was by no means an enviable one, as the shot and shell were flying about us in every direction, and it was no joke to scamper away from a bursting shell just as we had sat down to dinner. Some were almost every day sent to 'Kingdom come' sooner than they expected. Our camp on the plain before the enemy's fort was picturesque enough; the officers only had tents or marquees, the sailors and soldiers made the most of their blankets. However, except when the dew fell heavily at night, these were quite sufficient. A few only suffered who were not of the strongest, and they were attacked by a low fever.

We had been before this fortress nearly three weeks, and were impatient to storm it, as what with casualties and the enemy's shot we were losing the number of our mess faster than we liked, and, although our fire had been incessant, we had not been able to effect a breach of any considerable consequence. To give more facility to the operations the *Boyne* landed some of her guns, and a party of sailors were ordered to draw them up, or rather they volunteered to do so. The guns were placed in an advanced fascine-intrenched battery, made by the pioneers and artillerymen during the night, within half a gun shot of the enemy. In getting them up they were either placed upon field carriages or sledges made out of the trunks of trees. The sailors, who were harnessed by twenties, soon had them in their places, and when they were mounted they gave three hearty cheers, which must have astonished the enemy. The guns soon after opened a most destructive fire on the nearest work, as we could see quantities of the wall fly like showers of hail. During the night we expected a sortie from the fort, and were provided for such an event. A constant fire from all the batteries was kept up all night; the shells were well directed, and an explosion took place in the enemy's fort. At daylight we perceived that the advanced sailors' battery had effected a considerable breach in the fort, and a consultation was held among the superior officers. When over, they acquainted the sailors and soldiers that they were determined to storm it the following night. The three cheers which followed this speech must have been heard for miles. At 10am we discerned a flag of truce advancing towards our lines, and shortly after a French superior officer with his aide-de-camp requested to speak to the commanding officer. As the enemy had ceased firing, we did the same. The purport of the flag of truce was that General Rochambeau, finding it useless holding out any longer, wished to treat on terms, and requested a cessation of hostilities for twenty-four hours. The following morning the capitulation was arranged. At 10am the enemy marched out of the fort under arms, with drums beating and their colours flying, when we marched in and soon hoisted the colours of Old England on the flagstaffs. The island was now entirely in our possession. The French garrison marched to Fort Royale, where they grounded their arms in the market-place. Their superior officers were met by the Admiral, Sir C Gray, and the Duke of Kent, as well as other officers of the Navy and Army. In a few days afterwards they were embarked on board some of the transports and sent to France, the officers on parole, and the men not to serve until regularly exchanged.

CHAPTER 3

RETURN TO ENGLAND

On the 14th of April, 1794, we were ordered to receive on board a superior officer of the Navy and Army with the despatches for England, also several wounded officers and the colours taken from the forts and churches. In the evening we saluted the admiral and left the bay for England.

On our passage, during a middle watch, I beheld a splendid and most perfect lunar rainbow. It extended from the stern of the frigate to some considerable distance. These bows are generally more distinct than the solar, owing to the glare of light not being so great.

We were followed for some days by a fish with two regular tails. It was about three feet long, of a bluish colour, and shaped like a salmon. We endeavoured by every possible stratagem to take it, but it was either too shy or too cunning to be caught. Fifteen days after quitting Martinique we anchored at Falmouth. The officers in charge of the despatches left the ship to proceed to London.

After having taken on board water and refreshments we repaired to Plymouth, ran into Hamoaze, lashed alongside a receiving hulk, unrigged and got the guns and stores out, and were afterwards taken into dock to have the copper cleaned and repaired.

Now, reader, I hope you will not think me unreasonable when I make known to you that I wished to see my mother, but I might as well have asked for a captain's commission. The time was too precious, and we were of too much use to be spared to see our mammas, so the second lieutenant said, and that was a sufficient damper. He had his wife in snug lodgings at Dock; he neither felt for us nor our mammas, so one of the youngsters remarked.

Whilst the frigate is refitting, I will describe some of our sailors' frolics on shore. Returning one afternoon from Plymouth, I met two hackney coaches driving very rapidly. The first of them contained one of our boatswain's mates and the coxswain of the launch with their delicate ladies. On the roof was another of our men playing the fiddle. I expected to see him fall off every moment, but, like a true sailor, he had learnt to hold fast. The second coach contained the mens' hats and their ladies' bonnets. As they were not allowed to go farther than Plymouth, they had been driving from Dock to that place and back again for the last two hours. On their coming on board they brought with them the sign of Whittington's cat, which belonged to the public-house in North Corner Street, where they had dined. They gave the landlord fourteen shillings for it, and two days after gave it to him back for nothing. On another occasion twelve of them took six coaches, into which they stowed with their ladies, to drive backwards and forwards from Plymouth to Dock six times. The sternmost to pay for a dinner, of which the whole were to partake, each kept bribing the coachman to go faster; the consequence was that the money they gave for this task amounted to more than the hire of the vehicles. When they made their appearance on board they were decorated with shawls tied round them like scarfs, and three of them had portraits of their females as large as an ordinary picture fastened round their necks with a piece of a bell rope.

I prithee, reader, censure them not too harshly. Sailors possess shades like other men; but when you reflect that they are on board their ships for months in an open sea, exposed to all weather, privation, and hardship, which they bear with philosophic patience, you will agree with most people and admit that they deserve indulgence when they get on shore; but you may wish for their sakes that they knew the value of money better. You cannot change the Ethiopian's skin without boiling him in pitch, which you know is a dangerous experiment. Sailors seldom arrive at the age of reflection until they are past the meridian of life, and when it is almost too late to lay by anything considerable to make them comfortable in their old age.

I have known a boatswain's mate who a few months after he had joined the ship received about twenty pounds. One of his messmates asked him to lend him a few shillings. 'That I will, my hearty,' was his generous reply; 'here's a fist full for you. Pay me a fist full when you are able.' The master at arms who observed the action desired the borrower to count it; it amounted to twenty-nine shillings.

The frigate now came out of dock and warped alongside the hulk, and in five days she was ready for sea. On the seventh day we sailed to cruise off Cherbourg, and to join a squadron of frigates under Captain Saumerez. The enemy had three large class frigates fitting out at Havre de Grace and two others at Cherbourg. Our squadron consisted of five frigates and a lugger.

At this period, 1794, Cherbourg, although a strong place, was nearly an open roadstead, and we frequently stood in so close as to oblige the outer vessels at anchor to run farther in.

Having cruised along the French coast for five weeks watching the progress of the enemy's frigates, which appeared very slow, we, in carrying sail after a small vessel, sprung our fore and mizzen top-masts, and were ordered to Guernsey, where we shortly after anchored in Castle Cornet roads. Whilst we remained here some of the mids and myself had permission to go on shore. After rambling about the town without meeting with any object worth attention, we crossed over to some small, rocky islands, and having two fowling-pieces with us we shot four large rabbits; their hair was very soft and long. The inhabitants, who are neither English nor French, but speak both languages in a corrupt manner, fabricate gloves and socks from the fur of these animals. I bought two pairs of the former, but they did not last long; the hair constantly came out on my clothes, and when once they are wet they become useless.

On the fifth day after quitting the squadron we rejoined them in Cancale Bay. At daylight next morning our signal was made to chase an enemy's lugger in shore. We were gaining rapidly on her when she ran in between some rocks; we then prepared the boats to attack and bring her out, but as we stood in for that purpose we found the water suddenly shoal, and a battery we had not perceived opened its fire on us. We were obliged to haul off, but not before we had fired several shot at both lugger and battery. The latter again fired and knocked away our mizzen topgallant mast. We bore up and gave it a broadside, and could see pieces of rock near it fly in all directions. The signal was made to recall us, and soon after we rejoined the squadron. For more than two months had we been tantalized by cruising in this monotonous manner, with little hope of the sailing of the frigates we were blockading, when the commodore ordered another frigate, ourselves, and the lugger to Guernsey to refit and procure live bullocks. Having got on board what we wanted, we made sail out of the harbour through the Little Vessel passage; the pilot, thinking the tide higher than it was, bumped the frigate on shore on the rock of that name. She struck violently, but soon floated off as the tide was flooding. On sounding the well we found she was making water rapidly. The pumps were soon at work, but as the leak gained on us, we made the signal of distress and want of assistance. It was soon answered by the frigate and lugger, who came within hail. We requested them to see us as far as Plymouth, as we could not keep the sea in consequence of our mishap. Fortunately the wind was in our favour, and we reached Plymouth Sound in the afternoon, ran into Hamoaze the same evening, lashed alongside a receiving ship and had a party of men to assist at the pumps.

At daylight we got out the guns and the heavy stores, and the ship into dock. On examining her, it was found that part of the main keel and bottom were so much injured that it would be a fortnight before the repairs could be finished. In three weeks we were ready for sea, and were ordered to join a squadron of nine sail of the line, under the command of Rear-Admiral Montague. We sailed with the intention of joining the Channel fleet under Lord Howe, but were much mortified on receiving intelligence from a frigate we spoke that the action between the English and French fleets had taken place on the 1st of June, and that the latter were defeated with considerable loss. In the sanguine hope of meeting with some of the enemy's lame ducks, we made all sail for Brest water. The next morning we saw the Island of Ushant, and soon after eight sail of the enemy's line of battle ships and five large frigates. They were about three leagues on our weather beam. We made all sail in chase of them, but they being so near Brest, and in the wind's eye of us, we only neared them sufficiently to exchange a few shots. In the evening they anchored in Brest roads. On this mortifying occasion there was a grand cockpit meeting, when the middies declared the French were a set of cowardly, sneaking rascals. 'Let me,' said one of the youngest amongst them, 'command a squadron of eight sail of the line against ten of the enemy, I would soon take the gloss off their sides, and show them the way into Portsmouth harbour.'

On the afternoon of the following day we fell in with the defeated enemy's fleet which had escaped Lord Howe. They, unfortunately, were to windward of us standing for Brest, but the nearest of them was not more than two leagues distant. We made all possible sail to get between them and the land. Fourteen sail of their effective ships of the line perceiving our intention took their stations between us and their disabled vessels. Towards sunset we exchanged some shot with the nearest without effect.

The night was now setting in with dark, squally weather from the W.S.W., when we reluctantly gave up the chase. I will not shock my reader's ears with what the mids said on this occasion. Suffice it to say, that they offered up their prayers most heartily: in this, they, like obedient young officers, only followed the example of their gallant captain and most of the lieutenants.

Six weeks after remaining with this squadron we were ordered to Plymouth to fit for foreign service. The captain went on shore, and we did not see him until his return from London with a commission in his pocket to command a seventy-four-gun ship, into which, shortly after, we were all turned over. We regretted leaving the frigate, for although she was one of the small class, we were much attached to her. Not one of us mids had ever served in a larger vessel than a frigate. On board this large ship we were for some days puzzled to find out each other, and for the first time in our lives we messed and slept by candle-light. In a few days we received on board four additional lieutenants, six mids, a captain of marines, a chaplain, school-master, and two hundred more men, besides forty marines. As my former messmate, the gunner of the frigate, did not join this ship, I had to find another mess. One of the master's mates asked me if I would join him and six other midshipmen, which I did. Our berth, or the place where we messed, was on the orlop deck, designated by the name of cockpit, where open daylight is almost as unknown as in one of the mines of Cornwall. The mids' farthing candles and the sentinel's dark, dismal, not very clean lanthorn just made a little more than darkness visible. When the biscuits are manned, that is, infested by 'bargemen', they may be swallowed in this dark hole by wholesale, as it is next to an impossibility to detect them, except they quit their stow-holes and crawl out, and when they do, which is but seldom, they are made to run a race for a trifling wager. On the home station bargemen are scarcely known; it is only in warm climates where they abound. Another most destructive insect to the biscuit is the weevil, called by the mids purser's l – e.

While walking down Fore Street one morning with one of my messmates we came up with two well-dressed females, when he exclaimed, 'By Job! what a well-built little frigate she is to the left! How well she carries her maintop-gallant sail! What a neat counter, and how well formed between the yardarms! I'll heave ahead and have a look at her bow chasers, head rails, and cut heads, for I think I have seen her before somewhere. You,' said he to me, 'can take the one on the starboard hand.' He then let go my arm and shot ahead. He had no sooner done so than the youngest of them exclaimed, 'Why, my dear George, is that you?' 'Yes,' he replied, 'my dear Emily, and my dear mother, too; this is, indeed, taking me aback by an agreeable surprise. How long have you been here?' They were his mother and only sister, who had arrived that morning and were going to the Admiral's office to gain information respecting the ship to which he belonged. His mother was a genteel woman, to whom he introduced me; but what shall I say of his sister! She won my heart at first sight. She was a beautiful, delicate girl of about nineteen. Her figure haunted me for months afterwards. They were at the 'Fountain', and intended staying there until we sailed. 'You will go on with us,' said his mother. 'Yes,' said he, 'that I will, my dear mother, but after I have conveyed yourself and my sister to your anchorage I must make all sail I possibly can on board, and ask the first lieutenant for fresh leave. I hope to be with you in about an hour. Having seen them both to the inn, we made our bows and repaired on board. On explaining to the lieutenant his reason for wishing to go again on shore he obtained further leave, put on a fresh set of rigging, jumped into the boat that had brought us off, and was soon in the fond arms of his mother and sister. Shall I say I envied him? No, I did not; I only wished my mother and sister – for I had, like him, only one – were at the 'Fountain' and I alongside of them.

In less than a month we were ready for sea, and when we were all a *taunto* I was proud to belong to such a commanding and majestic-looking vessel. Before sailing, I will indulge my reader with a little sketch of the officers of our noble man-of-war.

The most noble captain I have before described, except that they had given him in the cockpit (he being a very dark-complexioned man) the name of 'Black Jack'; his praying propensities seldom quitted him, but, notwithstanding this fault, he had many good qualities. The first lieutenant of the frigate we left had gone to his family. The second, in consequence, had become first. He was a thorough seaman, and carried on the duty with a tight hand. Woe betide the unfortunate mid who was remiss in his duties: the masthead or double watches were sure to be his portion. When the former, he hung out to dry two and sometimes four hours. The mids designated him 'The Martinet'. The second lieutenant was an elderly man, something of the old school, and not very polished, fond of spinning a tough yarn in the middle watch if the weather was fine, a fidgetty, practical sailor with a kind heart. He informed us he was born on board the *Quebec*, that his father was gunner of her when she blew up in the action with the French frigate *Surveillante*, when all on board except fourteen of the crew perished. Among the number saved were his father and himself. The former jumped overboard from the fore-channels with the latter, who was only seven years of age at the time, on his back, and swam to the Frenchman's foremast, which was floating at a short distance, having been shot away by the English frigate. He added that had not this unfortunate accident occurred, the French frigate must have struck her colours in less than ten minutes. He spoke most indignantly of the conduct of an English cutter that was in sight at the time. His nickname was 'Old Proser'. The third was a gentlemanly person, but more the officer than practical sailor, fond of reading and drawing, and he frequently gave some of us instruction in the latter. He had been in the East India Service, and was a good navigator. We named him 'Gentleman Jack'. The fourth had been third in the frigate we left. I have already handed him up. His right leg was rather shorter than the left; he was called 'Robin Grey'. The fifth was a delicate-looking man, fond of dress and the ladies, almost always unwell; he was something of a sailor, but thought it a horrid bore to keep watch. Strange as it may appear, this officer left the ship a few months afterwards, and was made commander, post captain, and retired admiral without serving afloat! We named him 'The Adonis'.

The sixth was a stout-built regular man-of-war's man, an officer and a sailor, fond of conviviality, of gaming and a stiff glass of grog, but never off his guard. He went by the name of 'Tom Bowline'. The seventh was as broad as he was long; the cockpitonians dubbed him 'Toby Philpot'. He was an oddity, and fond of coining new words. He knew the ship had three masts and a sheet anchor. He was a strict disciple of Hamilton Moore, fond of arguing about dip and refraction, particularly the former, as he put it in practice on himself, being sometimes found with his head and heels at an angle of 30 degrees in consequence of dipping his head to too many north-westers. He was, however, good-natured, knew by rule how to put the ship in stays, and sometimes, by misrule, how to put her in irons, which generally brought the captain on deck, who both boxhauled the ship and him by praying most heartily, although indirectly, for blessings on all lubberly actions, and would then turn to the quarter-master and threaten him with a flogging for letting the ship get in irons, poor Toby looking the whole time very sheepish, knowing the harangue was intended for him. The master was a middle-aged, innocent west-country-man, a good sailor, knew all the harbours from Plymouth to the Land's End, and perhaps several others, but he was more of a pilot than a master, and usually conversed about landmarks, church steeples, and crayfish. The surgeon was a clever little dapper man, well-read, shockingly irritable, fond of controversy on ethics, etymology, and giving the blue pill. I need not acquaint my reader he was from York. The purser was the shadow of a man, very regular in his accounts, fond of peach-water, playing the flute, of going on shore, receiving his necessary money and taking all imaginable care of number one. The captain of marines was a soldierly-looking, little, strong-built man, very up-right, fond of his bottle of wine, of holding warm arguments with the surgeon, which always ended without either's conviction – sometimes to the annoyance, but more frequently to the amusement of the wardroom, and he always appeared an inch taller when inspecting his corps. In his manner he was always on parade, and he thought it a condescension to notice a mid. The first lieutenant of marines was a tall, slight man, knew the manual by heart, was fond of reading novels, presumed he was a great man among the ladies (question, what sort of ladies?). He was a great puppy, and when he passed the mids he regarded them with an air of patronage, which they returned by a look of sovereign contempt. The second lieutenant of marines was quite a different character. He was as playful as a kitten, and never happier than when skylarking with the mids in the cockpit. He was not a bad soldier, and a promising officer. When at sea he always worked the ship's reckoning for his amusement. The mids, with the exception of three, were fine-looking lads from the ages of fifteen to eighteen, fond of fun and mischief and of their half-pint of rum; were frequently at watch and watch, mast-headed, pooped, and confined to their half-farthing candle-lighted mess-holes. But, notwithstanding all these complicated miseries, they were wicked enough to thrive and grow, and when on shore forgot all their troubles and enjoyed themselves like princes.

The first surgeon's assistant was a tall, slight young man, with his head filled with the Pharmacopœia, bleeding, blistering and gallipots. We dubbed him 'The Village Apothecary', and sometimes 'Snipes'.

The second assistant was a coarse Scotsman, full of pretension and conceit, who assured us that if any of us should have occasion to have our legs or arms amputated he could do it without any pain. He used to feel our pulses after dinner with ridiculous gravity, and after examining our tongues tell us we should take great care and not eat salt junk too quickly, for it seldom digested well on young stomachs, and, added he with great consequence, 'I have a specific for sair heeds if ye ha' any.' As he was much pitted with the small-pox, we called him 'Doctor Pithead'.

With every feeling of reverence to the revered chaplain, I will tread as lightly over him as a middy's clumsy foot encased with boots is capable. Dear man, he came all the way from the Emerald Isle to join our ship, and brought with him an ample supply of pure brogue, which he spoke most beautifully. He was very inoffensive, perfectly innocent, and never ruffled in temper, except when the wicked youngsters played tricks with him while he was composing his sermon. One day he was much alarmed by the following adventure, got up expressly by the mids. Some of these incorrigible fellows, among whom I blush to acknowledge I was one, had laid a train of gunpowder to a devil close to his cabin, whilst they presumed he was very busy writing for their edification. The train was fired from the cockpit hatchway, and soon caught the devil. As soon as the dear, good man saw the sparks, he rushed out of his cabin, crying out, 'Oh, shure, byes, the ship's on fire! Och! what shall I do now the ship's on fire? Och! what will I do?'. On seeing that he was really alarmed, one of the master's mates went up to him with a comically-serious face, and informed him that the first lieutenant finding, when looking round after breakfast, that there was something which smelt unpleasant in his cabin, had ordered it to be fumigated with a devil, but as he knew it was about the time he composed his sermon, he was unwilling to disturb him, and the devil had in consequence been placed as near his cabin as possible to effect the purpose intended. His reverence was quite bewildered – an unpleasant smell in his cabin, and a devil to drive it away was to him incomprehensible; until the mate requested him to calm himself, and assured him there was no danger, that the devil was perfectly harmless except to unwholesome smells. 'There,' added he, 'is his infernal majesty,' for he was ashamed to say devil so often before the chaplain, 'nearly exhausted,' pointing to the shovel which contained the lump of gunpowder mixed with vinegar. 'Now, sir, I hope your alarm has subsided, and that you will not be more disturbed.' During this ridiculous scene, worthy of the pencil of Hogarth, the youngsters with their laughing, wicked heads up the hatchway, were enjoying themselves most heartily. The following day was Sunday; prayers were read, but no sermon, as the poor man was too much agitated afterwards to make one, and whenever his messmates thought his sermon too long, they threatened him by a visit from another devil.

The captain, on being informed of this trick, sent for the whole of the mids and admonished them as to their future conduct.

CHAPTER 4

OFF USHANT

We were now destined to make one of the Channel fleet, which we joined off the Island of Ushant, consisting of thirty-six sail of the line and seven frigates.

At daylight on the 6th of October, 1794, our signal was made to chase three suspicious vessels in the S.W. On nearing them we made the private signal, which they did not answer. We beat to quarters, and as they were under the same sail as when we first saw them, we neared them fast, and when within gunshot the nearest yawed and gave us a broadside, running up a French ensign, as did the other two. The shot fell short of us; we opened our main-deck guns and brought down her mizzen top-mast. The other two fired from time to time at us with little effect. They did not support their companion as they ought to have done. In a short time we were nearly alongside the one we had engaged, and gave her another broadside which she returned, and struck her colours. She proved the *Gentille*, of forty-four guns and three hundred and eighty men. The other two, also French frigates of the same size, made all sail to the southwards. The enemy had eight men killed and fifteen wounded; we had four men wounded. We soon exchanged the prisoners; put the second lieutenant, a master's mate, three midshipmen and fifty men on board her, and sent her to Portsmouth. We immediately made sail in chase of the others, but as they had gained a considerable distance from us during the time we were exchanging the prisoners, there was little chance, without a change of wind, of overtaking them. In the middle watch we lost sight of them, and the day after rejoined the fleet. In five days afterwards we were again in chase of a ship, and after a severe tug of fourteen hours we captured her. She proved a French twenty-four-gun ship, with one hundred and sixty-five men. We also sent her into Portsmouth. After having cruised off and on near Ushant for about eight weeks, we were ordered to Portsmouth, where we arrived shortly afterwards and completed our stores for six months. Before sailing we received some prize-money, which produced, from stem to stern, little wisdom, much fun, and more folly. We were again ready for sea, and received orders to repair off Plymouth and join part of the Channel fleet and a convoy consisting of more than two hundred sail, bound to different parts of the world. In a few days we joined the rest of the fleet off Cape Finisterre, where some of the convoy parted company. The day following a most tremendous gale sprung up from the S.W., and in the night a transport with two hundred Hessian troops on board went down on our weather beam. The shrieks of the poor fellows were distinctly heard. As it was impossible to render them any assistance, every soul on board her perished. In the morning the convoy were much dispersed; the gale continuing, they were ordered to leave the fleet for their destinations. After the gale abated the signal was made for our captain. An hour afterwards he came back looking as black as a thundercloud. As soon as he reached the quarter-deck he stamped with rage, and when it had nearly subsided he informed the officers that we were to proceed to the West Indies without delay. This was an unexpected shock to many of the officers as well as himself, as they had left some of their clothes behind; however, there was no remedy for this mishap. As for myself, I anticipated a merry meeting with the many copper-coloured dignity ladies I formerly knew, provided the land-crabs had not feasted on their delicate persons.

In the afternoon we gave a long, lingering look at the fleet, and parted company with two other seventy-fours who were in the same scrape. Our noble captain did not get rid of his angry looks for some days, and actually wept at what he termed the treacherous conduct of the Admiralty. We understood afterwards that he was under an engagement of marriage to the sister of a nobleman, which was to have taken place in three months. Nothing worth notice occurred during the passage, except the visit from Neptune and his wife, and the shaving and ducking all his new acquaintances, who were rather numerous. We saw several tropical birds, which the sailors call boatswains, in consequence of their having one long feather for a tail, which they term a marlin-spike – an iron instrument sharp at one end and knobbed at the other, used in splicing ropes, etc.

The captain of marines also shot an albatross or man-of-war bird, so called from its manner of skimming through the air after other birds, which the seamen compare to sailing. It measured seven feet from pinion to pinion. On the fifth week of our separation from the fleet we made the Island of San Domingo, and on the day after anchored with the squadron in Cape St Nicholas mole. We found here the *Sampson*, of sixty-four guns, the *Magicienne* and the *Thorn*, and some transports. This mole, or harbour, is formed by the high land of the island on the right hand going in, and on the left by a peninsula, joined by a narrow sandy isthmus to the island at the head of the mole. It is strongly fortified. The harbour is a fine one, and would contain the whole British fleet. The town has a common appearance and has nothing remarkable in it. We remained here three weeks, at the end of which period we ran down to Jamaica, and anchored off Port Royal. This town is built on a small peninsula, joined to the island by a long, narrow neck of sand called the Palisades. Here all unfortunate whites who depart this life become feasts for crabs of all descriptions, as it is the place of burial for the town and men-of-war. This isthmus is the dam which secures the harbour of Kingston from the inroads of the sea. The houses of this town are generally not more than a single storey high, constructed of wood with overhanging shingled roofs, and verandahs in front, which prevent the sun entering the rooms.

One evening, being on shore at Port Royal, seated on a bench, I overheard a grey, woolly-headed black man relate the following story. I will give it in good English. In the year 1788, said he, the harbour of Port Royal was much troubled by a very large shark, which drove all the fish out to sea and distressed a number of fishermen. Every attempt had been made to catch him, but without success. He at length became so constant a visitor that they named him 'Port Royal Tom'. At last, continued old Sambo, for that was the narrator's name, a young friend of mine, who was a very strong, courageous fisherman, said if the magistrates of the town would give him a doubloon, he would engage the shark and try to kill him in single combat. The magistrates consented, and two mornings after, before the sea-breeze set in, the dorsal fin of 'Port Royal Tom' was discovered. The black fisherman, nothing dismayed, paddled out to the middle of the harbour where the shark was playing about; he plunged into the water armed with a pointed carving knife. The monster immediately made towards him, and when he turned on his side (which providentially sharks are obliged to do to seize their prey, their mouths being placed so much underneath) the fisherman, with great quickness and presence of mind, dived, and stabbed him in the bowels. The shark, in agony, gave a horrid splash with his tail, and disappeared for a short time. He then rose again and attempted to seize the man a second time, but the latter once more dived and gave him his death-blow; he then regained his canoe almost exhausted. The shark soon after turned on his side, discolouring the water with his blood. Four men in a canoe threw a rope over his tail and towed him on shore, where all the town came to meet the courageous fisherman, with the magistrates at their head, who presented him with his well-merited reward and his liberty. The shark was dissected and the skeleton sent to Spanish Town, where a few years afterwards it fell to pieces for want of care. This unfortunate town has been twice destroyed by an earthquake; the ruins on a clear day may be seen in three-fathom water.

We had been refitting and amusing ourselves on shore by dancing at dignity balls given by the upper-class copper-coloured washerwomen, who are the quintessence of perfection in affectation, when we were obliged to bid adieu to these interesting copper and coal-skinned ladies, as the ship was reported ready for sea, and the following morning we weighed and stood out of the harbour. As we passed the point we saw handkerchiefs without number waved by our dear, motley-coloured damsels as a farewell. We beat up to St Domingo and anchored in Cape St Nicholas mole, where we found the *Leviathan*, *Raisonable*, *Sampson*, and several frigates. We remained a week, and sailed with the above-named ships on a cruise round the island. On the third night after sailing, which was very dark with a fiery sea-breeze, the *Sampson* (sixty-four) ran on board of us. She came with such force that she, by the shock, carried away her fore-mast, bowsprit, main-top mast and figure-head. She fortunately struck us abaft the main channels; had she done so amidships, it would have meant the destruction of both ships and of about a thousand lives. Her larboard bumpkin dismounted the eighteen-pounder in the foremost lieutenant's cabin in the wardroom, and in falling clear she swept away both quarter galleries from the side, one of which was fitted up as a library for the first lieutenant, who lost all his books. Some of the mids who loved him were wicked enough to say that it was a punishment inflicted on him for mast-heading them so often. I say nothing!

The *Sampson* was towed to Jamaica by the *Success* frigate to repair her damages, and a fortnight afterwards we followed. The heroes of the cockpit declared the commodore was ashamed of our appearance. As we had only galleries on one side, we looked like a pig with one ear.

We anchored at Port Royal in the afternoon, and before the sails were furled we were surrounded by a number of boats and canoes filled with dignity and first and second-class dingy damsels, some of them squalling songs of their own composition in compliment to the ship and officers, accompanied by several banjos. When the ropes were coiled down they were admitted on board, when they began dancing round the quarter-deck and making love to the officers for their washing. Having accomplished the purpose of their visit, they departed, promising that we should 'hab ebery ting berry clean by Saturday ebening, and dat he lib in hope for see massa at him house berry soon.'

The carpenters from the dockyard soon repaired the quarter galleries, and made good all other defects, when that fatal scourge, the yellow fever, made its appearance among the ship's company. The schoolmaster, a clever, intelligent young man, who had been educated at Christ's Hospital, was the first victim. This was quite sufficient to alarm the nerves of our gallant captain, who never joined the ship afterwards; he, having obtained permission from the admiral to return to England by a lugger going with despatches, took French leave of the whole of us – that is, no leave at all. In a few days afterwards Captain B joined us as acting-captain. He was a young, active, and smart officer. The yellow fever was now making lamentable havoc among the crew. Six were either carried to the hospital or buried daily. After losing fifty-two men, one of the lieu-tenants, the captain's clerk, and four mids, the captain requested the admiral's permission to go to sea, for, although we had more than thirty cases of the fever on board, the surgeon thought the pure sea-breeze might be the means of preserving their lives. Alas! he was fatally mis-taken, for nearly the whole of them were thrown over the standing part of the fore-sheet before we returned from our cruise. We were one hun-dred and sixty short of our complement of men, besides having about fifty more in their hammocks, but the captain wished to persevere in keeping the sea. We had been from Jamaica three weeks, cruising on the south side of St Domingo, when we captured a French brig of war of fourteen guns and one hundred and twenty-five men, and two days afterwards a large schooner privateer of one long eighteen-pounder on a traverse, and six eighteen-pounder carronades, with seventy-eight men. We now had nearly two hundred prisoners on board, and thought it prudent to retrace our steps to Port Royal, when on the following morning we fell in with two more schooner-rigged privateers. The first we captured mounted a long brass twelve-pounder and two six-pounders, with sixty-eight men. The other during the time we were exchanging prisoners had got consid-erably to windward of us. Fortunately towards the evening it fell calm, when we manned and armed three of the boats. I had command of the six-oared cutter with eight seamen and three marines. In the launch were the lieutenant, a mid, and eighteen men, and in the other cutter as many as my boat held. We were two hours on our oars before we got within musket-shot of her. She had several times fired at us from her long gun charged with grape-shot, but without effect. We cheered and gave way, when her last charge knocked down the coxswain of the cutter I was in, who died a few hours afterwards, being shot in the head. The lieutenant and one man were slightly wounded in the launch. We were soon under the depression of her gun and alongside, when, on boarding her, one half of her motley crew ran below. The captain and the remainder made a show of resistance, when we ordered the marines to present. As soon as they saw we had possession of her decks and were advancing with our pistols cocked and our cutlasses upraised, they threw down their arms and surrendered. She proved a French privateer with a long six-pounder on a traverse and eight one-pound swivels, with fifty-two men. We took her in tow and soon regained the ship. We made all sail for Port Royal with our four prizes, and on our arrival next morning astonished our black and yellow-faced acquaintances, who, as before, came off with boats and banjos to welcome our return, not a little by our success. The following morning we sent fifty men to the hospital. We had buried during the cruise forty-three seamen, besides two mids and another of the lieutenants. The most healthy were the first attacked, and generally died on the third day. Out of the five hundred and sixty men we brought from England, we had only now two hundred to do the duty of the ship.

CHAPTER 5

WEST INDIES AGAIN

On the fourth evening after our arrival it was thought necessary to despatch two armed boats to Kingston to procure seamen either by entering or impressing them. Finding there was no chance of the first, we entered on the unpleasant duty of the last. We boarded several of the vessels in the harbour, but found only the mates and young boys, the seamen having on seeing our boats gone on shore. We had information of three houses notorious for harbouring seamen. To the first of these we repaired, where, after strictly searching the premises, we were unsuccessful. A sailor we had recently impressed, and who the day after entered, informed us that it was the fashion for the men of the West Indian and Guinea ships, when on shore, to disguise themselves, sometimes as American women, at other times as tradesmen, such as coopers, shoemakers, etc.

On entering the second house, the scene was laughably ridiculous. At a table sat three slovenly-dressed females with old, coarse stockings in their hands, which they appeared to have been mending, and on the table near them were some children's shirts, with needles, thread and a small basket. Not far distant from them was a cradle of a large size, half-covered by a thick mosquito net. The bed in the room had also a net, and in it was lying a person in the last stage of illness. Another female, who appeared to be a nurse, was near the head of the bed, persuading the invalid to take the contents of a bottle of some red mixture. At the foot of the bed stood a man dressed in the uniform of the town militia, who acquainted us that the woman in bed was his wife in the last stage of consumption; that in consequence he had sent for all her friends to take leave of her before she died, and to attend her funeral; and that the person dressed in black standing near him was the doctor. This last, with a countenance full of gravity, assured the lieutenant that he did not think his patient could live more than an hour, and begged him to examine the house as quietly as possible, as he had another sick patient in the next room who had arrived from the other side of the island, and from fatigue and distress had been seized with a fever. The lieutenant, who really was a humane man, listened to his mournful story with much attention, and replied he was sorry to disturb a dying person. Then turning to the women, he assured them it was with much reluctance he entered on the duty he had to perform, but as he had information of seamen frequenting the house he must be under the necessity of searching it. One of the persons sitting at the table, who was most like a female in appearance, rose and said they had only the room they sat in and the next, which was occupied at present by the other sick female. 'But I guess,' said she, 'your notion of there being British seamen in the house must be false, as we are not acquainted with any.' During this speech, uttered with as much grace as a Yankee lady of the seventh magnitude is capable, the coxswain of one of our cutters, who had been searching the features of one of those dressed as a female sitting at the table mending a shirt, exclaimed, 'If I ever saw my old shipmate, Jack Mitford, that's he.' Another of our men had been cruising round the cradle, and whispered to me that the baby in it was the largest he had ever seen. After the coxswain's ejaculation, all the party appeared taken aback and began to shift their berths. Perceiving this, we immediately locked the door and insisted on knowing who they were; but when they spoke we were convinced that they were all men except the American, who began to scream and abuse us. I approached the bed, and on looking closely at the sick person I discovered a close-shaved chin. The lieutenant, who had followed me to the bed, desired two of our men to move the clothes a little, when we found the dying person to be a fine young seaman about twenty-six years of age, and who, on finding he was detected, sprang out of bed, and joining the doctor and nurse, who had armed themselves with hangers, attempted to resist us. As we were sixteen in number, and well armed, we told them it was useless, and the constable who was with us desired them to be peaceable and put their weapons down. As they saw they were on the wrong tack, they surrendered. The dear little sleeping infant in the cradle proved a fine lad sixteen years old. The over-fatigued female in the next room turned out a young seaman, whom we secured with the pretended sergeant, the nurse, and the doctor, making in the whole eight good seamen. This was a good haul. We got them without accident to the boats. The delicate American female followed us screaming and abusing us the whole way. We could hear her voice for some time after leaving the wharf. The men a few days after being on board, finding the boatswain's mates did not carry canes, entered. The nurse, sergeant, doctor and his dying patient were rated quartermaster's and gunner's mates, and the remainder topmen. We had been a month refitting when we made another attempt to procure seamen at Kingston, but only sent one boat with a lieutenant, myself, and twelve seamen. On landing, we made for the house we had not entered on our last visit, where we knocked at the door, and had to wait some short time before it was opened, when a mulatto man appeared and asked 'What Massa Buckra want? He hab nutting for sell; he no hab any grog.' 'Why, that copper-skinned rascal,' called out one of our men, 'is the fellow who deserted from the *Thorn* sloop of war when I was captain of the mizzen top.' 'Take hold of him!' said the lieutenant; but before this could be done he slammed the door against us; this was the work of a moment. Three of our seamen instantly set their backs against it, and with a 'Yo-heave-ho,' they forced it in. We now entered the house. After passing through two small rooms, which, as an Irishman might say, had no room at all, for they were very small, dirty and barely furnished, we came to a door which was fastened. We attempted to open it, when an elderly, dingy white woman made her appearance and informed us the house belonged to herself and sons, who were coopers, and at work in the cooperage. 'That door,' said she, 'leads to it, but I have the key upstairs; wait, and I will fetch it.' The old woman, on going out, turned the key of the room we were in. I remarked this to the lieutenant, who, apprehending some treachery, ordered the men to force the door we had endeavoured to open. It soon gave way, when we suddenly came on four men dressed as coopers. Two of them were knocking a cask to pieces, the other two drawing off a liquid which had the appearance of rum. They did not desist from their occupation, nor were they surprised at our visit, but told us very coolly we had mistaken the house. So should we have thought had we not seen our copper-faced acquaintance who had in such unmannerly fashion shut the door in our faces. 'Come, my lads,' said the lieutenant, 'there's no mistake here; you must leave off drawing rum for your old mother, who wished to take great care of us by locking us in, and go with us, as we want coopers.' 'Rum,' said one of the boat's crew, who had tasted it, 'it's only rum of the fore-hold. A fellow can't get the worse for wear with such liquor as that, sir. It's only Adam's ale.'

'Oh, oh!' cried out some of our men, 'is this the way you work to windward, my knowing ones? Come, come, you must be more on a bow-line before you can cross our hawse; so pack up your duds, trip your anchors, and make sail with us.'

The old woman again made her appearance, and asked us if we were going to take her sons. 'If you dare do it,' said she, 'I will prosecute the whole of you for breaking through my premises, and have you all put into gaol.' 'Hold your tongue, mother,' said one of the men we had taken, 'what's the good of your kicking up such a bobbery about it? You only make it worse. If you don't see us to-morrow, send our clothes to Port Royal.' They then quietly submitted. We returned through the rooms entered, and on turning into the passage leading to the street, we encountered Master Copperskin. Two of our men immediately seized him; he struggled violently, and attempted to draw a clasped knife, which on the coxswain perceiving he gave him a stroke on his calabash with his hanger, which quieted him. He was then pinioned with one of the seamen's neckhandkerchiefs. On getting into our boats a party of about twenty men and women of all colours came down to the wharf in the hope of rescuing the mulatto man, but they were too late. When we put off from the shore we found it no joke, as they fired into our boat and seriously wounded the man who pulled the stroke oar. Luckily the awning was canted towards them, or they would have shot several of us, as it had seven shots through it. We were obliged to fire in self-defence, killing one man and wounding several others. I remarked the man we killed jumped a considerable height from the ground and then fell prostrate. Finding they had had enough fighting, they marched off with their killed and wounded. The day after we were summoned to Kingston to explain our adventure before the magistrates, who, finding we were first attacked, acquitted us of wilful murder as we had been compelled to act in self-defence, but informed us it was necessary to appear before a jury next day for the satisfaction of the townspeople. This was vexatious.

The day following, after rowing about three hours in a hot sun, we were examined by twelve very wise and common-looking bipeds, who, after questioning us in a most stupid and tiresome manner, found a verdict of justifiable homicide. On returning to the boat we were followed by a number of women and boys, who made a most horrible squalling, and some stones were thrown at us on our pushing off. The yellow fever was still making havoc amongst the officers and crew. We had lost five lieutenants, the surgeon's mate, captain's clerk, and eight midshipmen, one of whom died singing 'Dulce Domum'. It was at length my turn. I was seized with a dreadful swimming in my head; it appeared so large that it was painful to carry it. I was much distressed by a bitter nausea in my mouth and sudden prostration of strength. The doctor gave me an emetic, and soon after I ejected a quantity of bitter bile. It tried me exceedingly, and when I put my head down I thought I was not far from 'Kingdom come'. The second morning I knew no one, and was in a high fever. The third was much the same until about noon, when I slept for about two hours. On awaking I found the pain in my head less, and was perfectly sensible. I requested something to drink, when the sentinel gave me some orange-juice and water, which refreshed me. About dusk, one of the mids who had just come on board from Port Royal, came to me with a cup filled with some sort of herb tea mixed with rum. He requested me to drink it off. This I refused to do. He assured me he had been on shore on purpose to procure it for me, that old Dinah, who was a grey-headed washerwoman, had made it, and I must drink it. I was so weak that I could scarcely answer him, when he put it to my mouth and forced more than half of it down my throat. With the exertion I fainted. He told me the following day he thought he had killed me, and had called the doctor, who gave me a draught. On the morning of the fourth day I was considerably better and in a gentle perspiration, and had passed a quiet night. My three messmates, who alone survived out of eleven, came to cheer me. He who had given me the tea and rum told me he was certain they had cured me, and I really believe it caused the pores to open and in a great measure drove the fever from the system. I was removed to the gunroom, and in a few days was able to sit up and eat oranges.

A week had now elapsed since the doctor had reported me convalescent, when I was painfully distressed by seeing my open-hearted, generous messmate brought in his hammock to the gun-room, attacked by the fatal malady. As he was placed near me, I watched him with intense anxiety. On the fourth morning he died. He was a very florid and robust youth of sixteen. He struggled violently, and was quite delirious. When the sailmaker was sewing him up in his hammock he gave a convulsive sigh. I immediately ordered the stitches to be cut, but it availed nothing. He was gone. Poor fellow! I felt his loss.

In the fifth week I began to crawl about. The boatswain's wife was very kind to me and brought me fresh fruit every day. The doctor, who although a little hasty, was a clever and excellent character, paid me great attention. The kindness and care I experienced, and the affectionate letters I received from my mother, informing me of the happy marriage of my only sister and of the appointment of my youngest brother in India, all these possibly contributed to my recovery and cheered my spirits. Our acting-captain, who was a good and active officer, was appointed to a frigate. He was superseded by an elderly, farmer-looking man, who, we understood, was what a black man considers a curiosity – a Welshman. When in harbour we never saw him, and at sea very seldom. He left everything to the first lieutenant. He appeared to have too much pride to ask an humble mid to dine at his table, so that when he departed this life, which he did four months after he joined us, of yellow fever, he died unregretted. Having received a draft of men from the flagship, we were ordered to our old station, Cape St Nicholas mole, it being considered more healthy than Jamaica, although the yellow fever was carried from thence to the other islands in 1794 by the vessels captured at Port-au-Prince.

We arrived there three weeks afterwards, having captured on our passage a French brig laden with coffee. We completed our water, and took on board a Capuchin friar and two mulatto officers, for what purpose we never could find except to give them a cruise. The friar, who was a quiet, fat, rather good-looking man, messed in the cabin. The wicked mids said to 'confess' the captain.

One afternoon we anchored in a bay to the west-ward of Cape François. The carpenter was directed to go on shore and cut some bamboos for boats' yards. The pinnace was despatched with himself, a master's mate and nine men. They landed and had cut about nine poles when they were fired on from the bushes. They, not being armed – for the mulatto officers assured us there was no danger – attempted to reach the boat, but before they could do so the carpenter was killed and two men seriously wounded and taken prisoners. The rest jumped into the boat and came on board. The captain appeared to feel he had done wrong in placing confidence in people who were strangers to him. After cruising on the north side St Domingo without capturing anything, we returned to the mole. Our worthy, hasty-tempered skipper was taken unwell about a month after our arrival, and took apartments on shore, where he in a fortnight afterwards died.

The captain who stepped into his shoes was a dark, tolerably well-built, good-looking man, who had a very good opinion of himself, and by his frequently looking at his legs, imagined there was not such another pair in the West Indies. This gallant officer proved the quintessence of gallantry. He loved the ladies, loved a good table, loved the games of crabs and *rouge-et-noir*, was a judge of hock and champagne. He had seen much of high and low life, had experienced reverses, he said, through the imprudence of others, and had been detained in a large house in London much longer than he wished. He had run through two handsome fortunes, and was willing to run through two more. He had the misfortune, he told us, of being a slave to the pleasures of the world, although he knew it was filled with rogues. Whilst I was with him his memory was rather impaired, for he forgot to repay several sums of money he borrowed, although he was frequently written to on the subject. In short, he was a libertine, liked but by no means respected. He brought with him six mids and his clerk. The first were complete scamps, picked up from the scrapings of London; the last was a fine young man. Our martinet mast-heading first lieutenant, who had outlived all the others save one, was promoted as commander into a sloop of war, in which he died a few months after of apoplexy in consequence of repletion. The only one remaining of those who sailed from England with me was a few months afterwards also promoted as commander into a brig sloop, and he, poor fellow! was drowned on his second cruise. The six lieutenants who came from England were now no longer living, and out of eighteen midshipmen only another and myself were in existence. The lieutenants who had superseded those who died were rather commonplace characters. The discipline of the ship was totally changed. The first lieutenant was a disappointed officer and a complete old woman, and the ship was something of a privateer.

CHAPTER 6

TOUGH YARNS

We generally had about seventy men in the sick list, and were at anchor nearly four months – half the crew doing nothing and the other half helping them. They generally amused themselves by dancing, singing, or telling tough yarns. I was much entertained by hearing some of them relate the following stories, which they declared were true.

'My brother,' said one of these galley-benchmen, 'belonged to the *Unicorn*, of Shields, which traded to Archangel in the White Sea. I suppose,' said he, 'it is called the White Sea because there is much snow on the shore, which throws a kind of white reflection on the water. Well, the ship had anchored about a mile from the town, when my brother, who had the middle watch, saw something like the ship's buoy close to the vessel. At first he took little notice of it until it raised itself about three feet out of the water and opened a mouth wide enough to swallow a Yankee flour-barrel. He was very much afeared, for he was only a young chap without much experience. He immediately jumped down to the chief mate's cabin and told him what he had seen. They both went on deck, the mate armed with a loaded pistol and my brother with a cutlass. By this time the serpent – for it was a sea-serpent – had twisted itself round the bowsprit of the vessel, and was about twenty feet long. Its eyes were about the size of the scuppers and shined like the morning star.' 'Why, Bill,' said one of the listeners, 'clap a stopper on that yarn; those sarpents are only seen on the coast of Ameriky, and nobody but Yankees ever seed them.' 'Avast, Bob,' replied the narrator, 'don't be too hasty; it is as true as the mainstay is moused, for I never knew Jack tell a lie (meaning his brother), and now I'll fill and stand on. The boatswain, hearing the noise, came on deck. The mate pointed to the monster, and told him to get an axe. The beast had bristled up like an American porcupine and was ready to dart at them when the mate got abaft the foremast and fired at its head, which he missed, but struck it in the neck. The animal, finding itself wounded, darted with its jaws wider than a large shark's at the boatswain, who was the nearest. Luckily for him, the mate was ready to fire his pistol again.

The ball struck its lower jaw and broke it. It then made a stern-board, but before it could reach the bows the boatswain gave it a stroke with the axe which nearly gullyteened it; you know, shipmates, what that is. Why, mayhap you don't; so I'll tell you. It's a kind of gallows that cuts off Frenchmen's heads. But I must heave-to a bit and overhaul my reckoning, for I almost forget. Did ever any of you see a port-go-chaire?' 'We never heard of such a port,' said some of his auditors; 'you're humbugging us.' 'I have been to America, the West and East Ingees, but I never heard of such a port,' said another. 'Why, you lubbers,' said the story-teller, 'if you go to France, you'll see thousands of them. It's what they drive the coaches under into their yards.' I was inclined to correct the word, but I thought it better not to interrupt them. 'Where did I leave off?' 'Come, Bill, heave ahead and save tide; your yarn is as long as the stream cable; they'll be piping to grog presently,' said one of his impatient listeners. 'Well,' said Bill, 'to make short a long story, I left off where the boatswain cut off the head of the sea-serpent. By this time all hands were on deck; they threw a rope over the beast and secured it to the cablebits, but not before they had got several raps over their shins, as it kept twisting about for almost an hour afterwards. Next morning, said my brother, the magistrates having heard of it, came on board to know all about it, as no one in the town had ever seen such a serpent. A man with a cocked scraper offered to buy it, but the mate wanted to stuff it and carry it to England. The captain who had come off with the magistrates said it could not remain on board, as it would bring on an infection. At last it was agreed that if four dollars were given to the ship's crew, he might have it. The money was paid to the mate, and the serpent towed on shore, and before they sailed Jack saw it in a large room, stuffed and the head spliced on, among a great many more comical-looking animals. And if any of you go there,' added he, 'you may see all for nothing.' The boatswain's mates now piped for supper, and the party left the galley-bench.

The following evening I found another set on the bench. Their tales were rather marvellous. The captain of the waist of the starboard watch was the teller. He began by asking the others if they had ever been in the Baltic, to which they answered in the negative. 'It is now,' said he, 'five years since I sailed in the *Mary*, of Newcastle, to Bremen. We had been lying there a fortnight, taking in hemp and iron, when two old, ugly women came on board in a small boat paddled by themselves. They had with them two small leather bags full of wind. They went to the chief mater, for the captain was on shore, and asked him if he would buy a fair wind, and pointed to their bags. "How long will it last?" asked the mate. "Two days," said the hags; "but if you want it for four, we will to-morrow bring you off a larger sack." "And what do you ask for it?" said he. "Oh, only eight dollars," replied they.'

I must inform my reader that the greater number of the sons of the sea, although fearless of the enemy and of the weather, however stormy, are superstitious and have implicit faith in ghost-stories, mermaids, witches and sea-monsters, as well as in the flying Dutch ship off the Cape of Good Hope. This rough son of the north was a hardy sailor, but he had his share of credulity. He told them the captain was on shore, but if they would come off in the morning, as they were to sail the following afternoon, it might be settled. The weather at this time was anything but fair, which made him the readier to enter into the witches' bargain. Here I must first inform my reader that these women are exceedingly cunning, and can not only scan the mind of the person they deal with, but can also, from keen observation, calculate on the wind and weather for the next twenty-four hours, and, as what they prognosticate generally proves true, they frequently meet with ready customers. Next morning the captain came on board, and shortly afterwards was followed by the hoary fair-wind sellers. After some consultation with the mate, the captain gave four dollars for a bag of fair wind for three days from the time he was to sail.

'The wind,' continued the captain of the waist, 'remained foul until four o'clock next day, when it veered round and became favourable. The believing captain and mate thought they had made a good bargain. The bag was to be untied after three hours.' I reflected on this narrative, and was astonished to find that people who are Englishmen, and who, generally speaking, imagine themselves the most free from superstition and the most intellectual of any nation, should be so easily deceived and cheated by a set of old women.

It was now the turn of another to spin his yarn. He began by entreating his shipmates not to disbelieve what he was going to say, for it was about mermen and mermaids. He did not see it himself, but it had been told him two years before by his uncle, who was mate of a ship that traded to the North Sea. 'The ship,' said he, 'was the *John and Thomas,* named after the owner's two brothers, and bound to Stockholm for flax and iron. One day they were becalmed near the Island of Oland, and let go the anchor in twelve-fathoms water, when soon afterwards they saw, as they supposed, two men swimming towards the ship. They soon after came alongside, and made signs for a rope to be thrown to them. On their getting on deck the crew found they were mermen. One of them, who appeared to be about twenty-six years old, told the captain he had let go his anchor through his kitchen chimney, and begged him to weigh it again, as it had knocked down the kitchen-grate and spoilt his dinner. "It has happened very unfortunately," said he, "for we have some friends from the coast of Jutland, who have come to attend the christening of our infant." Whilst he was speaking four young mermaidens appeared close to the ship's side, making signs for the mermen on board to join them. The sailors wished them to come on board, and threw them ropes for that purpose; but they were too shy. The mermen requested the captain to give them some matches to light their fire, and a few candles. This being complied with, they shook hands with him and the mate, and jumping overboard, rejoined the females, swam round the ship three times, singing some kind of song, and disappeared. The wind becoming favourable, the crew got the anchor up, on which, when catheaded, they found part of the chimney and the fire-tongs astride on one of the flukes!'

When this improbable tale was told, I asked them if they believed it to be true. 'Yes,' said two of them, 'we do, because we have had shipmates who lived with some of the mermaidens for several years and had children; but as for their having combs and glasses, that's all nonsense. One of the children was sent to London to be educated, but not liking so many double-tailed monsters, as he called the men, nor their manner of living, he crept down to the Thames, and in a few hours rejoined his parents.'

During the time we were at anchor at this place I was ordered, with four seamen and two marines, to take the command of a block-house on the Presqu' Isle to watch the movements of the enemy, whose advanced post was about four miles on the other side the isthmus, as well as to make signals to the commodore whenever strange ships appeared near the land. I remained a month, shooting guanas and gulls and other birds, catching groupers, snappers and sometimes rock-fish, living principally on salt junk, midshipman's coffee (burnt biscuit ground to a powder), picking calelu (a kind of wild spinach), when we could find it, snuffing up a large portion of pure sea-breeze, and sleeping like the sheet anchor. Oh, reader, I blush to inform you that I was envied by the greater part of the mids of the squadron who loved doing nothing. The life I now led was too independent to last much longer; my month expired, when I gave up my Robinson Crusoe government to a master's mate belonging to a ship which had come in to refit. We at length up-anchored, as the mids declared if we remained longer the captain feared we should ground on the beef-bones we threw overboard daily! Three days after sailing we captured a Spanish schooner from Cuba, bound to Port-au-Paix, with nine French washerwomen on board with a quantity of clothes. We presumed, with some reason, these copper-faced damsels – for they were all mulattos, and some of them handsome – had taken French leave of their customers, or possibly they were going on a voyage of discovery to find

out whether the water of St Domingo was softer for washing linen than
that of Cuba. We did not ask them many questions on the subject, and as
the vessel was nearly new, and about seventy tons, we put a mid and five
men on board her and sent the ladies for a change of air to Jamaica.

We had been cruising between Cuba and Cape François a fortnight,
when we saw a roguish-looking black schooner about nine miles to the
westward of the cape, close to a small inlet. We tacked and stood to sea, to
make her imagine we had not discovered her. At dusk we stood in again,
and at ten we armed the barge and large cutter. The fifth lieutenant, who
was a great promoter of radical moisture (*ie*, grog), was in the barge. I
had, with another mid, the command of the cutter. We muffled our oars
and pulled quietly in shore. About midnight we found the vessel near the
inlet, where she had anchored. We then gave way for our quarter. She
soon discovered us, and hailed in French. Not receiving an answer, she
fired a volley of musketry at us. The strokesman of my boat fell shot in
the brain, and two others were seriously wounded in the arm and leg. We
had three marines, two additional seamen and my volunteer messmate in
our boat. This last had smuggled himself in without the first lieutenant's
leave. We cheered and stretched out. The killed and wounded were
placed in the bottom of the boat, and the extra men took their oars. The
barge was nearly alongside of her, and we boarded at the same time, she
on the starboard quarter and we on the larboard side. The marines kept
up a constant discharge of their muskets, and fired with much effect on
the foremost of the enemy. We soon gained her deck, and found about
twenty-five of her crew ready to oppose us abaft her mainmast. The man
who appeared to be the captain waved his cutlass and encouraged his men
to attack us; at the same time he sprang forward, and about twelve followed him, when the conflict became general. I was knocked down on
my knees. I fired one of my pistols, which took effect in my opponent's
left leg, and before he could raise his arm to cut me down with a toma-
hawk, the coxswain of my boat, who had kept close to me, shot him in the
head, and he fell partly on me. I soon recovered and regained my legs. I
had received a severe contusion on the left shoulder. The lieutenant had
shot the captain, and the marines had knocked down nine men. The rest
now called for quarter and threw down their arms. She proved to be the
French privateer *Salamandre*, of twelve long brass six-pounders and forty-
eight men. She had also on board nine English seamen, the crew of a
Liverpool brig, who informed us they had been captured in the Turk's
Island passage three days before. The privateer's loss was eleven killed
and seven severely wounded, ours three men killed and five wounded.
On our drawing off from the shore, a small battery opened its fire on us

and wounded the boat-keeper of the barge. We discharged the guns of the privateer at it, and as it did not annoy us a second time, we supposed our shot had rather alarmed their faculties and probably subdued their courage. By 3am we rejoined the ship. Our mates gave us three hearty cheers, which we returned. We soon got the wounded of our men on deck and the prisoners out. I was ordered to go as prize-master, taking fourteen men with me, and carry her to Cape St Nicholas mole, where I arrived the same evening. I found myself stiff for some days afterwards and my shoulder painful, but in a short time I was quite myself again. After remaining idle and half-dead with *ennui* for three weeks, the ship arrived, bringing in with her an American brig laden with flour. False papers were found on board her, and she was shortly afterwards condemned as a lawful prize. The captain of her, who was a regular-built Bostonian, declared we were nothing 'but a parcel of British sarpents and robbers, and it was a tarnation shame that the United States suffered it. But,' said he, 'I calculate that in two years we shall have some three-deckers, and then I have a notion you will not dare to stop American vessels without being called to account for it.'

The yellow fever had now taken its departure, but in consequence of the scanty supply of fresh provisions and vegetables, it was succeeded by a malignant scurvy, and one hundred and forty of the seamen were obliged to keep their beds. Their legs, hands, feet and gums became almost black, and swollen to twice their natural size. Some we sent to the hospital, which was miserably fitted up, for it was only a temporary one, and several died on being removed. As the cases were increasing, the commodore ordered us to Donna Maria Bay, near the west end of St Domingo, where the natives were friendly disposed towards us. The day after we arrived there, having taken on board all our sick that could be removed from the hospital with safety. Immediately, on anchoring, by the advice of the surgeon, we sent a party on shore with spades to dig holes in the softest soil they could find for the purpose of putting the worst scurvy subjects into them. The officer on shore made the concerted signal that the pits were dug. Twenty men, who looked like bloated monsters, were removed on shore, and buried in them up to their chins. Some of the boys were sent with the sufferers to keep flies and insects from their faces. It was ridiculous enough to see twenty men's heads stuck out of the ground. The patients were kept in fresh earth for two hours, and then put into their hammocks under a large tent. On the fourth day they were so much benefited by that treatment and living on oranges, shaddocks, and other antiscorbutic fruits, that they were able to go on board again. At this place I rambled with some of my messmates through orange and lime groves of some leagues in extent, as well as through several cocoa plantations. We were at liberty to take as much fruit as we chose, and sent off several boats filled with oranges and limes, as well as a vast quantity of yams, sweet potatoes, cocoanuts and cocoas, besides fresh calelu (wild spinach), which is considered a fine anti-scorbutic. We found some arrowroot, which was also of great service. In one of our rambles we met a party on mules going to the town of Donna Maria, which was not far distant. It consisted of two young mustiphena-coloured men, an elderly mulatto woman, with an infant on her lap, and a black manservant. They saluted us in passing, when we remarked that the men had delicate European features, and that the infant was white.

A short time afterwards we stumbled on a burying-ground, and seated on one of the graves we found the two persons we had taken for men, the eldest of whom was suckling the infant. They proved to be the wife of the Governor of Donna Maria, who was a native of France, and her sister. The old woman was the nurse, and the black man their factotum. They spoke French, which some of our party understood, and we spent a very agreeable half-hour in their company. After having given us an invitation to their house, they bade us adieu and proceeded on their journey. I afterwards found it was a common custom for the better class of females in this island to ride and dress like men when they made any distant journey, as the greater part of the island is too mountainous to admit of travelling in carriages.

One of the lieutenants, who was fond of voyages of discovery, had permission to take one of the cutters to survey a deep inlet about three miles from where we anchored. He asked me if I should like to be one of the party. I thankfully said yes. 'Well,' said he, 'to-morrow morning at daylight I intend going round the Cape Donna Maria (which has the shape of the mysterious helmet of Otranto), and exploring a river which runs into a large lagoon, and we shall be away most likely two days. I shall find prog, but don't forget your great coat and drawing apparatus.'

At four o'clock the following morning we left the ship, and after pulling for two hours we entered the river, which was narrow and enclosed between two thickly-wooded hills. The noise of our oars startled a vast number of large and small birds, which made a horrible screaming. I fired at one of the large ones and broke its wing; it fell ahead of the boat, and we picked it up. It was twice the size of a gull, a dark brown colour on the back, a dirty white underneath, long, reddish legs, and rather a long, pointed bill; it was shaped like a heron. We had been rowing about an hour when we entered the lagoon, which was about a mile long and three-quarters of a mile wide. The country to some extent was low, and covered with mangrove trees, whose branches take root when they touch the ground, and one tree forms a number of irregular arches. Those nearest the water are covered with a profusion of small oysters, which are taken by the natives and pickled with spice and vinegar, and sold in small jars. They are considered good eating. We observed several large ants' nests formed on the branches of these trees; they were about the size of a bushel measure. The insect is half an inch in length; its bite is severe, but not very venomous. We could only make good our landing at one spot, covered with long, coarse grass, which the natives twist into ropes for the rigging of their canoes, and the finest of it they clean, stain with different colours, and fabricate into hammocks, which are made like a net with large meshes.

I had strolled from the boat with one of the men, when he called out, 'There goes a large water-snake! Take care, sir!' It came close to me, when I made a stroke at it with my hanger. I struck it on the body, but not sufficiently, for before I had time to give it another blow, it had wound into a kind of jungle, and I lost sight of it. It was about five feet long, speckled yellow and black; its tongue, which it kept in continual motion, was forked; its eyes were small, and not projecting. Finding myself in company with gentry of this description, I retraced my steps to the boat, where I found the whole party with their hands and mouths in full activity. I soon was as well employed as themselves. The lieutenant told me whilst we were at dinner that one of the men had found some alligators' eggs; two of them were broken and the young ones alive. They were about half-a-foot long, of a dirty brown. The eggs were oblong, and larger than a swan's, of a brownish-white colour.

The evening was now drawing on, when we pulled the boat to the middle of the lagoon and let go the grapnel for the night. One of the boat's crew, who sung in the style of Incledon, entertained us with several sea songs until we fell asleep, which was not, however, very refreshing, in consequence of the multitudes of mosquitoes. I positively believe some of us lost two ounces of our best blood. About three o'clock in the morning, the man who had the watch pulled me by the arm and pointed to something dark floating near the boat. I awoke the lieutenant, who, after yawning and rubbing his eyes, for he had taken an extra strong northwester the evening before to make himself sleep sound, took up his fowling-piece; but he might as well have fired at the best bower anchor – the swan-shot with which it was loaded glanced from the object at an angle of twenty-five degrees. We weighed the grapnel, and were soon in pursuit, when we saw two other black-looking objects. We steadily gave chase to the first, the lieutenant, myself and the coxswain firing at and frequently striking it, but without any visible effect. At length it landed, when we found it was an alligator about fifteen feet long. It soon ploughed up the mud in which it buried itself; our musket-balls were unavailing. The other two had also landed. On turning the boat round, we saw another, and as he was with his head towards us, we had a better chance. We stretched out, and when within a few yards of him, let fly our muskets at his head. One of the balls struck him in the left eye, which stunned him, and he lay insensible on the water until we reached him. We threw a rope round him and towed him astern, after having given him another ball in the throat, which despatched him. He was a young one, nine feet four inches long. After rowing round the lake in search of fresh adventures, and finding none, we amused ourselves by cutting off several branches of the mangrove trees strung with oysters, and being tired of rowing where there was so little novelty, we turned the boat's nose towards the river, on reaching which we again startled numerous flocks of screaming birds, five of which we shot; but as they were only noddies and boobies, we did not take the trouble to pick them up. At 4pm we joined the ship, with our prizes, the alligators, their eggs, the heron, and the oysters. The doctor, who was something of a naturalist, asked for the alligator we had shot, one of the young ones, and the bird, and shortly afterwards he had them stuffed. We had now but five slight scurvy cases, and had only buried three seamen and one marine, who died two days after our anchoring. The boats were employed nearly two days in bringing up oranges, limes and yams, besides other fruit.

CHAPTER 7

CRUISING OFF PORTO RICO

The officers gave a dance to the inhabitants of the town of Donna Maria, which was attended by the Governor, who was a well-bred, gentlemanly old Frenchman, his wife and sister-in-law (whom I had seen dressed as men when we first arrived). The quarter-deck was filled with mustiphenas, mustees, mulattos, Sambos, and delicate, flat-nosed, large-mouthed and thick-lipped black ladies. Had Vestris been present, she might have taken some new hints in dancing. The waltzing was kept up with so much spirit that four couples were hurled to the deck one over the other, and it was truly laughable to see the melange of blacks and whites struggling to be the first on their legs. At one o'clock in the morning they took their departure, highly pleased with their entertainment.

The following day I was sent with another midshipman with two boats to haul the seine in a bay about a mile to the westward. On the first haul we caught about four bucketsful of rays, parrot-fish, snappers, groupers, red and white mullet, John-dories, some crabs and two electric eels. One of the boat's crew hooked one of the latter by the gills with the boat-hook, when his arm was immediately paralysed, and he let it fall, calling out that someone had struck him. The man near him laid hold of the fish again as it was making for the shore, and the shock he received threw him on his knees. I ran up to him, for he appeared in great pain. However, he soon recovered, and before the ill-fated eel could reach its element, he caught up a large stone and made it dearly atone for the pain it had inflicted. We made another haul, but were not so successful, as we only caught some ray, crabs, and an alligator three feet long, which had torn the net. We stunned him by a blow with one of the boat's stretchers, threw him into the boat, and after taking in the net, repaired to the ship.

In one of my excursions at this place I found a large manchineel tree. The fruit is nearly the size of a pippin, of a light yellow colour blushed with red; it looked very tempting. This tree expands its deadly influence and poisons the atmosphere to some distance. We in consequence gave it a wide berth. I also found a number of sponges, and some beautiful shells and sea-eggs. We had been enjoying ourselves for nearly three weeks at this agreeable place, when a sloop of war arrived with orders from the commodore to join him off the east end of Porto Rico, as he had information that a French squadron had been seen by an American schooner off the Caicos Islands steering for St Domingo, which report in the sequel proved a tarnation Yankee lie. When near the Platform we experienced a heavy squall, which carried away the foretop-mast and jib-boom, and, most singular to relate, although some miles from the shore after the squall had passed, we found some scores of very small crabs on the decks. I leave this phenomenon to longer heads than mine – although mine is not the shortest – to explain. We had seen two waterspouts in the morning between us and the land. It might possibly have happened that the suction which forms them drew up these unfortunate crabs and crabesses, and discharged them with unrelenting fury, through the medium of a dark, lowering cloud upon our decks. They being too small to eat, were given to the Muscovy ducks, who found them a great treat, and soon made mincemeat of them. We soon got up another topmast and jib-boom out, and the following morning signalled the ships lying in the mole.

Five days after we joined the squadron near the Mona passage, when the commodore acquainted the captain that the intelligence he had received respecting the French squadron was all an American humbug. The next morning we spoke three ships bound to Jamaica, from whom we took seven good seamen, and procured a newspaper, which informed us of the gallant action off Camperdown, and that Bonaparte had frightened men, women and children by his threatening to invade England, take up his residence in Portland Place, turn the royal palaces into stables, make a riding-school of St Paul's and a dancing academy of Westminster Abbey! The cockpitonians said he might whisper that to the marines, for the sailors would not believe him. Here, reader, I beg you will pause and reflect that you must die; and may your departure be like that of our worthy captain of marines, who died as he lived, in charity with all his frail fellow men. His loss was much regretted by nearly all on board. His messmates declared they could have spared another man, looking hard at the purser whilst they uttered it; but 'Nip-cheese' would not take the hint, and lived to return to England, where he took unto himself a better half, and I hope he is happy, for who is not so when they take a fair lady for better——I dislike adding anything further, so, reader, finish it yourself. I hope to get spliced myself one of these fine days, and I sincerely trust it will be a long splice. But we must keep a good look-out that in veering the cable does not part in the hawse, for if it unfortunately does, ah, me! the separation most likely will be a permanent one.

Whilst I am on the tender subject of connubial felicity, I will relate a short dialogue which passed between two of my messmates. The eldest was a Benedict, the other about twenty, who wished to be initiated, as he thought he had a kind of sidewind regard for the innkeeper's sister at Port Royal. 'Why,' said the first, 'I met my wife at a hop in the country among a parcel of grass-combers. I asked her to dance, which she at first refused, giving for a reason that, as I was a sailor, I could not know how to lead down the middle and cast off at top. "If that's all," said I, "my dear, I know how to do that as well as anybody in the room." I was now pushed aside by a lubberly, haymaking chap, who led her out, but who as much knew how to dance as the captain's cow. After they all sat down, I asked the catgut scraper if he could play the fisher's hornpipe. He said yes. I told him to play away, and I would dance it. After veering and hauling on his instrument for a short time, he brought it out. I then struck out, with my hat on one side, my arms a-kimbo, and a short stick under one of them. The bumpkins all stared, and Nancy began to awake and find out that a sailor knew how to cut a caper. After I had finished, I ran up to her to pick up her handkerchief, which I thought she had dropped, but found it was only the tail of her gown. She smiled and gave me her hand. I thought this a good beginning, and was determined to follow it up. I observed her plough-tail admirer did not half like seeing me on such a good footing with her. I had not forgotten his push, and if he had interfered I should have knocked him down, for I began to feel that I was already over head and heels in love. About midnight all the clodhoppers took their departure. As the dance, or merry-making as they called it, was given at her father's house, I remained as long as I could, and as the old governor was fond of sea songs and tough yarns, I served them out freely until the clock struck 2am, when, after taking a good swig out of a large tankard of strong ale, which had frequently been replenished, I took Nancy's hand and kissed it, and wished her good-night. The father, who was a hearty old farmer, asked me to call in again before I sailed, for at this time I was master's mate of the *Savage* sloop of war. She was just commissioned at Chatham, and as we did not expect to sail for three weeks, I had plenty of time to make love.' 'But did you think it prudent to marry, knowing that you could scarcely support yourself, much less a wife?' demanded the younger. 'That's all true,' replied he; 'but don't put me in mind of my misfortunes. I was in love, you know, and when a man is in love, why, he's two-thirds a woman. I only thought of the present – the future I sent packing to the devil.' 'Well,' asked the other, 'how long were you backing and filling?' 'About a fortnight,' replied he. 'Her mother said it was too short a time, and the marriage had better be put off until I returned from a cruise. "That will never do," replied I; "I may be popped off the hooks. There is nothing like the present moment, is there?" said I, appealing to Nancy and her father. "Why," said she, "dear mother, I think William" – for that, you know, is my Christian name – "is right; is he not, father?" "Do as you like, girl," said he. "I only wish to see you happy." It was now settled that in two days we were to be spliced. All the clodhoppers and grass-combers I had met before, who were mostly her relations, were asked to the wedding, and among the rest her clownish admirer, who, I understood, was her cousin. He was rather sulky at first, but seeing everyone around him in good humour, he came up to me and offered his hand, which I took and shook heartily. The farmhouse not being more than three miles from Chatham, we hired two coaches from that place, and with the addition of two chay-carts belonging to the farmers, we made a numerous (for there were twenty-six of us), if not a respectable, appearance. After pairing off and pairing in, we weighed and started with a pleasant breeze. The church soon hove in sight, and the bells struck up merrily. We hove to, all standing before the altar. The parson read the articles of marriage, and I was hooked. Nancy piped her eye, and I looked nohow. We made a man-of-war's cruise there and back again, and took in our moorings at the farm, where I had leave to remain four days. I had asked two of my messmates to the wedding, who were obliged to be off next morning by daylight. The same day my good old father-in-law took me aside and told me he would allow Nancy forty pounds a year as long as he lived and did well, and that she might remain with her mother, who did not like parting with her, as she was their only child, as long as I liked. I thanked the old governor most sincerely, and informed him that the Secretary of the Admiralty was a relation of my mother's, a ninety-ninth cousin far removed – but that's nothing – and that I was certain of a lieutenant's commission in two years, when my time would be served. Here I counted my chickens before they were hatched, for I have now served three years over my time, and here I am, with not much a day, except the good farmer's forty pounds, to keep myself, my wife and a child. You see,' said he, 'how I am obliged to keep close hauled, and can't afford to sport my figure on shore as some of you do. No,' added he, 'don't be after splicing yourself until you have a commission, and if you do then, you will have as much business with a wife as a cow has with a side pocket, and be, as a noble First Lord of the Admiralty used civilly to tell married lieutenants, not worth a d——n.'

My messmate's narrative brought me up with a round turn, and I felt my heart working like the tiller-ropes in a gale of wind. 'Well,' said I, after a pause, 'how did you back out when you parted with your wife?'

'You may well say "back out,"' said he. 'I was taken slap aback – it came over me like a clap of thunder. I was half inclined to play the shy cock and desert, and had it not been for the advice of the good old man, I should have been mad enough to have destroyed my prospects in the Service for ever. Now,' said he, 'how do you feel?' 'A little qualmish,' said I, 'and I'll take a good stiff glass of grog to wash it down. But you have not finished. How did she behave when you were ordered to join your ship?' 'Nobly,' said he; 'just as I thought she would. After a good fit of crying, she threw herself on her mother's shoulder, and after fondly embracing me, "Go," said she. "William, may that God who has a particular providence over our sailors always be with you! If your duty will not prevent you, come again to-morrow, and get leave to remain until the ship sails."

'I joined the sloop, and the first lieutenant and my messmates told me I looked more like a person who had been doing something he was ashamed of than a happy Benedict.

'When I got below, my mates informed me the sloop was to fit foreign and going to the West Indies. My mind was like a coal-barge in a water-spout when I heard this, and I was determined to cut and run; but when I reflected next morning on the probability of my gaining my commission shortly after our arrival, as I should go out on Admiralty promotion, I clapped a stopper on my determination, and held on. We were to sail in two days, and I contrived to get leave to go every evening to the farm, and return by 8 o'clock next morning. I told my wife our destination, and the probability of my promotion. "Never mind me, William," said she, with her sweet voice; "go where duty calls you. When in that path you cannot be wrong. The hope of your promotion cheers me. Let us do all we can to merit the blessings of a gracious Creator, and the good-fellowship of our fellow-creatures, and we shall not be very unhappy, although far distant from each other." The last morning I spent with my wife was a mixture of cheerfulness and grief. At last I tore myself away. I have now given you the whole history, from the main-royal truck down to the kelson.'

'Come,' said I, 'let's have another glass of grog, and I'll drink your wife's good health and speedy promotion to yourself.' 'That's a good fel-low,' said he, giving me his hand, and brushing away a tear. 'Should you ever be spliced, which I hope for your own sake will not be for some years, may you anchor alongside just such another saucy frigate as mine.' I am truly happy to inform my reader that my good-hearted messmate was shortly afterwards promoted into a frigate going to England.

After cruising with the squadron for some days, we had permission to go in search of adventures, and next morning, as we were running down along the coast of Porto Rico, we discovered five sail of vessels in a small bay. The water not being sufficiently deep to admit the ship, we manned and armed three boats and sent them in. I had the six-oared cutter, with nine men; we were soon alongside of them. They proved Spanish vessels, four small schooners and a sloop laden with fruit, principally oranges and shaddocks, and a quantity of yams and plantains. We sent them all down to Jamaica – why, you must ask the captain, as by the time they reached their destination almost the whole of the fruit was rotten, and the vessels did not pay the expenses of their condemnation. Shortly after this affair, two of the boats, with a lieutenant, a master's mate, and myself, were sent in shore near Cape François, St Domingo, on a cruise of speculation. No object being in sight when we left the ship, about 10pm we came suddenly on three dark-looking schooners, who on seeing us gave us a warm reception. The night, fortunately for us, was very dark, and we were nearly alongside of them without our perceiving them, as they were anchored so near the land. I was mid of the lieutenant's boat, and he determined on boarding the largest of them. I knew, or rather I could foresee, the result; but he had taken in the course of the last two hours three north-westers, and was half-seas over, my advice availed little. The other boat was at some distance from us. On we went, when three of our men were seriously wounded and I received a musketball through the left side of my hat, which slightly wounded my ear, taking part of the hair, and I felt a distressing whirling noise inside my head, and was so giddy I was obliged to sit down, not before, however, I had shot a man in the main-channels who I thought had fired the shot at me. We had kept up a brisk firing, and must have killed several of their men, when they got long spars with a spike at the end over the side, and endeavoured to drive them through the bottom of our boat. The lieutenant, who was now more himself, found boarding her impracticable, as she had her boarding netting up, her decks filled with men, and nine ports in her side. We reluctantly pulled off. We had unfortunately taken the bull by the horns – that is, pulled for her broadside. The lieutenant and myself, for I recovered sufficiently to load my musket, kept firing at her decks as we retired. She paid us the same compliment, and slightly wounded another of the boat's crew. Had the night not been so cloudy, and without a moon, we should have paid dearly for our temerity. We rowed in a straight line for her stern. The two other vessels were well armed, and they saluted us with a few shot as we pulled off, which, however, went far over us. We soon after joined the other boat, which had lost sight of us when we attempted boarding the enemy's vessel. We learnt a few days afterwards, from a New Providence privateer, that they were three guardacostas, as the captain of her called them – in other words, Spanish government vessels,

commanded by lieutenants, well armed, manned and equipped. We
joined the ship next morning, and gave a Flemish account of our cruise.
One of the wounded men, through loss of blood, died soon after coming
on board. The other three having received flesh wounds, soon returned to
their duty. The surgeon examined my ear, and found the tympanum rup-
tured. It destroyed my hearing on that side for ever, and for years after I
was distressed with a loud roaring noise on the left side of my head. A
fortnight later we fell in with a Spanish eighty-gun ship, a large frigate
and a heavy-armed store ship. We were soon alongside the former, having
beat to quarters previously. We asked her where she came from. Her
answer was, 'From sea'. We then asked her where she was bound to. Her
answer was, 'To sea'. Our skipper then jumped upon one of the quarter-
deck carronades, with his eyes glistening like a Cornish diamond. The
muzzles of our guns were at this time almost touching her side. One of
our crew spoke Spanish. He was desired to hail her, and say that if she did
not answer the questions which had been put she should be fired into.
'From Cadiz' was the prompt answer, and 'Bound to the Havannah.'
'You might have answered that before,' said the skipper; 'if I had given
you a good dressing, you richly deserved it.' 'I do not understand what
you say,' was the reply. 'You be d——d,' said our man of war, and we
turned off on our heel. The same evening a court of inquiry was held by
the mids, who were unanimous in declaring that the captain of the line of
battle ship ought to be superseded and made swab-wringer, and that their
own captain had acted with that spirit which became a British commander of a man-of-war, and that he deserved to have his health drunk in a
bumper of grog, which was accordingly done. Here the court broke up,
hoping the mate of the hold would bring with him, after serving the grog,
an extra pint of rum to make up the deficiency. The captain, having heard
of our proceedings, sent his steward to us with a bottle of the true sort as a
proof of his satisfaction.

CHAPTER 8

MUTINY ON HMS *HERMIONE*

On the evening of the next day the boatswain's wife invited me to take tea. I could not refuse so kind an offer, and at the vulgar hour of six, behold us sipping our Bohea out of porringers, with good Jamaica stuff in it in lieu of milk. 'Do you like it?' said the boatswain to me. 'Have you enough rum in it? Take another dash.' 'No, thank you,' said I; 'no more splicing, or I shall get hazy, and not be able to keep the first watch.' 'That rum,' said he, 'is old pineapple, and like mother's milk, and will not hurt a child. Now,' said he, 'we are talking of rum, I'll tell you an odd story that happened to me in the last ship I belonged to. I had a capital case of the right sort given to me by a brother Pipes. One evening I had asked some of the upper class dockyard maties, for we were lying at Antigua, to take a glass of grog. When I went to the case, I found two of the bottles at low-water mark, and another a marine. "Ho! ho!" said I to myself; "this is the way you make a southerly wind in my case-bottles, and turn to windward in my cabin when I am carrying on the war on the forecastle, is it? I'll cross your hawse and cut your cable the next time, as sure as my name is Tricing." After the last dog-watch, I threw myself into my cot all standing, with my rattan alongside of me. About three bells of the first watch, I heard someone go very cunningly, as he thought, into my cabin. I immediately sprung out and seized a man in the act of kissing one of my dear little ones, for it was a case with nine quart bottles. "Who are you?" said I. "Nobody," replied he. "You are the fellow I have been cruising after since I entered the service five-and-twenty years ago, and now I have got you, by G–d! I'll sheet you home most handsomely for all past favours." I then gave it to him thick and thin. "Now, my lad," said I, "chalk this down in your log, that when you have the thievish inclination to take what does not belong to you, remember my cane, it you do not your God." This rum gentleman belonged to the after-guard, and I did not forget him.'

After cruising round Porto Rico and Hispaniola for two months, we bore up for the mole, where we found two sail of the line, a sixty-four and two sloops of war. In the course of our cruise we had sent in an American brig and a schooner laden with flour. The latter was condemned, half-barrels of gunpowder being found in the under flour casks. The former was let go, although we thought she ought to have been condemned, as her register was defective. We understood that the judge's wife, of the Vice-Admiralty Court, who was notorious for accepting presents, had received a purse from some of the masters of the American vessels detained by the cruisers to let them escape trial. How true this may be must be left to time and the curious to decide.

On overhauling the fore-shrouds and mainstay, we found them too much worn to be trustworthy. As we could not be refitted with lower rigging from the naval stores at this place, the senior officer gave us an order to proceed to Jamaica. We took leave of all the 'Ballaker ladies', as the mids chose to call them. Know, reader, that the fish called by that name is a most destructive and voracious one, and as I presume they thought the ladies were of that character, some of them had too much reason to call them so. We reached Port Royal on the afternoon of the following day, but remarked we were not received with that welcome as before; no boats filled with yellow-legged females came off with banjos. Why? Because we brought in no prize with us. And when we went on shore some of these delicate dames exclaimed when we accosted them: 'Eh, massa, you hab know me before? I no recollect you. What ship you belong to?' And we were seldom asked to the dignity balls. We were all now in tolerable health, when the packet from England arrived, bringing letters for the squadron, one of which I received, acquainting me that my sister's husband was appointed to command the *A.* frigate fitting for the Mediterranean, and that my youngest brother, in the India marine, had died in Bengal. He was a fine, spirited youth, nineteen years of age; we had not met since we were at school. Some of our seamen also received letters by the same opportunity, acquainting them with the mutiny at the Nore, and a few days afterwards a disaffected spirit broke out in the squadron, which we had some trouble in subduing. However, by reasoning with the petty officers and the best seamen, it terminated without open mutiny or bloodshed, although the crews of some of the ships had been mistaken enough to have delegates for their proceedings. To finally root out the trouble the admiral ordered the five line of battle ships fitting out at Port Royal to complete their stores and sail without delay for the Gulf of Mexico. Two days afterwards we stood out to sea. The squadron consisted of a ship of ninety-eight guns, four seventy-fours, and a frigate. The commander-in-chief had his flag on board the former. After touching at the Grand Caymans for turtle, we reached the Bay of Mexico, where, and off the Havannah, we cruised for some weeks without taking anything. One night, having the middle watch and looking over the lee gangway, I observed some black spots on the water. The moon, which was in her third quarter, was sometimes hidden by the dark scud, for it was blowing fresh, and when she shone in full splendour the spots appeared stationary. I lost no time in pointing this out to the lieutenant of the watch, who agreed with me that they must be the negro heads of some coral reef. We were with the squadron running directly on them. We immediately fired a gun and hauled our wind, and then fired a second to warn the ships astern of us of the danger. When we hauled off we could not clear them, and it was more than an hour before we got an offing. They were the 'Double-headed shot' keys. Our signal was made for the captain and master to repair on board the admiral. The latter, we understood, was well hauled over the coals, and he came on board looking like a boy who had been whipped. He thought it was 'moral impossible' (for that was always his favourite way of speaking when he thought he had anything of importance to relate) that the admiral should find fault with him as a navigator; he could not account for counter currents and under-tows, and he knew how to navigate a ship as well as any man in the fleet.

The inhabitants of the cockpit, as usual, held a court of inquiry on his conduct, when they declared on summing up what they had remarked of his character, that he was too conceited to be clever, that he was a very indifferent navigator, and they wondered who the devil gave him his warrant as master, for they would not trust him to navigate a barge in the New River. After cruising till the mids declared they were *ennuiéd* of seeing the Havannah, the dry Tortugas, Cape Antonio, and the low land near Mississippi so often, and that they had worn their chemises twice over and had only soiled sheets for table-cloths; that they were obliged to get one of the marines to pipe-clay their stockings and the collar of their shirts when they were asked to dine in the cabin; that it was a horrible, hard case to eat biscuits filled with bargemen and purser's lice; that the water was full of jenny jumps – all these miseries, concluded they, ought to be made known to the admiral, and that if he did not order the squadron in again he ought to be tried by a court of mids and reduced to the humble rank of a cockpitsman and feed off bargemen for a month.

We had now been out for two months when we bore up for the Gulf of Florida. In making the Havannah for a departure, we fell in with four Spanish brigs laden with quicksilver, which we captured. When near Cape Florida we experienced a white squall which carried away the fore-top-gallant mast and split the foresail. The ninety-eight gunship, which led the squadron, heeled so much over before she could shorten sail that she appeared to be turning the turtle. At last her foreyard went in the slings, and her main-topsail in ribbons, and she righted.

When off New Providence the wind was light and the clouds heavy and low, and in less than half an hour seven waterspouts had formed, two not far from us on our weather beam, the largest of which was nearing us rather fast. We got two of the main-deck guns ready, and waited until we could see its suction. The cloud which drew up and contained the water was in the shape of a reversed cone with a long point at the bottom of it: this was something like a corkscrew. We now thought it high time to fire, when down it came, discharging a sheet of water which must have contained many tons. The shock it gave the water drove it in breakers to some distance, and we partook of the motion, as we rolled for at least ten minutes before the swell subsided. The other waterspout passed some distance astern. In this gulf some years ago a dreadful catastrophe occurred to a West Indiaman homeward bound, caused by one of the sucking clouds or waterspouts. Several had formed very near her, one of them so near that the master of her was afraid to fire as it might endanger the vessel. It appeared to be passing when a flaw of wind came, and being heavily surcharged with water, broke it. Fortunately the hatches were on, and only the master, mate and four men on deck. The immense body of water it contained fell with such violence that it carried away all her masts, boats, spars and hen-coops, with all the live stock, as well as washing the master and three of the men over-board. The mate and the other man were saved by jumping into the caboose which held on, although they were half-dead with fright and half-drowned with water. After we had cleared the islands forming the Bahama group, we fell in with a low, rakish-looking schooner, which gave us a chase of seven hours, although our shot went over her. At length two of her men were killed, and the spyglass knocked out of the skipper's hand, when he, finding it was useless holding out any longer, hove to. She proved a Spanish privateer of six guns and forty men, with a number of sheep on board, but the mids declared they were more like purser's lanterns. When killed, one of them weighed only fifteen pounds. Nothing further occurred during the remainder of our passage to Jamaica, where we anchored two days after with our prizes. Before the sails were furled, half the inhabitants of Port Royal were round the ships making a most hideous noise with their squalling and banjos. Our five prizes made their eyes shine like a dollar in a bucket of water, and their mouths water like a sick monkey's eyes with a violent influenza. The last time we had anchored we returned prizeless, and no boat came off but an old washerwoman's; we now paid them off in their own coin, and desired all the canoes with the exception of two to paddle to some other ship, as we should not admit them on board. After lingering for about half an hour in the hope that we should change our minds, they paddled away looking blacker than their skins. Soon after our arrival we heard that the *Hermione* frigate had been taken and carried into Porto Bello on the Spanish Main by her crew, after having killed their captain and all the officers. This dreadful news gave me real concern, as one of my late messmates was third lieutenant of her. Captain Hamilton, of the *Surprise* of twenty-eight guns, offered to bring her out from where her rebellious crew had anchored her, and a few days after he sailed for that purpose. We were refitting very leisurely, and had been in harbour nearly five weeks, when one afternoon we saw the *Surprise* towing in the *Hermione*. Captain Hamilton had kept his word to the letter. He was three days before the port where she lay before he attempted his purpose. She was at anchor very close in shore, protected by a heavy half-moon and triangular battery. On the evening of the third day Captain Hamilton made his will, and after consulting with the officers he armed and manned the boats, and took with him the lieutenants, surgeon, a proportion of mids, and the lieutenant of marines, besides sailors and marines, making in the whole a hundred. He left the master and the remainder of the crew in charge of the ship, and ordered him when the boats shoved off to stand out by way of feint. The night was very dark. After a short pull they were alongside of the *Hermione*, which was evidently taken by surprise. On seeing the crew of the *Surprise* board them, they seized their boarding-pikes and cutlasses, and made a resistance which would have done them credit in a better cause. The conflict was severe and fatal to many of them; several jumped overboard. The struggle had continued about half an hour when her cables were cut and her topsails loosed. The remainder of the mutineers finding their numbers considerably decreased threw down their arms and surrendered, and at daylight the ship was in company with the *Surprise*.* Captain Hamilton received a severe contusion on the head, and had it not been for his surgeon, who was a powerful son of the Emerald Isle, he must have been killed. The loss on board the *Hermione* was considerable, that of the *Surprise* comparatively speaking trifling. Soon after they anchored I was sent on board the latter to learn the particulars which I have given above. The mutineers taken in the *Hermione* were but few, as the greater part were either on shore or had jumped overboard from her when they saw they should be overpowered. Before we sailed they were tried, and, with the exception of two who turned King's evidence, were hanged in everlasting jackets on the small islands without Port Royal harbour. I also

* See Appendix note (b).

learnt that my former messmate was lieutenant of the watch when the mutiny broke out, and one of the King's evidence mutineers gave me the following account:

'The captain,' said he, 'was very severe with the men, who were all good seamen, and they were determined to either run the ship on shore and desert, or else take her by force. This had been in their minds for months before it happened. At last,' said he, 'on a dark night, when the young lieutenant had the watch, our minds were made up. A party went to the cabin-door, knocked down the sentry, and entered it. The captain was in his cot, and he was soon overpowered. We threw him out of the cabin-window. Another party threw the officer of the watch over the larboard quarter, but he, being young and active, caught hold of the hammock-stanchion, when one of the men cut his hands off, and he soon dropped astern. The first lieutenant had been ill and keeping his cot, but on hearing the noise, he came up the hatchway in his shirt, when one of the carpenter's crew cut him down with an axe, and he was sent overboard with several others.' Captain Pigot, who commanded her, was no doubt a severe disciplinarian, but this was a most unheard-of, cruel and bloodthirsty mutiny; all the officers, both guilty – if there were any guilty – and innocent shared the same untimely fate, and surely if the crew found themselves oppressed and ill-used, they ought to have represented their complaints to the senior officer or the admiral, and they, in justice, would have been listened to; at least I hope so. I am sorry to state here that I have seen men sometimes flogged for trifles where a minor punishment would have been more appropriate. Caprice and partiality should never govern an officer's conduct; young lieutenants are too prone to make complaints to their captain without reflecting on the character of the offender. A thorough-bred seaman is very seldom in fault, and should he unfortunately trespass a little on the discipline of the ship, his offence should be visited as lightly as possible. Well-timed admonition will make a surer impression than half-a-dozen cats. I speak from experience. Before we sailed I had occasion to purchase some stockings, as I found on inquiry that my dingy-faced washerwoman had supplied her 'lubing bruder' with several pair belonging to me, to dance with her at a banjo hop, and took care I should not have them until the day before we sailed, which was Saturday. On examining them I found they were so worn into large holes that I could not put them on. Having obtained permission to go on shore, I repaired to the magazine. All shops in the West Indies are called magazines or stores, although some of them are so small that you are not able to turn round without hurting your elbows. The said shop, magazine or store was kept by a worthy, said to be honest, Israelite. I acquainted him with my wants. 'I can't sell you nothing-to-day,' he said; 'it is my Sabbath; but I will tell you what I can do. I will lend you six pair, and you can pay me to-morrow.' 'Thank you,' said I; 'where's your conscience? Tomorrow will be my Sabbath.' 'Ah,' said he 'I forgot that. Then you can pay me on Monday.' 'No,' said I; 'I'll pay you off with the foretopsail.' He laughed. 'Here, take the stockings, and pay me when you please.' This I did not do until I had given him a little note promising to pay him when we returned from our cruise.

We sailed the following morning, to cruise off the windward passages, where we fell in with two American sloops of war, cruising for an appetite. We were now tolerably well manned. Yellow fever and scurvy had taken their departure, and the only evil which remained with us was the blue devils, in consequence of the monotony so prevalent in a long cruise. We boarded several American vessels, and from one of them we procured some long, lanky turkeys. They stood so high that they appeared on stilts; they were all feather and bone, and Jonathan asked four dollars apiece for them, but we got him down to two by taking nine, which was all he had. I asked him if he had any dollar biscuits. 'No,' said he; 'but some of the men have a pretty considerable quantity of notions.' Here he called to one of them, and said, 'Nathan, I guess you bought some notions at Baltimore; bring them up, and let the officer see them.' Nathan was soon down the hatchway, and as quickly up again with his venture, or notions. They consisted of two pounds of infamous Yankee tea, three pounds of tobacco made into a roll, a jar of salt butter, a six-pound ham, and a bag of hickory nuts. The tea and ham I bought, and one of the boat's crew had the tobacco. The first proved too bad for even a midshipman's palate; and the ham, when the cover and sawdust were taken away, was animated by nondescripts, and only half of it eatable. I was tried by a court of inquiry by my messmates for want of discernment, and found guilty; and the Yankee who had cheated us was sentenced to be hanged, but as he was out of sight, the penalty was not carried into execution. We once more anchored at the mole, after having reconnoitred Porto Rico and part of Cuba, without any addition to our riches.

On the fifth evening of our arrival we heard the drums at the town beating to arms. We manned and armed three of our boats, and sent them on shore to inquire the cause of the alarm. The soldiers were forming to march, when one of our mids exclaimed: 'Look what a vast number of large fire-flies there are in the bushes over the town!' 'Are you sure those lights are fire-flies?' said a captain of one of the companies. 'Yes,' said the mid; 'I'll convince you in a jiffy.' Away he flew into the bushes, and in about five minutes returned, with his hat swarming with them, which produced a pale, bright light equal to several candles. The adventure produced much laughter at the expense of the piquet who had given the alarm, and the retreat was beat.

At particular periods of the year these little insects meet in the same manner that birds do on St Valentine's Day. The soldiers who formed the piquet had never seen anything of the kind before, and as the sentinel at a small fort at the entrance of the harbour had been shot by the enemy a few nights previously, they were determined not to be taken by surprise.

CHAPTER 9

A MOCK COURT-MARTIAL

After completing our water and stores, we sailed, and made the circuit of St Domingo, and a month afterwards returned to Port Royal, where we found the dignity ladies looking as blooming as black roses, and as it was understood that we were to be paid prize money, a general invitation was given to all the wardroom officers to a grand ball two days after our arrival; for be it known to you, gentle reader, that humble mids are never invited to dignity balls of the first class, which are given by the mustees and quadroons. Some of these ladies are beautifully formed, with handsome features. The second class generally consist of mulattos and blacks; these last are the most numerous; the mids at their balls are quite at home, and call for sangaree and porter-cup in first style.

At this period I had served my six years within a few months, when the captain sent for me, and told me he intended sending me on board the flagship on promotion. 'I send you there,' added he, 'beforehand, that you may have the opportunity of becoming known to the commander-in-chief, that at the expiration of your time you may be more immediately under his notice and be sure of your promotion.' I thanked him sincerely for his kind intention, and the following morning behold me, bed and traps, ensconced in the starboard midshipman's berth – one of the darkest holes of a cockpit I ever was yet in – on board the *Queen*, a ninety-eight gun ship. My messmates, ten in number, were the poorest of all poor mids. I was welcomed to the mess by the master's mate, who held in his hand a dirty, empty bottle, with a farthing candle lighted in the neck of it. 'Take care,' said he, 'you don't break your shins over the youngsters' chests.' 'Thank you,' said I; 'but I always thought a flag-ship's cockpit too well regulated to have chests athwartships.' 'Why, to tell you the truth,' replied he, 'those d——d youngsters are so often changing ships, being here to-day and promoted to-morrow, that it is impossible to keep either chests, mess or them in anything like order. I wish they were all at the devil.' 'Amen,' responded a person in the berth, whose nose was looming out of a hazy darkness, 'for, d——n them,' he continued, 'they have eaten all the cheese and have had a good swig at my rum-bottle, but I'll lay a point to windward of them yet.' These two hard officers were both old standards. The last who spoke was the mate of the hold, and the other of the lower deck. One had seen thirty-five and the other thirty-nine summers. The hope of a lieutenant's commission they had given up in despair, and were now looking out for a master's warrant. They were both brought up in the merchant service, and had entered the Navy at the beginning of the war as quarter-masters, and by their steady conduct were made master's mates, a situation which requires some considerable tact. The greater portion of my hopeful brother officers were from eighteen to twenty years of age. Their toast in a full bumper of grog of an evening was usually, 'A bloody war and a sickly season.' Some few were gentlemanly, but the majority were every-day characters – when on deck doing little, and when below doing less. Books they had very few or none; as an instance of it, we had only one, except the Hamilton Moore's and the Nautical Almanack, among ten of us, and that was 'Extracts from the Poets.' One of the mates above mentioned, seeing me moping with the blue devils, brought it me. 'Here,' said he, 'is a book nobody reads. I have looked into it myself, but there is so much dry stuff in it, that it makes my grog go too fast; but,' added he, '"Dry" is put under that part, so you can skip over it.' Now, reader, the most beautiful passages of this neglected book were from Dryden. The mate, happy, ignorant man, imagined, in his wisdom, that where the abridgment of this poet's name was placed, it was to indicate to the reader that the poetry was dry and not worth reading. Oh, Ignorance, thou art sometimes bliss, but in the present instance it were not folly to be wise! I attempted to take the Irish half-crown out of his mind by comparing some of Dryden's passages with the others, and he was as much convinced as a cable-tier coiling and stowing-hold officer is generally capable of being, that the 'Dry' poetry was the best.

The captain of this ship was from the north, I believe, strictly moral and as strict in discipline, admirably economical, and as regular in his habits as any old-clothes man in Monmouth Street. He kept all the cockpitonians on the *qui vive*, and as every recommendation went through him to the admiral it was but good policy for the mids to be on the alert. As all the lieutenants were constantly changing, those promoted making room for others, I shall not describe their characters, except noticing that the generality of them were good officers and gentlemen. A month after I joined we were ordered to sail, and on going out of Port Royal Roads we struck with great force on a sand bank called the Turtle Head. The master, who was as ignorant as he was conceited, had taken charge of the ship before she was out of pilot water, and in less than half an hour after the pilot left us she struck. As we were still in sight of the vessels at Port Royal, we made the signal for assistance, and soon afterwards saw a frigate and a store ship coming out towards us. The sea breeze began to set in, which drove us more on the shoal, notwithstanding that we had carried out two anchors ahead. At length she thumped so violently that we jumped at least a foot high from the deck. I could not refrain from smiling to see the captain and officers with serious, long, anxious faces, cutting capers against their will. The rudder and false keel soon parted company, and we all expected to see the masts jerked out of their steps. On sounding the well we found the ship making water rapidly. The pumps were set to work, but in vain. She soon sank in three fathoms and a half water, and we had eighteen feet of water in the hold. The frigate and store ship, with some smaller vessels, had anchored as near us as they could with safety. The small craft came alongside and took out our guns and stores, and one hundred additional men were sent on board us to work the pumps. Pumps were also sent from the dockyard, and were introduced into the hold through the decks, which had been scuttled for that purpose. On the morning of the third day we had got everything, except the lower masts and bowsprit, on board the lighters, and by the exertions of the men at the pumps, which had been incessant for three days and nights, we had lightened her, and she floated off the shoal. The frigate took us in tow, and in three hours afterwards we were lashed alongside the dockyard. The fatigue and want of rest, for not a single hammock had been piped down during the time the ship was on shore, threw about fifty men into the sick list, and several of them died at the hospital afterwards. The seamen of the fleet in general had a great aversion to go to the hospital, and when ill used to entreat the doctor not to send them there. It was said of the matrons, which did not redound to their credit if true, that when a seaman died, and was reported to them, they exclaimed: 'Poor fellow! bring me his bag, and mind everything belonging to him is put into it.' This they considered their perquisite. Surely this is wrong and robbery! Ah, Mr Hume! why were you a puling, helpless babe at that time? Had you been a man and known it, you would have called for reformation and been the seaman's friend.

We had now a difficult and arduous duty to perform, which was to heave the ship down keel out. I was stationed on the lower deck with a party of thirty seamen to keep the chain pumps going as long as they would work – that is, until the ship was nearly on her side. In about twenty minutes she was nearly on her beam ends, when all the temporary stanchions which had been fixed to keep the deck from yielding gave way like a regiment of black militia in chase of Obie, or Three-fingered Jack in the Whee Mountains, when they are in full retreat. I was standing at this time in no enviable position, my feet rested on the combings of the main hatchway with my back against the deck. I expected every moment to have my brains knocked out, but this apprehension was soon superseded by a cry from the shore of, 'Make for the stern ports and jump overboard; the hawsers are stranded; there will be a boat ready to pick you up.' 'Sooner said than done,' thinks I to myself; 'I wish with all my heart that the first lieutenant who ordered me here was in my place, and he would find the order practically impossible.' Another cry was then heard: 'Hold all fast on board!' 'You are a wise man,' thinks I again for that order; 'it is the very thing we are determined to do.' 'All's safe,' was the next squall through the trumpet, 'the mastheads are secured to the beams.' 'Thank you for nothing,' said I to myself, 'it's more good luck than good management.' When the ship was hove down, we got some of the pumps to work on the side next the water, as it had gone from the well, and in a few hours kept her clear. On the fourth day we righted her, as the dockyard maties had botched her up.

We had now to wait about six weeks for the rudder; in the meanwhile we got on board the water, provisions and stores, and fresh powder, the last having had a ducking. From the time the ship came to the yard we had slept and messed in the capstan house, consequently we had not an opportunity of holding a cockpit inquiry on the master's conduct for running the vessel on shore. The second day after getting on board we put on our scrapers and toasting-forks, and assembled in the larboard berth, which was illuminated for the occasion by four farthing candles. The court consisted of fourteen members. I was chosen president; a black man who waited on our berth was to personate the master. After taking our seats according to seniority, we declared we would show neither favour nor partiality to the prisoner, but try him fairly by the rules of the cockpit. I began, as president, by asking him the reason he let the pilot quit the ship before she was clear of the shoals.

Prisoner: ''Cause, massa, I had berry good opinion of myself, and I tink I sabby de ground better den dat black scorpion who call himself pilot.'

President: 'If you knew the channels better than the pilot, how came you to let the ship get on shore on the Turtle Head shoal?'

Prisoner: 'Ah, Massa President, me no tink Turtle Head lib dere; me tink him lib tree legs more west. De chart say him moral impossible he lib so near Port Royal.'

Here the chart was examined, and the shoal was in reality laid down in a wrong place. This saved the master, or he must have been smashed.

Here the court adjourned to consider the sentence. After laughing and joking some short time in the larboard wing, we again assembled looking as solemn as a Lord Chancellor, when I, as the noble president, addressed the prisoner as follows:

'Prisoner, this honourable Court having duly considered the unseamanlike and stupid blunder you have committed, do adjudge you to be suspended from your duty as master of this ship for six calendar months, in order to give you time to reflect on the mischief you have done and the great expense you have occasioned by running His Majesty's ship on a shoal called the Turtle Head; and they advise you not to be so self-sufficient in future, and, if it be not morally impossible, to clothe yourself with the robe of humility, and to put all your conceit into the N.W. corner of your chest, and never let it see daylight. And the Court further adjudges you, in consequence of your letting the pilot quit the ship before she was in sea-way, to be severely reprimanded and also admonished as to your future conduct, and you are hereby suspended, reprimanded, and admonished accordingly. I dissolve this Court. Master Blacky, get dinner ready as fast as you can, as we are very sharp set.'

'Yes, massa,' was the answer; 'to-day you hab for dinner salt junk and bargeman biscuit, and to-morrow you hab change.' 'What do you say, you black woolly-headed rascal?' said one of the mids. 'Why, I say, massa, you hab change tomorrow – you hab bargeman biscuit and salt junk.' 'Why,' said another horrified mid, 'I heard the caterer order you to get some fish from the canoe alongside.' 'Yes, massa, dat berry true, but de d——d black scorpion would not sell 'um to massa midshipman, cause he no hab pay for fish last time.' 'If you mention that again,' said one of my messmates, 'I'll crack your black cocoa-nut, and if you do not get some to-morrow, I'll take care your grog shall be stopped.' Here the caterer of the mess interfered by promising the mess should have some fish for their dinner next day, and the contest ended. Master Blacky started up the ladder to stand the wrangle in the galley for our dinner, and shortly after we attacked a tolerably good-looking piece of King's own, with the addition of some roasted plantains, which our black factotum had forgotten to mention in his bill of fare.

Having procured our rudder we sailed to prove, the middies said, 'Whether promotion should be stopped or not by the ship's sinking or floating?' Fortunately for us, by the aid of the chain pumps twice a day, she did the latter. We continued on a man-of-war's cruise there and back again for five weeks, and then returned to our former anchorage. During this short cruise I had prepared myself for passing, and soon after our arrival, my time being served, I requested the first lieutenant to speak to the captain that I might pass for a lieutenant. 'Go yourself,' said he, 'and tell him. He is in his room at the capstan house. I'll give you the jolly boat.' I was soon on shore and at the door of his room. I knocked. 'Enter,' said a voice not at all encouraging. 'What do you want, any orders?' 'No, sir,' said I, with one of my best quarter-deck bows, which appeared to soften him. 'I hope I am not intruding; I have taken the liberty of waiting on you, sir, to acquaint you that I have served my time.' He was half-shaved, and my visit appeared unfortunately ill-timed, and I began to apprehend by the expression of his countenance, and the flourishes he made with his razor, he intended making me a head shorter. 'Who sent you to me at this inconvenient time?' asked he. 'The first lieutenant, sir,' said I; 'he thought it was better for me to inform you before you went to the Admiral's pen.' 'Oh, very well; you may go; shut the door, and let the barge come for me at seven o'clock.' On board I repaired, and delivered the message. I kept pondering whether my hardy, half-shaven captain's manner was favourable to the information I had given him or not. My messmates were anxious to know how I was received. 'Not very graciously,' was my reply. Next morning, to my agreeable surprise, I was ordered to take the barge, and go on board the *Alarm* frigate, where I met my old captain, who shook hands with me, and two others. 'Well,' said the former, 'are you prepared to prove you are an able seaman and an officer?' 'I hope so, sir,' said I. He introduced me to his two brother officers, and informed them I had sailed with him some time, and that I had frequently charge of a watch. We all descended to the cabin, where Hamilton Moore's 'Epitome,' a slate and pencil were placed before me. I was first asked several questions respecting coming to an anchor, mooring, tacking, veering, and taking in sail. I was then desired to find the time of high water at different places, and the variation of the compass.

They appeared satisfied with my answers and solutions, and before I left the ship they presented me with my passing certificate. On the following day I took the oath of allegiance, abused the Pope – poor, innocent man – and all his doctrines, and received my commission for a twenty-four gun ship which I joined the day after. I left some of my messmates with regret, as they were made of the very stuff our Navy required.

CHAPTER 10

MORE CRUISING

On introducing myself to my new captain, who was a short, corpulent, open-countenanced man, he informed me he had conversed with my former captain respecting me. 'We lost both the lieutenants by the yellow fever the latter part of last cruise,' said he, 'and if you like to be first lieutenant, I will request the Admiralty to give me an acting officer.' I thanked him for his good opinion, but begged leave to decline being first. About a fortnight afterwards, during which time no other lieutenant had joined, the captain again asked me if I had altered my mind. 'And,' added he, 'the time you have been on board has given you some insight respecting a first lieutenant's duty. Your early rising I much approve, and your regularity with the duty pleases me. Let me write for an acting lieutenant.' I made him due acknowledgments but still declined, pleading the want of experience. 'Well,' said he, 'if you will not, I must ask for a senior officer,' and soon afterwards he was appointed. Another fortnight expired, when we sailed for the Gulf of Mexico. I will now rest on my oars a little, and as I have the watch below, I will amuse myself by sketching the outline of the gun-room inmates.

The first lieutenant knew his duty, but was too fond of the contents of his case-bottles of rum, which made him at times very irritable and hasty; in other respects he was a sociable messmate. The second was a kind of nondescript; he was certainly sober, and I hope honest, fond of adventure, and always volunteered when the boats were sent on any expedition. He was sociable, and frequently rational, although too often sanguine where hope was almost hopeless. Three-and-twenty summers had passed over his head, but still there was much to correct. He was generous and open-hearted, and never could keep a secret, which often got him into a scrape with ladies of all colours. The value of money never entered his head, and when he received a cool hundred, he spent it coolly, but not without heartfelt enjoyment. The master comes next. He was a little, natty man; we presumed he had been rolled down Deal beach in his infancy, where pebbles without number must have come in rude contact with his face, for it was cruelly marred. He had made some trips in the East India Service, which had given him an air of consequence. He was not more than twenty-four years of age, and certainly clever in his profession. I will now bring forward the doctor, who appeared to doctor everybody but himself. He was every inch a son of Erin, could be agreeable or the reverse as the fit seized him, fond of argument, fond of rum, and sometimes fond of fighting. To see him put his hand to his mouth was painful; it was so tremulous that half the contents of what he eat or drank fell from it, yet he was never tipsy, although the contents of three bottles of port wine found their way very glibly down his throat at a sitting.

Now I will have a dead-set at the purser, who was generally purseless. He was the gayest of the gay, very tall, very expensive, and always in love. The first fiddle of the mess and caterer, fond of going on a boat expedition, very fond of prize-money, and as fond of getting rid of it. He used to say, 'It was a terrible mistake making me a purser. I shall never be able to clear my accounts,' and this was literally the case. Some years afterwards he was appointed to a large frigate, but by the irregularity of his conduct, although his captain was his friend, he was by a court-martial dismissed the Service. When I heard this I was much concerned, as there were some good points about him. I have now handed up all the gun-room officers. Other characters in the ship I shall not describe; some were good, some bad, and some indifferent, but I am happy to remark the first-named preponderated. We made the Grand Cayman, and sent a cutter to the shore to purchase turtle and fruit. In about an hour and a half she came off with three turtle, some yams, plantains, cocoa-nuts, and a few half-starved fowls. I had cautioned the purser not to buy any grunters, as those poor animals blown out with water we had purchased from these honest islanders in days of yore, were still fresh in my memory.

The same evening we made Cape Antonio, and cruised between that cape and the Loggerhead Keys for some days without seeing anything but two American vessels from New Orleans. One of them gave us notice of a Mexican armed zebec ready to sail with treasure from Mexico for the Havannah. This news elated us. We were all lynx-eyed and on the alert. The youngsters were constantly at the masthead with glasses, in the sanguine hope of being the first to announce such good fortune. Alas! we cruised from the mouth of the Mississippi to the Bay of Campechy for five long weeks, at the period of which we saw a vessel we made certain was that which was to make our fortunes, and our heads were filled with keeping our kittereens and having famous champagne dinners at Spanish Town. After a chase of seven hours, we came up with her, but judge of our chagrin! She was the same rig as the American captain described. I was sent on board her, and expected to have returned with the boat laden with ingots, bars of gold and silver cobs. Oh, mortification! not easily to be effaced! On examining her, she proved, with the exception of four barrels of quick-silver, to have no cargo of any value. I really was so disappointed that I was ashamed to return on board, and when I did, and made my report, there was a complete metamorphosis of faces. Those that were naturally short became a fathom in length, and those that were long frightful to behold. The order was given to burn her and take out the seven Spaniards who composed her crew. On interrogating the patroon, or master, of her, he informed us that the vessel with the precious metal had sailed from Mexico two months before, and had arrived at the Havannah. The Yankee captain who had given us this false information, and made us for five weeks *poissons d'Avril*, was remembered in our prayers; whether they ascended or descended is a problem unsolved. We remained in the Gulf of Mexico jogging backwards and forwards, like an armadillo in an enclosure, for ten days longer, and then shaped our course for the coast of Cuba, looked into the Havannah, saw nothing which appeared ready for sailing, and made all sail for the Florida shore. The following morning it was very foggy, when about noon we had the felicity of finding that the ship had, without notice, placed herself very comfortably on a coral reef, where she rested as composedly as grandmamma in her large armchair. We lost no time in getting the boats and an anchor out in the direction from whence we came. Fortunately it was nearly calm, otherwise the ship must have been wrecked. The process of getting her off was much longer than that of getting her on. The mids, I understood, declared she was tired of the cruise and wished to rest. In the afternoon it became clear, when we saw an armed schooner close to us, which hoisted English colours and sent a boat to us. The captain of her came on board and informed us that his vessel was a Nassau privateer, and he tendered all the assistance in his power to get us afloat. As the ship appeared disinclined to detach herself from her resting-place, we sent most of the shot and some of the stores on board this vessel, when we began to lift, and in a short time she was again afloat, and as she did not make water we presumed her bottom was not injured. On examining the chart, we found it was the Carisford reef that had so abruptly checked the progress of His Majesty's ship. Nothing dismayed, we cruised for a week between Capes Sable and Florida, until we were one night overtaken by a most tremendous thunderstorm, which split the fore and maintop-sails, carried away the jib-boom and maintop-sail yard, struck two of the men blind, and shook the ship fore and aft. It continued with unabated rage until daylight.

We soon replaced the torn sails and got another yard across and jib-boom out.

The following day we were joined by a frigate, and proceeded off the Bay of Matanzas. Towards evening we perceived three dark-looking schooners enter the bay. As it was nearly calm, we manned and armed four boats, two from the frigate, under the direction of her first lieutenant and my senior officer, and two from our ship, under my orders. We muffled our oars and pulled quietly in. The night was very dark and the navigation difficult, owing to the numerous coral reefs and small mangrove islands. At length we discovered them anchored in a triangle to support each other. We gave way for the largest, and when within about half pistol-shot they opened their fire on us. Two of the boats were struck and my commanding officer knocked overboard, but he was soon afterwards picked up, and, except a slight wound in the knee, unhurt. We persevered and got alongside the one we had singled out. She received us as warmly as if she had known us for years. I took the liberty of shooting a man in her main rigging who was inclined to do me the same kind office, had I not saved him the trouble. We attempted cutting away her boarding netting, and in so doing three men were severely wounded. Her decks appeared well filled with men: some of their voices were, I am certain, English. After a struggle of some minutes, in which one of the boats had not joined, my senior officer, who had five of his men wounded, ordered the boats to pull off. Shall I say I was disappointed? I most assuredly was, and my boat's crew murmured. I desired them to be silent. The boat which had lost her way now came up, and received a broadside from the vessel we were retreating from, which almost sank her, and killed and wounded four of her crew. The order was again given to pull off as fast as possible. As the senior officer neared me in his boat, I asked him, as we had found the large schooner so strong, if it were not desirable to attempt the others. His answer was yes, were they not so well armed and so close to each other. 'But,' said he, 'it is my orders that the boats repair on board their own ships, as my wounded men are dying, and I am suffering the devil's own torments.' 'So much for a broken-down expedition,' thinks I to myself. 'If the bull had not been taken by the horns, something might have been effected.'

On joining my ship I reported the wounded men, who were sent to their hammocks, after having been dressed by the doctor, who declared their wounds, though severe, not to be serious. 'Well,' said the captain, 'what have you done?' 'Worse than nothing,' replied I. 'I never was on so sorry or so badly planned an expedition. The enemy's armed vessels were on the alert, whilst we were half asleep, and they were anchored so close under the land that we were nearly on the broadside of the largest before we perceived her, and she gave it us most handsomely, and I give her credit for her spirited conduct.' 'You are a generous enemy,' said my skipper. 'Not at all,' returned I; 'it is my opinion that the man who commands that vessel, who has given us such a good trimming, deserves well of his country.' I then made him acquainted with all the particulars. 'My opinion of the officer who had the management of this boat affair has been hitherto favourable,' said the captain. 'He is certainly a young man, but his captain is perfectly satisfied with his method of carrying on the duty in the ship.' 'Yes,' said I; 'but ship duty and boat duty are different.' Here the conversation, which was irksome to my feelings, terminated. A few days floated away, when the first lieutenant had a dispute with the captain, and he was suspended from his duty. I was sent for into the cabin, when the captain told me he was happy in the opportunity of again offering me the situation of first lieutenant. 'For,' added he, 'Mr G and I shall never accord after what has happened, and if he does not effect an exchange with a junior officer to yourself, I will try him by a court-martial.'

Two weeks more finished our unsuccessful cruise. We bore up for the Florida Stream, ran through the Turks' Island passage, made St Domingo and Cuba, passed over the Pismire shoal of the N.E. end of Jamaica, and anchored at Port Royal. The morning following we received letters from England. I must here relate an incident which was most feelingly trying to one of the youngsters. He had, among others, received a letter from his mother, and to be more retired had gone abaft the mizzen-mast to read it. The sea-breeze was blowing fresh, when, just as he had opened it and read the first words, it blew from his hands overboard. Poor little fellow! The agonised look he gave as it fell into the water is far beyond description. He was inclined to spring after it. Had he known how to swim he would not have hesitated a moment. Unfortunately all the boats were on duty, or it might have been recovered. Mr G, the first lieutenant, effected his exchange, and a fine young man joined as second. I was now positively fixed as first. I was invited to dignity balls without number, and had partners as blooming as Munster potatoes.

My servant was of a shining jet colour, and a fiddler. I took lodgings on shore, and after the duty of the day was performed, about half after six o'clock in the evening, I went to my *château*, taking with me Black George and his fiddle, where my shipmates and a few friends of all colours amused themselves with an innocent hop and sangaree, for I had now grown too fine to admit the introduction of vulgar grog. Even the smell of it would have occasioned the ladies to blush like a blue tulip. After amusing ourselves on shore and performing our duty on board, we were ready for sea the fifth week after our arrival, and on the sixth we sailed for the south side of St Domingo. We had been cruising a few days off the port of Jacmel, when the *Nimrod* cutter and the *Abergavenny*'s tender joined us. The lieutenants of both vessels came on board, and related the following fact in my hearing: – The former vessel had detained an honest trading Yankee brig on suspicion, and had sent her to Jamaica to be examined. The latter vessel caught a large shark the morning after, and found in its maw the false papers of this said American brig, which she had thrown overboard when the *Nimrod* chased her.

'Will you oblige me by a relation of the circumstance?' said our skipper to Whiley, who commanded the cutter. 'It happened in the following manner: I had information of this Charlestown vessel before I left Port Royal, and I was determined to look keenly after her. I had been off the Mosquito shore, where I understood she was bound with gunpowder and small arms. At length I fell in with her, but could not find any other papers than those which were regular, nor any powder or firearms; but as I had good information respecting her, I was determined to detain her, even if I burnt my fingers by so doing. The morning after I sent her for Jamaica I fell in with Lieutenant Fitton, who hailed me, and begged me to go on board him. When I got on the quarter-deck of the tender I saw several large sheets of paper spread out on the companion.

"'Hulloa!" said I; "Fitton, what have you here?" "Why," said he, "I have a very curious story to relate; for that reason I wished you to come on board me. This morning we caught a shark, and, singular to tell you, on cutting him up we found those papers (which you see drying) in his maw. He must have been preciously hard set, poor fellow. I have examined them, and find they belong to the *Nancy*, of Charlestown." "The *Nancy*, of Charlestown," said I. "That is the very brig I have sent to Jamaica.' 'Well, then,' said Fitton, 'they are yours, and I congratulate you on the discovery and your good fortune.'" 'This is singularly remarkable,' said our captain; 'I hope you have taken care of the jaw of the shark. It must be sent to the Vice-Court of Admiralty at Jamaica as a memento of the fact, and a remembrancer to all Yankee captains who are inclined to be dishonest.' 'A good hint,' said Fitton; 'it shall be done, sir.' And it was done, as I well recollect its being suspended over where the American masters of detained vessels stood when they desired to make oath.

In the evening these gentlemen, after having dined on board us, repaired to their respective vessels, and we soon after parted company. The following day we anchored off the Isle de Vâche, near Port au Paix, St Domingo, and sent the two cutters in shore on a cruise of speculation, under my orders. On quitting the ship we all blacked our faces with burnt cork and tied coloured handkerchiefs round our heads, in order to deceive the fishing canoes. On nearing the shore we discovered a schooner sailing along close to the beach. In a short time afterwards we boarded her, and found she was a French vessel in ballast from Port au Paix, bound to Jacmel. She was quite new, and not more than fifty tons burden. We took possession of her, but unfortunately, when we were in the act of securing the prisoners, the enemy fired at us from the shore. We had three men severely wounded and the schooner's crew one. We lost no time in getting the boats ahead to tow her off, and although the enemy's fire was frequent, it did no further mischief. On nearing the Isle de Vâche we found the ship gone, and, notwithstanding we were without a compass, I was determined to bear up before the sea-breeze for Jamaica. Fortunately we fell in with the *A.* frigate, who took out the wounded men, and wished me to burn the prize. This proposal I rejected. The following evening we reached Port Royal, and I sold her for £140. In a fortnight afterwards the ship arrived. On joining her the captain informed me that three hours after we had quitted her two vessels hove in sight, and as they looked suspicious he got under weight and chased, with the intention of again returning to his anchorage after having made them out. This he was not able to effect, as in point of sailing they were far superior to the *Volage*, and after a useless chase of a night and a day, they got into the port of St Domingo. The ship regained the anchorage the day afterwards, and fired guns, hoping we were on the island; but after an interval of some hours, without seeing the boats, the captain despatched an officer with a flag of truce to Port au Paix, thinking it likely we had been in want of provisions, or overpowered by gunboats. The officer returned with the information of our having been on the coast, but that we had not been seen for two days. The ship again put to sea, and after a short cruise came to Port Royal, where happily they found us.

CHAPTER 11

A JAMAICA PLANTATION

Soon after we arrived I was invited to spend a few days in the mountains. We were mounted on mules, and started from Kingston at four o'clock in the morning. Some part of the road was very narrow and wound round the mountain we were going to. At one of the angles, or turns, the purser, who was one of the party, had got his mule too near the precipice, and in a few seconds was rolling down the declivity, the mule first and he afterwards. Fortunately for both animals, there were several dwarf cotton-trees about half-way down, which brought them up with a severe round turn. The planter, who, I presumed, had seen exploits of this kind before, lost no time in procuring from the nearest estate some negroes with cords, and in a few minutes they were extricated from their perilous situation. The purser was much cut about the head, and both his arms severely contused. The poor animal had one of his legs broken, and it was a charity to shoot him on the spot.

As we were not far from the estate we were going to, the black men, who manifested much willingness and humanity, procured a hammock, which they suspended to a pole, and carried with much ease my poor unfortunate messmate, who, notwithstanding his bruises, kept joking on his misadventure. Another hour brought us to a delightful pavilion-built house surrounded by verandahs. It was like a Paradise; the grounds were highly cultivated and produced sugar-canes, coffee, cotton and pimento. The air was quite embalmed, and the prospect from the house was enchanting. I could see the ships at Port Royal, which appeared like small dark dots. The estate belonged to a young lady, a minor, residing in London, and it was managed by her uncle. The number of slaves it contained was three hundred. They appeared to me, the four days I remained among them, as one happy family. I visited, with the surgeon of the estate, several of the cabins or huts; each had a piece of ground to grow plantains, yams, sweet potatoes, cocoas, etc. Some grew a few melons, nearly all had fowls, and several had two or three pigs. The whole of Sunday and the Saturday afternoon were their own, on which days they repaired to

Spanish Town or Kingston markets to sell their vegetables, fruit and poultry. The pigs, the doctor informed me, were generally bought at the market price by the overseers. 'This estate,' resumed the doctor, 'is very well conducted, and during the five years I have been here we have only lost three slaves, and two of those were aged. I need not say that the manager is a man of humanity – you know him as a gentleman. The whip is seldom used, and only for theft, which scarcely ever occurs. And I do not think that, were they free to-morrow, they would leave Mr W, who is an Englishman.'

On the second morning of my residence here I rose at four o'clock, and the view from a kind of field called the Park was most remarkable and picturesque in the extreme. Below me in all the valleys was a dense fog, resembling a white woolly-looking could, stretched out like an immense lake. The lower mountains appeared like so many islands. At first I stared in astonishment at so novel a sight, and it reminded me of the picture of the Deluge, when all the lower world was under water.

At breakfast I mentioned to Mr W the extraordinary scene I had witnessed. 'To you,' said he, 'it may appear strange, but for at least four months in the year we have those settling clouds or fogs. They first form on the higher mountains, and then descend into the valleys. About seven o'clock, as the sun gains force, they disperse. But,' added he, 'they are very necessary to the young plantations, which they moisten profusely.'

The purser was now sufficiently recovered to join us in our rambles of an evening, in one of which we came near a large tamarind-tree, where a number of humming-birds were flying around. 'I would not hurt any of those little creatures for a trifle,' said Mr W. 'Were I to do it in the presence of any of the negroes, they would immediately conclude I was wicked. They consider them sacred, and, although they might fetch a good price, I have never known one to be sold.'

On the fifth morning the mules were ordered at an early hour, and we bid adieu to our kind and hospitable friend, who promised to spend a day with us on board on our return from our cruise. We arrived at Kingston at eleven o'clock without accident, and were on board by dinner-time. On the following Sunday we put to sea, and a week afterwards were on our old cruising grounds in the Mona passage and off Porto Rico.

We again sent two boats away on a speculative cruise with the second lieutenant, who a few hours after returned with a very handsome Spanish schooner, about forty tons, in ballast. We now put all our wise heads together, whether to send her to Jamaica or make a tender of her. As I was the first consulted, I voted for the last, 'As were she to be sent to Jamaica,' said I, 'the expenses of her condemnation will most likely exceed what she may be sold for. In this case, we should not only lose our prize, but have to pay for capturing her.' 'That is very true,' said the captain, 'and I have experienced the fact, which I will relate in a few words:

'I took a French ship from Antwerp bound to Caen, laden with salt. I took her into Portsmouth. A few months afterwards I received a letter from my agent to inform me that the vessel and cargo had been sold; but in consequence of the duty paid to Government on the salt, she had not covered the expenses of her trial by eight pounds, which my agents were obliged to pay for me to the Proctors.'

'It is a hard case,' said we all. 'After risking our lives and distressing the ships by sending officers and men away in captured vessels, we are sometimes informed, as a reward for the risk, anxiety and trouble, that instead of receiving we have to pay money.' This most certainly cries aloud for reform, and it appears monstrous that sailors find so little support either in the House of Commons or at the Admiralty. Soldiers have many advocates in the former, but sailors few, and those few not worth having. The first Secretary of the Admiralty is generally a member of Parliament, but he only concerns himself with the affairs of the Admiralty; but ask him respecting the habits of sailors, he may tell it to the marines, for the captain of the main-top will never believe him. It is true the Admiralty have now given orders for captains to make a quarterly return of all punishments inflicted on seamen. This I think quite right, as it must in a great measure strike down the hand of tyranny. Nor do I find fault with the encouragement and respectability which has lately been given to the petty officers. I am only astonished it was not given years ago, but we are still in our infancy.

Before I quit this subject, I am compelled in justice to ask both Admiralty and Lower House the reason why old and meritorious officers are so shamefully neglected. The commanders above the year 1814 may, I hope, expect promotion in heaven, as I fear they never will meet with it on earth. One would suppose the Admiralty were ashamed of having such old officers, and wish to forget them altogether, or probably they think they are too well paid and deserve, after spending the best part of their lives in toil and service, nothing more. As for the old lieutenants, God help them! – they must contrive to hang on by the eyelids until they slip their cables in this, and make sail into another world. Is the hand of interest so grasping that the Lords of the Admiralty cannot administer justice to old officers and promote four or six from the head of the list on a general promotion as well as those very young officers, who most likely were not in being when their seniors entered the Service, nor have many of them seen a shot fired except in a preserve? It has been said that the patronage for the promotion of officers in the Navy is entirely in the hands of the First Lord, who is a civilian. If this be true, interest and not service must be his order of the day. He cannot know the merits or demerits of officers but from others. Possessing this ignorance, it is but a natural conclusion, though no consolation, to those who suffer from it, that he should only promote those who are recommended to him, and this accounts for so many officers who entered the Navy at the conclusion or since the termination of the war being made post-captains or commanders. We read that promotion comes neither from the east nor the west. In a recent instance it came from the north. It may be advisable for some old officers to make a trip to the coast of Nova Zembla, get frozen in for two or three years among the Nova Zemblians and Yakee Yaws, come home, present themselves to the Admiralty, who would undoubtedly promote them, then they would have an audience and receive knighthood from a higher personage. This, as we all know, has occurred, and may occur again, more particularly so if they should be able to add to the important information the last persevering and gallant adventures brought to England. The French beg a thousand pardons when they have committed any little indiscretion; an Englishman says simply, 'I beg your pardon.' As such, gentle reader, I sincerely beg yours, for having led you such a Tom Coxe's traverse.

To resume my narrative. We came to a conclusion that the schooner should be fitted up as our tender, and as we had all taken a fancy to her she should be called the *Fancy*. We put on board her a twelve-pounder carronade and mounted four half-pound swivels on her gunwales. The second lieutenant, as he captured her, was to command her; he took with him one of the senior midshipmen and sixteen good seamen. After receiving his orders and provisions he parted company for the north side of Cuba, and was desired to rendezvous every Sunday afternoon off Cape Maize. This was Tuesday. In the meanwhile we sent a boat into a small bay to the westward of the Cape to fill some small casks with water from a fall we saw from the ship. Three hours afterwards she returned, not only with water but also with three large pigs, which the master, who had direction of the boat, had shot. At last Sunday arrived; we were off the Cape, but no *Fancy*. The weather had been very squally, and we thought it probable she might have got to leeward. The following morning we spoke an American brig from St Jago, who informed us that she had passed a Spanish schooner laden with tobacco at anchor at the mouth of the river. We stood in, and discovered the ship with the glass. In the evening I volunteered to cut her out, and at dusk we started in a six-oared cutter. By eleven at night I was within the mouth of the river and under the Moro Castle and another large fort. Our oars being muffled prevented any noise. We pulled round the entrance twice, but to no purpose, as the vessel had removed and we could not discover her. Daylight was breaking as we cleared the shore, when we saw a vessel which appeared like our ship standing towards us, but were with reason alarmed at seeing three more. I immediately concluded they were enemy's privateers. My fears were soon confirmed by their hoisting Spanish colours, and the nearest began firing at us. I had eight men and a midshipman with me, and we all did our utmost to escape. Unfortunately our ship was not in sight, and after a fatiguing and anxious pull for three hours and having two of the boat's crew wounded, I was, in consequence of the nearest privateer being within pistol shot, obliged to surrender. We were taken possession of by the *Gros Souris*, a Spanish zebec with a long eighteen-pounder and seventy-five men. The other vessels were a three-masted zebec with an English sloop which she had captured and a schooner. Two hours afterwards we were all at anchor in the river, and the next day proceeded to St Jago, where I had, with the crew, the felicity of being put into the gaol. In the afternoon I received my parole, as also did the youngster who was with me. The American Consul, Mr B, very handsomely sent a person to conduct me to the American hotel. This said tavern was kept by a Boston widow, who was really a good sort of person. The *table d'hôte* was very tolerable, and I had the honour of being acquainted with some of the American skippers. Some were very *outré*, coarse and vulgar, but two of them were agreeable and very civil. The morning after my arrival the Governor sent for me. On being introduced he requested me to take a seat, a cup of coffee and a cigar. The two former I accepted, the latter I refused, at which he expressed some surprise, as he imagined all Englishmen smoked. He then requested me to relate through an American interpreter the manner in which I had been made prisoner, if I had been treated well on board the privateer, or if any of my clothes had been taken. I answered him very promptly to the last question by informing him that I had nothing to lose, as I left the ship only in the clothes I stood in. After a pause he sent for his secretary, and desired him to write a note to the American Consul, who in a short time after made his appearance. 'Here,' said he, 'is a British officer who has been unfortunately taken by one of our vessels; as you speak his language, tell him from me that I am very sorry for his accident, and that I have requested you to let him have any money he may require, for which I will be responsible.'

I made suitable acknowledgement for so noble and disinterested an offer. I told him in my own language, for he understood it, and spoke it imperfectly, that it was out of my power to thank him sufficiently for his generosity to an enemy and a stranger. 'The first, I am sure,' replied he, 'you are no longer; the last you are, and call forth my sympathy and protection,' offering me his hand, which I took respectfully. 'Now,' continued he, 'we understand each other, and I shall be happy to see you without ceremony whenever you like to come.' Here he turned to the Consul, and after some complimentary conversation, he said, 'Take this officer with you and treat him as a friend, for he has found one in me.'

We made our bows and withdrew. In our walk to his house I could not forbear speaking of the great kindness the Governor had evinced towards me. 'I am not astonished at it,' said the Consul; 'I do not think since he has had the government of this place he has ever seen a lieutenant of your Navy, and as he considers you an officer of rank, he is determined as an act of policy to make the most of you. His character is that of the high Spanish, and I may add Irish, school, for his grandfather was an Irishman, and died ennobled and a general officer in their service. His name is O'B.'

This conversation brought us to the Consul's residence. 'Walk in,' said he, 'and rest yourself.' After having conversed on the unprofitable service and risk of boating, he asked me if my purse wanted replenishing. I answered in the affirmative. He gave me what I required, for which I gave him an order on my agent at Kingston. Before we parted, he invited me to ride out and spend the evening, which I accepted. At three in the afternoon we were on horseback. 'Sailors,' remarked he to me, 'are not generally considered Nimrods. They ride too fast and sit too much over the horse's shoulders; but probably,' continued he, 'you British sailors ride much better than the Americans, for they certainly do not make much figure on horseback.' 'I frankly acknowledge,' said I, 'that I am no horseman, for the last time I was mounted was with a party of landsmen who had asked me to dine at Rock Fort, but I blush to relate that when we had reached the Parade at Kingston, my horse took fright at the black soldiers who were exercising. I, finding I could not manage him, gave him the bridle, when he ran into the ranks, knocked down one of the sergeants, and would have knocked my brains out against the upper part of the stable door, if fortunately a man had not been there, who threw up both his arms, which stopped him from entering.'

'How did you proceed afterwards?' inquired he; 'Did you lose your dinner?' 'No,' said I, laughing, 'that would have been very hard on the rest of the party, whose mouths were anxious to devour the fish ordered at the tavern. I procured a more quiet horse, and we proceeded at a parson's trot, and did ample honour to our feast, for we were very hungry on our arrival.' In our ride I found the country in this part of Cuba highly cultivated. Large patches of sugar-canes, cocoa, orange and lime groves met my eye in every direction, and in some places near lagoons or pieces of water rice was cultivated. I also observed some plantations of tobacco. Three and four times a week I rode out with the Consul, and found him and our excursions very agreeable. He informed me he had been several times in England, and was much pleased with his visits. 'I found,' said he, 'the men prompt and regular in business, as well as hospitable; but,' added he, 'the greater part of your women have the minds of angels, and make the best wives in the world. In saying this I only allude to the society I moved in – the merchants of the higher classes. I much regret,' continued he, 'that the better sort of my countrymen have not the polish of yours. As long as they give up all their time to dollar-making they cannot be anything more than what they are.'

One morning at an early hour I was called to attend the Governor. On my seeing him, he appeared agitated; he had a kind of despatch in his hand.

'I am sorry to say,' said he, 'I have bad news for you. I have received accounts from the coast that another of your boats has been taken. The officer and three men have been shot, and five taken prisoners. I have reprimanded my people severely for firing on them, as they were much superior to yours in numbers. The officer who commanded our party assures me he could not prevent it, as the natives near where your boat landed had been plundered of most part of their live stock, and several of their pigs were found shot near their huts.' By the description given I knew it to be the master, who had before brought off pigs which he had shot. I told him then he would, I feared, try once too often, at which he only laughed. I made as many lame excuses for the conduct of those who ought to have known better, as I thought prudent, and assured the Governor that the officer must have exceeded his orders, as I was convinced the captain would be very much grieved to hear that he had lost his life and the lives of others on so worthless an occasion.

'No,' said he, 'by what I can learn, his purpose was to procure water; had he quietly restricted himself to that employment he would not have been interrupted.' Here the interview ended; I withdrew, and went with my mind disquieted to the tavern, where I met some of the Yankee captains, who would have drawn me into a conversation on what had happened, but I was determined to be silent, and retired to prose in my chamber.

On the second day after this sad event I received an invitation for myself and Mr S, the mid who was with me, to a ball given by the

Governor. About eight o'clock in the evening Mr B, the American Consul, called for us, and we repaired to the Government House, a large, square building in a spacious yard. We entered an ante-room, where the guard were stationed, and afterwards a lofty kind of hall, the walls of which were white-washed, and at the farthest end was an orchestra raised on a platform. About eighty well-dressed people were assembled, the greater part of whom were females; some of them were very pretty, and made my heart go pit-a-pat. I saluted the Governor, who shook hands with me, and introduced me to a lady, who, as he was a bachelor, presided for him, and whose fine auburn hair was so long that she had it fastened with a graceful bow to her side, otherwise it would have trailed on the ground. She was a native of Guadeloupe, and married to a relation of the Governor's. The ball was opened by four sets of minuets, which were danced with much grace. I figured off in one, but I fear, not gracefully. Country dances then began, which were kept up for about two hours. Waltzes were then the order of the ball, which continued until nearly daylight. I was heartily glad to reach my room, and did not breakfast until a late hour. I was spending my time very pleasantly, but not profitably. I was a prisoner, and that was sufficient to embitter a mind naturally active. I began to get tired of doing nothing, and longed to be free. I was shortly afterwards invited to two more balls, but as they were much the same as the one I have described, it is not worth while speaking of them, except that I lost my heart to three young females, who, alas! were perfectly ignorant of the fact.

On the day of the American Independence, Mr B invited me to his dinner-party, where I met the Lord knows who. A number of toasts were given replete with freedom and Republicanism, and guns were fired, and we were all very merry, until a person near me, in hip-hip-hipping, hipped a bumper of wine in his next neighbour's face. This disturbed the harmony for some minutes, when, on the friendly interference of the Consul, the offended and the offender shook hands, and all went on prosperously until midnight, at which hour we took leave of our kind host, some with their eyes twinkling and others seeing double. A few mornings afterwards the Governor asked me to breakfast at six o'clock. I found him taking his coffee on the terrace of the house, where he had one of Dollond's large telescopes, the view from which was magnificent and rich; but before I had been half an hour with him I found my eyes suffering from the great glare of light owing to the terrace being white. This he remarked. 'We will descend,' said he, 'and if you are fond of horses and mules, you shall see my stud.' On the landing-place of the stairs we met a servant. 'Go,' said he to him, 'and tell the grooms to bring all the mules into the yard. In the meanwhile you and I will enter this room,' pointing to a door on the right. 'This,' said he, 'is my retreat, and where I take my nap after dinner.' I remarked it contained no bed, but a Spanish silk-grass hammock hung low from the ceiling, over which was a mosquito net and a light punkah within it. 'Here,' said he, 'I lose sight of the world and all its absurdities for at least two hours every day by going quietly to rest, and as it is the custom of the country, there is little fear of my being disturbed.' The head groom came to announce that the mules were in the yard. 'Come,' said he, 'let us go and look at them; they are considered fine animals.' We were soon in their company, and I beheld eight beautiful cream-coloured mules of considerable height. 'These are my state mules, and are seldom used. I have eight others for common work. Horses,' continued he, 'are seldom in request, but I have three, which you shall see in the stable.' They were large-boned, with ugly heads and short necks. 'You do not admire them,' said he; 'they are not very handsome. They came from the Island of Curaçoa, and perhaps are rather of Dutch build. I use them for the family carriage.' After expressing my gratification which the sight of the beautiful mules had excited, and thanking him for his condescension, I took my leave. A week after this visit I was again sent for. 'I have now good news for you,' said the kind-hearted Governor. 'Your ship is close in to the Moro, and has sent in a flag of truce to request me to release you, and you are free from this moment, and,' added he, 'I will send every English prisoner with you, if you will say that an equal number of Spaniards shall be returned on your arrival at Jamaica.' This I did not hesitate to promise, as I was certain the commander-in-chief would do it on a proper representation. I took leave of this excellent man and the Consul with the warmest feelings of respect and gratitude.

CHAPTER 12

FIGHTING EPISODES

On going on board a boat provided for the purpose, I found with much joy the five men who had been taken when the unfortunate master lost his life, my own boat's crew, and seven other seamen. This addition was cheering. Five hours later we were shaking hands with some of our mess and shipmates, who appeared delighted to see us. The ship being close in with the shore, we soon reached her, and received a hearty welcome from all on board. I acquainted the captain with every circumstance respecting our capture, and with the great kindness and liberality of the Governor and American Consul, and that I had pledged my word of honour as an officer that an equal number of officers and men should be exchanged for us. 'For your satisfaction, and I hope for his,' replied the captain, 'a cartel is on her passage with a superior Spanish officer and twenty men, for immediately our liberal-minded commander-in-chief, Lord H Seymour, heard, by an American vessel, of our misfortunes, he ordered the cartel to be got ready, and desired me to proceed, before we had half refitted, to St Jago to reclaim you, having written a handsome letter to acknowledge the humane manner in which the Governor treated the English prisoners' – which letter was given to the Spanish officer to present to him on his arrival. 'Now,' continued the captain, 'have you heard anything of the *Fancy?* I am afraid she is lost, with all on board her. The morning after you went away,' resumed he, 'we saw a vessel in the offing much resembling her. I stood towards her, and found she was an American. The seabreeze became so strong that I could not fetch sufficiently to windward, and that accounts for your not seeing us. I was truly unfortunate, and the cruise was disastrous beyond credibility. You a prisoner, with a midshipman and nine seamen, the master and three men killed, and five others taken, and the second lieutenant, a midshipman and sixteen of the best seamen most likely drowned – for I think beyond a doubt she has upset.' This conjecture was a few days after unhappily confirmed by a Bermudian sloop, which informed us that she had passed a small vessel, as we described her, bottom up near the Island of Inagua. This intelligence threw a gloom over the whole of us. 'This is too tender a subject,' said I, 'to have any more tenders.' 'No,' replied the captain; 'all these unhappy circumstances combined are most deplorable. I do not think I will ever send the boats away again.' 'Not till the next time,' thinks I to myself. We repaired to one of our old cruising grounds, the Isle de Vâche, and although our noble captain had some days before come to a kind of secondhand determination of not sending boats away from the ship, on a large schooner heaving in sight towards the evening, I volunteered with the purser, if he would allow us the two cutters, as the wind had died away, to go after her. He, after a brown study of about half an hour, granted our request. 'But,' said he, 'be cautious, and if you find her heavily armed, try to decoy her off shore, but by no means attempt boarding her. We have suffered too much already.' Having prepared the boats, away we started, and after a most fatiguing pull, came up with her as she was making for Jacmel. Fortunately for us, the land-breeze was blowing rather fresh, which obliged her to make several tacks, and we boarded her whilst in stays. The people on board appeared astonished to see so many armed men so suddenly on her deck, as she had in the obscure light taken us for fishing canoes. She proved a French schooner, laden with bags of coffee. We soon rejoined the ship, quite elated with our prize, and sent her to Jamaica in charge of the purser. In the course of this cruise we fell in with two American sloops of war, which we chased, and as they did not shorten sail nor answer the private signal, we fired at the nearest; the shot passed through her cutwater. This event roused the minds and, I presume, the Yankee blood of both Jonathans, for they bore up, and we could hear their drums beating to quarters. We shortened sail, and they soon bowled alongside of us, with their sails spread like the tail of a turkey-cock. 'You have fired into me,' said the nearest. 'Have I?' said our skipper, very coolly; 'I intended the shot to go ahead of you. You must blame your superior sailing for the accident. You fore-reached so rapidly that the shot had not time to go ahead of you.' 'I don't know anything about that,' was the reply. 'We are American cruisers, and no one has a right, I guess, to fire into the United States men-of-war.' 'Then the United States men-of-war should have answered the private signal and hoisted their colours,' returned our captain, 'as we did ours.' Here they hailed each other, and soon afterwards hoisted their colours. Another boat adventure and the capture of a beautiful small schooner without any accident was the wind up of this cruise.

We anchored at Port Royal once more. About a week after our arrival I was again attacked with the yellow fever and removed to my lodgings, where I was nursed with unremitting attention by a quadroon female, who did not leave my bedside day or night. She was a most tender and attentive nurse. It was a month before I was sufficiently strong to go on board, and nearly another before I could resume my duty. I was so reduced that I was literally a walking skeleton, or, if my reader pleases, the shadow of a ghost, and, had a purser's candle been placed within me, I might have made a tolerably good substitute for the flag-ship's top light.

We were, in consequence of several of the crew being seized with yellow fever, ordered by the recommendation of the surgeon to Bluefields for change of air, and I am happy to state that from this judicious arrangement we did not lose a man. During the three weeks we remained here we amused ourselves by fishing. The water in eight fathoms was as pellucid as glass, and we could see the large conger eels twisting about between the stones at the bottom, as well as other fish, of which we caught several. I was regaining my strength rapidly, and was frequently invited to spend the day at several of the estates.

I enjoyed walking of an evening about an hour before sunset in the pimento groves, of which there were several, and when the land-breeze set in we were often regaled on board the ship by their balmy fragrance. Mr S, at whose house I frequently dined, was particularly kind, and his hospitality will not easily be effaced from my recollection. He had an amiable daughter, and had my heart not been lost in six different places, I think I should have sent it to cruise in her snug little boudoir. The captain, as the people who were ill had nearly recovered, thought His Majesty's ship should no longer lie idle. We bade adieu to our kind friends, and once more made the water fly before us. Three days more brought us off the Havannah, where we joined the *Trent* and *Alarm* frigates. Nothing worth noticing occurred until the *Trent*, which was in chase of a vessel, ran on a coral reef off Matanzas. The wind was light and the sea smooth, and we soon got her afloat again. The vessel she had chased ran on a sand beach under the protection of a martello tower. Two boats armed were soon in motion from each ship, to get her off if possible. I had the direction of our boats. The enemy's gun-boat, for such she was, under Spanish colours, hoisted her ensign and the red flag of defiance, and kept up a smart fire on our boats. Fortunately we escaped, but those from the *Alarm* had the lieutenant and three men wounded. Our boats were the first alongside of her, when I hauled down the red flag and her colours, and threw them into one of our boats, but the senior lieutenant claimed the former. This I refused, because as I was first on board and hauled it down I considered myself entitled to keep it. He said he should refer it to his captain, who was the chief officer. 'So be it,' I replied. On our boarding the enemy's vessel we found the crew had abandoned her, and were firing at us with muskets from the bushes. They had scuttled her, and she was full of water. We turned her guns on them, which soon dislodged them, and they scampered off as fast as their legs would carry them. More than half of our boat's crews had landed and were under my orders. We soon perceived about thirty horse soldiers in a full trot towards us. We formed in a body two deep, and when we were near enough gave them a sailor's salute with our muskets and three cheers. We knocked one off his horse, and set the others on a full gallop back from whence they came. They discharged their carbines at us, but they were too much alarmed to take good aim, and we escaped unharmed.

As it was impossible to get the gun-boat afloat, we tarred her sails and set fire to her. We should have blown her up had not her powder been under water. She mounted a long eighteen-pounder on a traverse, and six long six-pounders on her quarter-deck. She was of great length and a formidable vessel, and we much regretted our not being able to get her afloat, as she would have answered for the Service. She had also four brass swivels mounted on her gunwales, which we took in the boats. After waiting until she had nearly burnt down to the water's edge, we returned to our ships, taking with us the wounded Spanish dragoon. Soon after we were on our oars the martello tower began blazing away at us. It had hitherto been silent, but we supposed that when the run-away dragoons perceived we were withdrawing, they returned and mounted the tower to give us a parting salute. They might have spared themselves the trouble, as it had only one gun, and that badly served. We were on board our own ships before they fired the fourth shot. 'Well,' said the captain, on my reaching the quarter-deck, 'you were not able to get the vessel off.' 'No,' I replied; 'she was scuttled, and sank before we boarded her.' 'Were her guns brass or iron?' 'Iron,' said I, 'and not worth bringing on board; there were four brass one-pound swivels, but those were taken by the lieutenant of the commodore's boat, and he ungenerously claimed the red flag I had hauled down, but I refused to give it up.' Whilst this conversation was going on, a boat from the *Alarm* came alongside with a midshipman and a written order from the commodore for me to give up, no longer the flag of defiance but that of dispute. 'I think,' said the captain, 'you had better comply with the order.' On seeing my disinclination to do so, he said, 'It is not worth contending about.' 'I believe, sir,' I replied, 'you are right. It is of too childish a nature to contend about, although I cannot help considering it arbitrary, and I am surprised that a man like Captain D could ever give such an unjust order.' 'There are many men of various minds,' said he. There the disagreeable conversation ended. The mid received the piece of red bunting, and I walked the deck as surly as a bear with the Caledonian rash. The captain, who was going to dine with Captain A, told me he would explain to him anything I wished respecting what had occurred. This I declined, but I mentioned the swivels, and told him that they were very handy to mount in the boats when going on service. 'I will ask him for two of them,' said he; 'by doing this I probably may get one. You know,' continued he, laughing, 'he is from the Land of Cakes and bannocks, where the device is "To hold fast and not let go."'

In the evening the captain returned on board, bringing in the boat one of the swivels. 'I have laid a point to windward of the Highlander,' said he to me; 'but I was obliged to make use of all my best logic, for he chose to be distressingly deaf on the subject of giving. But when I mentioned that I had a canister of real Scotch which was of no use to me, as I had left off taking snuff, his ears became instantly opened. "You said something about two swivels, I think," said he; "I cannot spare you two, but I will give you one. Will you take it in your boat with you, or I will send it in our jolly boat, and as I am nearly out of snuff, you can spare me the canister you mentioned that you do not need."' 'This puts me in mind,' said I, 'of an Irish pilot who asked the purser of a ship I formerly belonged to, to spare him an empty barrel to make his pig a hencoop, and he would give him a sack of praters for nothing at all, at all.' 'The case is nearly in point,' replied the captain; 'I am afraid I have not gained so much on his weather-beam as I first imagined.' The signal was now made to weigh, and we were soon under sail. Next morning we parted company with the frigates, swept the Bay of Mexico, ran through the Turks' Island passage, and cruised between Capes Maize and François for three weeks; took a small French schooner with tobacco, and burnt a small sloop in ballast. Again our anchor found the bottom of Port Royal, and the crew their copper and jet-coloured ladies.

One afternoon, taking a glass of sangaree at the tavern, I was accosted by one of our late mids who had come on shore with some others to what he called wet his commission. 'Will you do me the favour to join us for a quarter of an hour. We have a room upstairs,' said he to me. I told him I would in about five minutes. On entering, I found a gallon bowl filled with strong punch, with his commission soaking in it, and eight jolly mids sitting at the table in full glee. They all rose as I approached, and one of them offered me a chair. 'Come, sir,' said the donor of the entertainment, offering me a bumper from the contents of the bowl, 'tell me if it will suit your taste.' 'Not quite,' replied I, 'you have spoilt it by putting your commission into it instead of your pocket, and it smacks too much of ink and parchment.' 'I told you how it would be,' said he, addressing a sly, roguish-looking youngster, who had persuaded him to put it in. 'I vote that he shall drink it himself, and we will have another.' 'Not on any account,' said I, 'without you will allow me to pay for it.' 'That will never do,' cried all of them. Another of a smaller size was ordered, out of which I drank his success. I remained nearly half an hour, during which time the large bowl was drained to the last dregs in spite of its parchment flavour, and the parchment was, what the mids called, returned high and dry to the owner of it, with the writing on it nearly effaced. I remarked they ought certainly to have a patent for wetting commissions, and wished them a pleasant evening.

On returning on board I found a note for me from the captain, to acquaint me that we were to sail in a few days for Black River, in order to collect a homeward-bound convoy, as we were ordered to England. I withdrew my heart from the different little snug rooms I had left it in, and placed it on the right hook. I was so much elated that my dinner went from table untouched. I kept conjuring up Paradises, Elysian fields, and a number of other places never heard of, inhabited by women more beautiful than Eastern imagery can possibly describe – so fair, so chaste, so lovely, and so domestic. 'Oh!' said I aloud, to the astonishment of my messmates, who were much occupied with their knives and forks, 'give me but one of those fair ones, and I will not eat my dinner for a month.' 'Hulloa!' said the surgeon, 'what's the matter with you?' 'Nothing,' replied I; 'the illusion is vanished, and I will take a glass of wine with you. I cannot eat, my mind is too full of England, and my heart crowded with its delightful fair ones. What unfeeling sea monsters you are all of you,' continued I, 'to be eating with such voracious appetites when you know we are going to glorious England – the land of freedom and genuine hospitality.' 'Not so fast,' said he, interrupting me; 'how long is it since you were there?' 'Nearly eight years,' said I. 'I fear,' resumed he, 'you will not have your dreams – for dreams they are – verified. I was there eighteen months ago, and found freedom in the mouths of the lower classes, who evidently did not understand the meaning of it, and when they did they only used it as a cloak to do mischief, for demagoguing – if you will allow the term – was the order of the day at that time, and as for hospitality that has, as you may express yourself, made sail and gone to cruise into some other climate. I had letters to two families from their relations in India; they asked me to dinner in a stiff, formal manner, and thought, I suppose, they had performed wonders. There our acquaintance ended. I am an Irishman,' continued he, 'and I assert without partiality that there is more real hospitality in my land of praters than in all Europe. Freedom we will not talk about; but as for the women, dear creatures, they are a mixture of roses and lilies, and such busts, like dairy maids, sure,' said he; 'don't say anything more about them, or I shall be what has never happened to an Irishman yet – out of spirits.' 'Now,' said I, 'doctor, we have found you out. You lost your heart when in England, and were not requited by the cruel fair one.' 'Fair or foul,' answered he, 'I would not give one Munster girl for a dozen English. To be sure,' added he to a young Irish midshipman, whose turn it was to dine in the gun-room, 'they are rather thick about the trotters, and their heels are to be compared to their red potatoes, but the upper part of their figures – say no more. Come, messmate, let's drink a speedy passage and soon, as a worthy alderman did at a Guildhall dinner.' 'You mistake, doctor,' said the second lieutenant, 'he gave for a toast, a speedy peace and soon.' 'Never mind,' said the doctor, 'it will be all the same a hundred years hence; an Irishman is always allowed to speak twice.' Our parting with our washerwomen and other friends was pathetic in the extreme; their precious tears were sufficient to fill several (but as I did not measure them I cannot say how many) monkeys.

'Oh, Gramercy, my lob!' said my lady to me, 'I neber shall see you no more; but I hope dat you member dat Julia lob you more den he can tell. No,' said she, turning aside, 'nobody can lob like poor me one, Julia.' She appeared overwhelmed with grief, and I felt my situation awkward and pathetically silly, as she had followed me down to the boat, and the eyes of several boats' crews with their young, laughing wicked mids, were on us. I shook hands for the last time and jumped into the boat with a tear rolling down my cheek from my starboard eye. Reader, I beg you will not pity me, for I was not in love. I was what an old maiden cousin would have called imprudent.

CHAPTER 13

HOME AGAIN

At daylight next morning we catted the anchors, made all sail, and were the next day reposing like a swan in a lake at Black River. As notices from the merchants at Kingston had been sent to the different ports round the island that two men-of-war were going to take convoy to England, we were soon joined by several West Indiamen. This place can scarcely be called even a village, there being so few houses, and those straggling. The first time I went on shore I was called to by a stout man wearing a linen jacket and trousers, with an immense broad-brimmed straw hat on his head, and his address was abrupt and by no means polished. 'What ship,' said he, 'officer?' 'The *Volage*,' replied I, not in love with the person's face, which was bluish-red, with a large nose. 'Then,' said he, 'you bloody dog, come and bow to my bishop,' pointing to the best house there. I stared with astonishment, and was turning away presuming he was a cloth in the wind or some madman escaped from his keeper. 'Ho, ho! but you can't go before you have bowed to my bishop,' he again called out; 'come with me to my house, and we shall be better acquainted.' He took my arm; I thought him a character, which I afterwards found he was, and gave in to his whim. On entering the verandah of the house, which was shaded by close venetian blinds and very cool, he stopped before an immense large jug in the shape of a bishop. It was placed on a bracket slab, so that to drink out of the corner of its hat, which was its beak or spout, you were obliged to stoop. This I found he called bowing to his bishop. It contained delicious sangaree, and I bowed to it without being entreated to do so a second time. 'Now,' said he, 'you bloody dog, you have complied like a good fellow with my first request. Your captain dines with me to-morrow; I must insist on your doing so too, and then I shall consider you an obedient officer and worthy to bow to my bishop whenever you are thirsty. My dinner-hour is five o'clock, and as I am the magistrate of this over-grown metropolis I admit of no excuse.' I could not help smiling at this rough urbanity. I accepted the invitation, and at the appointed hour repaired to his house with the captain and surgeon.

He received us with great good humour, and insisted, as we were bloody dogs – I understood afterwards he was very partial to naval officers and always called them by that pet name – that we should bow to his bishop before dinner. We met at his table our kind acquaintance Mr S, his daughter, another gentleman, his wife and two nieces, who were going to England in one of the ships of the convoy. The dining-room was entirely of cedar, and the floor like a mirror, very spacious, and it partly projected over the river. Above the dining-table was a large punkah, which was kept in constant motion during dinner by two young grinning black girls. The table groaned with good things, and we did ample justice to our host's entertainment. He was evidently a great humourist, and amused us at dinner by relating anecdotes of Lord Rodney and Admiral Benbow's time. 'There are,' said he, 'twelve tough old fellows, of which I am the chairman, who keep up the twelfth of April by an annual dinner, and as he never flinched from the enemy, we never flinch from the bottle, and keep it up till daylight, when we are so gloriously sober that we are carried home by our slaves.' 'Is it true,' said he, addressing the captain, 'that Sir Eyre Coote is to supersede the Earl of B as Governor of our Islands? Do you know anything of him?' 'Only from report,' was the reply; 'I think he distinguished himself by a brilliant victory over Hyder Ali in the East Indies.' 'Why, the devil,' said he, 'I beg your pardon, ladies, for swearing, do they send us soldiers as governors? We want something in the shape of a statesman with a lawyer's head, with his wig and litigation. I have no fault to find with the earl; he has governed us very fairly, and I hope his successor will do the same, although we prefer a civilian to a soldier.'

After dinner we were amused by the feats of one of his household slaves named Paddy Whack, who threw somersaults round the drawing-room, walked on his hands, and afterwards threw himself several times from the highest part of the bridge, about twenty-four feet, into the river. After coffee we took leave of our eccentric but warm-hearted host, who, on shaking hands, insisted on our bloody dogships dining with him once more before we sailed. We promised to do so conditionally. Eighteen sail of merchant vessels had assembled, and we expected seven more. The surf had been high on the bar, and we had not had communication with the shore for the last two days. A canoe came off from Mr C with Paddy Whack, who delivered a note to the captain. 'What is it about, boy?' said he. 'Paper peak, massa,' was the reply; 'Paddy only wait answer from Massa Captain.' The note was a pressing invitation to dine on shore the following day, and included the captain and officers. As I had dined with the worthy planter I persuaded the second lieutenant to go. The rest of the convoy having joined us, our sails were again swelling to a strong sea-breeze. The convoy of thirty sail of sugar-laden ships were hovering round us like chickens round the mother hen. Four others joined us at Bluefields, and off Negril Point we fell in with the S frigate, with the former Governor of Jamaica on board and three other West Indiamen. The captain went on board the S to pay his respects and to receive his orders.

After his return on board the signal was made to make all sail, and away we bowled for the Gulf of Florida. We touched at the Caymans for turtle, and were cheated as usual. Nothing particular occurred during our passage but our nearly being run down by one of the ships of the convoy, and my having my left shoulder unshipped by being washed off one of the weather guns by a heavy sea, which obliged me to keep my cot for more than a fortnight. The eighth week brought us in sight of the Land's End, when we repeated the signal for the convoy to separate for their respective ports. Those bound to London kept company with us as far as the Downs. I longed to be once more on my native shore, but I was doomed to be mortified for two days, as the surf on the beach was too high to admit a boat to land. On the third day I jumped on shore with a light heart and a thin pair of trousers, and repaired to the 'Hoop and Griffin.' I had a desperate desire to have a cruise on horseback. I rang the bell, which was answered by one of the finest formed young women I ever beheld. I was taken aback, and my heart, which I had brought from the West Indies, went like the handle of the chain pumps up and down. 'What do you please to want, sir,' said she, with a most musically toned voice. I blushed and modestly requested to have a horse as soon as he could be got ready. 'I am really sorry, sir,' answered she, 'that all our horses are posthorses, but' continued she, with the gentlest accent in this world and probably many more, 'we will procure you one.' 'Many thanks,' said I; 'and will you oblige me by sending up some bread and butter with some oysters, but not those which are gathered from the mangrove trees,' for I had the West Indies in my mind. 'Gathered from trees! – oysters from trees! I never heard of such a thing before,' said she, and she went laughing out of the room. The waiter soon appeared with what I had ordered, and a foaming tankard of ale which I had forgotten to order. During my repast I envied no one. I was as happy as a city alderman at a Lord Mayor's feast; I could not contain myself or believe I was in England; I could not sit quietly in my chair; I paced the room, jumped, rubbed my hands and head, and in one of my ecstatic fits I rang the bell. My beautiful maid (not Braham's) entered as I was cutting a caper extraordinary. 'Did you ring, sir?' said she with a smile becoming an angel. 'I believe I did,' I replied, 'but I am not certain. I scarcely know what I am about. I have eaten my oysters, and now I wish for my horse.' 'He is not quite ready yet, sir. You said something about oysters growing on trees, didn't you, sir. I told it to my mother, and she thinks I did not understand what you said. Will you be good enough to tell me if they grow in orchards like our apples?' 'I have seen thousands, and have eaten thousands that have grown on trees,' said I, 'but not in orchards. The tree that bears them grows close to the water side; its lower branches dip into it, and are clustered by the shell-fish, which are very small, and you may swallow a dozen at a mouthful.' 'Thank you, sir; my mother I am sure will believe me now. I will desire John to take away. Did you like our country oysters as well as those in foreign parts?' 'They are,' said I, 'like you, excellent.' 'I will see if the horse is ready,' said she, as she dropped a curtsey and quitted the room.

Shortly after up came John to announce my horse being at the door. 'Will you have a pair of master's spurs, sir?' said he. 'No, I thank you, my good fellow,' returned I. 'Lend me a whip, and I shall be able to manage without spurs.' Behold a sailor on horseback, gentle reader, to the admiration or astonishment of all the bystanders, of which there were as many as would man a king's cutter. I kept under moderate sail until I reached Middle Deal, when my companion brought up all standing at the door of a decent-looking house, nor could I make him again break ground until a maidservant opened the door. 'Lord,' said she, 'I thought it was the baker, sir, for you are on his horse.' 'That accounts,' I said, 'for his halting at your door. I wish, Betty, you would get him once more into plain sailing.' She most kindly took hold of the bridle and led him into the middle of the street. I now thought myself in the fair way, and I gave him a stroke with the whip, which I nearly repented, for he kicked up with his hind legs, and had not I seized the after part of the saddle I should have gone over his forecastle. I held on until he righted. After this freak, which was nearly knocking up my cruise, we jogged on steadily until we came to a narrow street, down which he turned in spite of all my endeavours to prevent him, and again hove to at the door of another house.

'This turning to windward,' thinks I, 'will never do. It reminds me of Commodore Trunnion making a Tom Coxe's traverse to fetch the church.' Whilst I was puzzling my wise noddle what I was to do next, a man passed me. 'I wish you would get this horse under weigh,' said I, 'for here have I been at single anchor for these five minutes at this door, and cannot cast him the right way.' 'Why,' said he, 'I knows that there horse; it be the baker's.' 'D——n the baker, and his horse too,' said I, not much pleased at his remark. 'You are close to the Canterbury road, and mayhap if I leads him he may go on.' 'You are the best fellow I have met for a quarter of an hour. Do get him into open cruising ground as fast as you can, for I have been on his back more than an hour, and have not gained half a mile.' He gave me a broad grin, and good-naturedly led the horse until I got clear of the houses. He then let go the bridle, gave the animal a smart slap on the flank, which set him off at a hand-gallop, and nearly jerked me over the taffrail. I kept him to his speed, and in about half an hour he stopped suddenly near a small farmhouse, and I was again nearly going over his bows. A slovenly kind of woman hove in sight. I hailed her, and asked her to bring me a tumbler of milk, but I might as well have spoken to a Porto Rico donkey. She showed me her stern, and brought up in a piggery. 'The devil take your hospitality,' said I. The weather was exceedingly warm, and I was very thirsty, which made me more hasty in my expressions to the Dulciana of the pigstye than I ought to have been. But show me the fair one who would not excuse a sailor thirsty and on the back of an animal as obstinate as a boat's crew when cutting out. After a fruitless attempt to proceed further on my voyage of discovery, I hove about. The animal answered stays as well as any frigate, and was round sooner than the captain of the forecastle could clap the jib traveller over the end of the jib-boom. I was heartily tired of my horse cruise, and was glad when I have to at the 'Hoop and Griffin.'

As soon as I had thrown myself on the sofa, my beautiful maid entered. 'Will you favour me with your name?' said I, addressing her with quarter-deck modesty. 'I am called Lucy,' said she. 'That's a very pretty name,' returned I. 'Pray, Miss Lucy, may I ask where the horse came from I have been riding? I have had a worse cruise than a dismantled Dutch dogger on the Goodwin Sands. I have, into the bargain, lost out of my waistcoat-pocket two two-pound notes and five new gloves out of six which I very stupidly stuffed into my coat-pocket.' 'I am very sorry, sir, indeed, for your misfortune,' answered she. 'The horse came from the "Royal Oak." We desired them to send a quiet one, as it was for a gentleman who was not in the habit of riding.' 'I wish they had sent me a donkey instead of the baker's horse,' said I; 'he took it into his head to stop at his master's customers' houses, nor could I make him leave them without assistance. No more cruising on horseback for me,' continued I. 'Pray do let me have plenty of oysters and bread and butter, with a tankard of ale as smiling as yourself, as soon as the waiter can bring them up, for I am very hungry.' 'We have a nice cold chicken in the house and some ham; shall I send them up too?' 'That's the stuff for trousers,' answered I. 'Let all be handed up in the turn of a handspike, and if I do not do ample justice to the whole, you are not the prettiest girl I have seen. I suppose it would be treason to ask you to partake of the good things I have ordered?' 'Oh, no, sir,' said she; 'that is not the fashion in our house, for me to sit down with a strange gentleman.' Saying this, she left the room, and as I observed the smile which dimpled her blooming cheeks had vanished, I began to think I had said too much. Whilst I was in a blue study, up came chicken, ham, oysters, bread and butter, with the ale. I drew to the table and began with a keen West-country appetite, and for the first ten minutes forgot Lucy, baker's horse, pound notes and gloves, and almost that it was growing dark, and that we were to sail by the next morning's tide. Before I had finished moving my under jaw, which had been in constant motion for the last twenty minutes, in came the purser and one of the mids to report the boat being on shore. 'You have saved me from a surfeit,' exclaimed I. 'Come,' said I to the youngster, 'sit down and finish the feast. As for you, Master Purser, I know you have been faring well elsewhere, therefore I shall not ask you to take anything.'

Having paid the bill and shaken hands with Lucy, I jumped into the boat, and was soon on board. On seating myself in the gun-room, 'Now, messmates,' said I, addressing the second lieutenant and surgeon, 'you commissioned me to buy you each a pair of gloves. I fulfilled it to the letter, but I have left them on the Canterbury road.' I then related my adventure, which elicited a hearty laugh. 'Now,' added I, 'we will have a glass of grog, and drink to fair Lucy at the "Hoop and Griffin," for she is a very pretty girl, and I have lost half my heart.' 'If we do not sail tomorrow,' replied they, 'we will go on shore and see whether she deserves the appellation you have given her.' 'Do,' said I, 'and give my love to her.'

At daylight our signal was made to remain at anchor until further orders. On sending the last boat on shore for the officers, I ordered the midshipman who had charge of her to acquaint my messmates not to bring off any strangers to dinner, as no boat would leave the ship after they returned. About 3pm the boat came on board, and, in contradiction to my order, brought off a stranger. The second lieutenant was first up the side, and the stranger followed. On his reaching the quarter-deck, he introduced him to me as a person sent off by the admiral as a broker to exchange English for foreign coin. He gave me his card, which I put into my pocket without looking at it. I began by telling him he had come on board at a very inconvenient time, and that, in consequence of the spring tide, the boat would not leave the ship until the morning. 'It is of little consequence to me,' said he, very coolly; 'I can remain where I am until that time.' 'Respecting the errand you have come on,' I resumed, 'I am afraid you will be disappointed, as two persons have already been before you.' 'How came you,' said I to the youngster who had charge of the boat, 'to disobey the order I gave you?' Before he could answer the surgeon came up and whispered to me, 'It is your brother.' I examined his countenance more closely. He gave me one of his schoolboy grins and his hand, and then I was convinced. We had not seen each other for nearly nine years, and he had grown entirely out of my recollection. I did not give him the fraternal hug, but I shook him affectionately by the hand and told him I should not part with him until we reached Deptford, to which he willingly consented. He acquainted me with all family concerns, and that my mother was waiting in London, anxious to see me. The following day we received on board eighteen French prisoners for the prison-ships in the river. We wished them at Jericho, where the man fell among those who used him worse than a Turk would have done. The same afternoon we daylighted the anchor, mastheaded the sails, crested the briny wave like a Yankee sea-serpent, and on the second day let go no fool of a piece of crooked iron off dirty Deptford. As orders were received to pay us off, we were fully occupied for nearly a week dismantling the ship and returning stores, etc. On the second day I ran up to London and saw my mother. She did not, luckily for both parties, shed a flood of tears, but received me with maternal affection, though she said she scarcely knew me – I was grown, as my sister was pleased to say, such a black man. On the sixth day after our anchoring I ordered the ship to be put out of commission, and the cook hauled down the pendant. We had a parting dinner at the 'Gun' Inn, shook hands and separated.

CHAPTER 14

A HOLIDAY ASHORE

After I had remained in noisy, bustling, crowded and disagreeable London a month, my mother wishing to go into Surrey, I was glad of the opportunity to accompany her and to breathe purer air, and left town without regret. I was now under my own orders, and was much puzzled to find out how I was to obey myself. For the last ten years I had been under the control of superiors. Now I had the whole of my crew within myself, and discipline I found was necessary. I knew no more of England than it knew of me. Men and manners were equally strange to me, except those on board the different men-of-war I had served in, and they were not the most polished. In the society of the fair sex I was exceedingly shy, and my feelings were sometimes painful when I had to run the gauntlet through rows of well-dressed women, some looking as demure as a noddy at the masthead. I was now in my twenty-third year, and an agreeable – nay, an old lady, whose word was considered sacred – declared I was a charming young man. My life passed as monotonously as that of a clock in an old maid's sitting-room. My habits were too active to remain long in this state of listlessness. I was almost idle enough to make love, and nearly lost my heart seven times. Caring little for the society of the men, I generally strolled over two or three fields to read my books, or to scribble sonnets on a plough, for I began to be sentimental and plaintive. Whilst meditating one morning in bed, I started up with a determination to have an interview with Sir J Colpoys, who was one of the Lords of the Admiralty, and ask him in person for employment, for I began to be apprehensive if I remained longer on shore I should think a ship was something to eat, and the bobstay the top-sail haulyards. Three weeks after my application I was appointed to the *Minotaur* of seventy-four guns lying at Blackstakes, and I found it black enough, for she not having her masts stepped, we were all obliged – that is the officers – to live at the 'Tap' at Shurnasty, commonly called Sheerness, where we spent thirteen out of six shillings a day, and until the ship was ready to receive us, which was nearly a fortnight, we drank elevation to the noble Secretary of the Admiralty, for, owing to his ignorance, we had been obliged to spend seven shillings daily more than our pay.

Two days after the ship was commissioned, and I had been carrying on the war, for I was the senior lieutenant, the gallant captain made his appearance. After touching his hat in return to my grand salaam, he said, 'Hulloa, how is this? I expected to find the ship masted. I will thank you to desire the boatswain to turn the hands up to hear my commission read, and quarter-master,' addressing a dockyard matey, 'go down and tell all the officers I am on board.'

'That is not a quartermaster,' said I to him, 'he is one of the dockyard men.' 'Then where are the quartermasters?' 'We have none,' replied I, 'nor have we a seaman on board except some one-legged and one-armed old Greenwich pensioners that were sent on board yesterday.' At this satisfactory intelligence he turned his eyes up like a crow in a thunderstorm, and muttered, I fear, something in the shape of a prayer for the whole Board of Admiralty. Whilst we were looking at each other not knowing what to say next, a man came up the hatchway to report that one of the Greenwich men had broken his leg. 'Where is the surgeon?' said the captain. 'He has not yet joined,' replied I. 'We must send him to the dockyard for surgical aid. Man the boat, and you, Mr Brown, take him on shore,' said I. Mr Brown made one of his best bows, and acquainted me that it was the carpenter who was wanted and not the surgeon, as the man had snapped his wooden leg in one of the holes of the grating, and the carpenter's mate was fishing it. After a pause of some minutes, 'So,' resumed the captain, 'this is the manner King's ships are to be fitted out. Why, it will take us a month of Sundays before the lower masts are rigged. What the devil did they send those old codgers with their wooden legs here for? I will go immediately to the Admiral, and point out the state we are in.' In the afternoon another lieutenant joined the ship, junior to me. I began to think I should be the first, when on the following day I was unshipped, for two others came on board by some years my seniors. The captain also sent four young mids on board and the Admiralty two oldsters, one of whom was a sprig of nobility. On the morning of the fourth day we were masted, and a lighter came alongside filled with riggers from London, and soon afterwards we received our complement of marines, with a captain and two lieutenants. We were now beginning to get animated and to make some show, when, as I was giving an order to the boatswain, Mr Brown, whom I ought to have introduced before as the gunner, reported a barge coming alongside with prisoners. 'That is surely a mistake,' replied I; 'I hope they do not take us for the prison ship.' Bump she came, stern on. 'Hulloa!' I called out; 'do you wish to try what the bends are made of?' Before I could say anything more, up came and stood before me, cocked-up hat in hand, a consequential, dapper little stout man dressed in black, with his hair in powder. 'Please you, sir, I have brought, by the order of the magistrates at Maidstone, fifteen men to belong to your ship. They be all of them tolerable good men, except five, who have been condemned to be transported, and two to be hung, but as they be contrabanders like, the Government have sent down orders for 'em to be sent on board your ship.' 'I am sure,' said I, 'I can in the name of His Majesty's officers offer many thanks to His Majesty's Government for their great consideration in sending men who deserve hanging to be made sailors on board His Majesty's ships.' He then, with a flourish, presented me a paper with their names and the offences of which they had been guilty. Nine of these honest, worthy members of society were stout, robust fellows, and had only taken what did not belong to them. Two of the remaining six had been condemned for putting brave citizens in bodily fear on the King's highway and borrowing their purses and watches. The other four were smugglers bold, who wished to oblige their friends with a few hundreds of yards of Brussels lace and gloves, as well as some tubs of brandy, but were unfortunately interrupted in the exercise of their profession by those useless sea-beach cruisers called the Coast Guard. 'Pray, sir,' said I, 'to whom may I be obliged to for the safe conveyance of these honest men?' 'I be the under-sheriff's officer, sir,' answered he, 'and I have had mighty hard work to bring them along.' 'You deserve to be rewarded, Mr Deputy Sheriff' (for I like to give every man his title), said I; 'you would probably like to have a glass of grog.' 'Why it's thirsty weather, and I shall be obliged to you, sir.' I called the steward, desired he might have some refreshment, and he soon after quitted the ship, admonishing the live cargo he brought on board, who were still on the quarter-deck, to behave themselves like good men. A month had expired by the time the top-gallant masts were on end. We had received all our officers and two hundred men from Chatham and the river. At length, Greenwich pensioners, riggers, and dockyard mateys took their departure, to our great satisfaction, as it was impossible to bring the ship's crew into discipline whilst they were on board. Our complement, including the officers, was six hundred and forty men. We had only three hundred and twenty when orders came down for us to proceed to Plymouth. The captain and first lieutenant looked very wise on this occasion, and were apprehensive that if the ship slipped the bridles she would be like an unruly horse, and run away with us, for there were only forty men on board who knew how to go aloft except a few of the marines. The pilot made his appearance, and soon afterwards down went the bridles, and we were fairly adrift. We reached the Nore, and let go the anchors in a hail squall, and it was with the greatest difficulty we got the top-sails furled. The admiral, having proof positive that we were as helpless as a cow in a jolly-boat, took compassion on us and sent fifty more men from the flag-ship, most of them able seamen. On the fourth day after quitting the Nore we anchored in Plymouth Sound.

I now had the delightful opportunity of once more breathing my native air, viewing beautiful Mount Edgcumbe, revelling in clotted cream and potted pilchards, tickling my palate – as Quin used to do – with John-dories, conger eels, star-gazey and squab pies, cray-fish, and sometimes, but not very often – for my purse was only half-flood in consequence of my expenses whilst on shore at the 'Tap' at Sheerness – I had a drive upon Dock. The flag-ship in Hamoaze was the *Salvador del Mundo*, a three-decker taken from the Spaniards in the memorable battle of the fourth of February. The day after anchoring I was ordered by the captain to go with him on board the *Sally-waiter-de-Modo*. I reflected a short time, and not knowing there was such a ship on the Navy List, turned to the first lieutenant and asked him if he had heard of such a man-of-war. 'No,' said he, smiling, 'the captain chooses to call her so; he means the flag-ship.' On repairing on board her, my commander said to me, 'You help me to look at those fellows' phizes,' pointing to a number of men who were toeing the seam on her quarter-deck. 'I am to take thirty of them; they are queer-looking chaps, and I do not much like the cut of their jib. But mind,' added he, 'don't take any one that has not a large quid of tobacco in his cheek.'

I went up to the second man, who had a double allowance of Virginia or some other weed in his gill, the captain following me. 'Well, my man,' said I, 'how long have you been to sea?' 'Four months,' was the reply. 'Why, you d——d rascal,' said our skipper – for observe, reader, he never swore – 'what the devil business have you with such a quantity of tobacco in your mouth? I thought you were an old sailor.' 'No, sir,' answered the man, 'my trade is a tailor, but I have chawed bacca from my infancy.' 'Question another,' was my order. I interrogated the next, who was a short, slight, pale-faced man. 'And pray,' said I, 'what part of the play have you been performing; were you ever at sea?' 'No, sir,' said he; 'I am a hairdresser, and was pressed a week ago.' 'D——n these fellows!' said my captain; 'they are all tailors, barbers, or grass-combers. I want seamen.'

'Then,' said Captain N, who was the flag-captain, and had just come on board, 'I much fear you will be disappointed. These are the only dis-posable men, and it's Hobson's choice – those or none.'

'The admiral promised me some good seamen,' returned my skipper, rather quickly. 'Then I fear the admiral must find them,' was the answer, 'as I have not more than twenty seamen on board besides the petty officers. The last were drafted a few days ago in the *Defiance*. Will you take any of these men, Captain W?' 'What do you think,' said my captain to me; 'shall we take any of them?' 'Suppose,' returned I, 'we take twenty of them and the tailor; they will all fit in in time.' I then picked out twenty of the best, who were bad enough, as they were the worst set I ever saw grouped. Their appearance and dress were wretched in the extreme. I reached the ship before the hour of dinner with my live cargo. 'What, more hard bargains,' said the first lieutenant, 'we have too many clodhoppers on board already. The captain told me we were to have seamen.' 'Captain N,' said I, 'assured our noble captain that the *Defiance* had taken all the A.B.'s.' 'D——n the *Defiance!*' replied he; 'I *defy* Captain N or anybody else to match those gentlemanly ragamuffins.' The master's mates were called, and they were given into their charge.

One of them, a tall, large-boned man, requested to remain on deck a little longer as he had a palpitation of the heart. 'What country man are you?' said I. 'Shure,' answered he, 'I'm all the way from dear ould Ireland, and I don't think I shall be arter seeing the bogs again; but good luck to her, wherever she goes!' 'What did you do there?' said I. 'Och,' said he, 'why do I give all this trouble and what business have I here? In Ireland, plase your honour, I planted praters and tended cows. In the hay season I came to England and was employed in stacking, when one day, as I was taking a walk in a field near Lunnen, I fell in with four men who asked me to join them as they were going to a public-house to have something to drink. I thought this was very civil to a stranger. After taking the first pot they told me they intended going in a boat on the river, and asked me if I could pull an oar. 'I'll try,' said I. 'Well,' said they, 'on Saturday, at five o'clock in the evening, be down at Wapping Stairs and you will see a green painted boat with six men in her. I will be ready to meet you,' said one of the most good-natured, 'and we will have a pleasant trip.' I little thought, your honour, that these spalpeens, saving your presence, intended anything more than friendship. I was at the place pointed out, and stepped into the boat. I took the second oar, but I caught so many crabs that I was desired to sit in the stern. We pulled up the river, which I thought very pleasant. In returning, the man who steered said he had a message to deliver on board a dark-looking vessel we were close to. We got alongside of her. 'Won't you go up, Pat?' said he; 'you never was on board so large a vessel; she is worth looking at.' I went up after him, when a man dressed in a blue coat with yellow buttons came up to me and told me to go below. Saying this, he called to another, who told me he would show me the way, which he soon did, and I was forced into a dark place where I found seven more half-ragged, half-starved looking animals. Two of them were countrymen. 'Who have we here?' said one of them. 'I am all the way from Ireland,' said I, 'and I have come to see this ship.' 'The devil you have, my honey; and what do you come here for?' 'Shure enough,' replied I, 'that's true. I'll go and see arter my frinds.' At this they all laughed. I went to the door, but found a sodjer there with a drawn sword. 'What do you want?' demanded he. 'To go, and plase you.' 'To-morrow, my lad,' replied he; 'to-night you stay where you are.' 'Why, what a bother you are making, Pat,' said one of my companions; 'you know you are going to serve the King.' 'And pray,' said I, 'who is the King? I never saw or heard of him before. How can I serve him?' 'That's a good one,' said the one who first spoke. 'Where were you born and baptized?' 'About the bogs of Ireland,' replied I, 'and I was baptized over a bowl of buttermilk and praters by Father Murphy in a stable among a parcel of cows.' 'You'll do,' said another; 'have you any dibbs?' 'Yes,' answered I, 'I have got two shillings and fourpence. 'That will do. Send for a pot of the right sort, and we'll drink a long life to Ireland.' I gave the one who spoke some money. We had our pot, drew ourselves up like pigs in a trough, and went to sleep. Next morning at daylight we were put on board a tender – not very tenderly, your honour, for I lost my waistcoat and my money, and when I complained I was forced over the ship's side. They said the boat could not wait, as the tender was under weigh. We arrived at Plymouth about a fortnight ago, and here I am, your honour.'

'Well,' said I, 'if you behave yourself well and endeavour to do your duty, you will be happy enough; and as I brought you on board, I will, if you deserve it, keep sight of you, and in time you may become a good seaman, and perhaps a petty officer.' 'Long life to your honour! I'll be shure and take your advice.' And so he did, and in a few months after was made captain of the waist.

We were now tolerably in order, and soon after joined the Channel fleet off Ushant. The second day after leaving Plymouth Sound we fell in with the *Franchise*, a large French frigate of thirty-six guns and three hundred and forty men, who, after exchanging a few shot without doing us any mischief, struck her colours. She was from St Domingo, with General F on board, bound to Brest. Her second captain appeared a very delicate young person, and during the four days he was on board he never slept in the cot provided for him in the captain's cabin, but always threw himself down on the sofa in his clothes. We all conjectured that, as a son of Erin might say, he was a woman, which idea after the prisoners left us, was confirmed by the captain's steward, who had been bribed to secrecy during the passage to Plymouth. The lady was the daughter of the captain of the captured frigate in disguise.

Having seen our prize into Hamoaze, and taken our officers and men out of her, we left her in charge of the prize agent, and repaired to our station off Ushant. We joined the fleet, consisting of thirteen sail of the line and two frigates. We looked into Brest roads, and could discover only eight sail of the enemy's line of battle ships, with their top-gallant yards crossed; nine others were coming forward. Four more sail of the line having joined our fleet, we were directed to part company and cruise off Vigo Bay. Soon after we fell in with the *Venerable*. Having the watch on deck, the captain desired the signalman to hoist the dog-a-tory pendant over the dinner signal. The man scratched his head and made wide eyes at one of the midshipmen, requesting him to tell him what the captain meant. 'By Jove!' said the mid, 'if you do not bear a hand and get the signal ready, he will make you a dog-of-a-wig instead of a Tory.' Seeing the man at a pause, I asked him if he had the signal ready. 'Yes, sir,' replied he; 'I have the telegraph dinner flags ready, but I do not know what the dog-a-tory pennant is; it must be in the boatswain's store-room, for I have never had charge of it.' I could not forbear laughing at the man's explanation. 'What's the signalman about?' inquired the captain; 'why does he not hoist the signal?' 'He did not know where to find the pendant you mentioned,' replied I. 'I have told him you meant the interrogatory pendant.' 'To be sure; I said so as plain as I could speak. The fellow must be stupid not to understand me,' continued our deeply-read skipper. A worthier, better or braver seaman than our noble commander never had the honour of commanding a King's ship. His zeal and loyalty were unimpeachable. To hear him read the Articles of War to us once a month was, if not improving, most amusing. He dogrogated God's honour with emphasis, and accused the ministers of the Church of being lethargic. Some of my messmates declared, although it was perfectly without intention on his part, that the captain in the last expression was right, for although the word was liturgy, he was justified in reading it lethargy. Respecting the other word, 'dogrogation,' they had all turned over the leaves of Bailey's ancient dictionary in vain; but they presumed the captain meant to read 'derogation,' as it respected God's honour, and they considered it as a *lapsus linguæ*. Two of the officers' names were Bateman and Slateman. For months after they had been on board our worthy captain did not appear to know one from the other, and we were sometimes much diverted, and they were much annoyed, by his sending for one when he meant the other. Although our cruising ground appeared a profitable one, and we were considered fortunate in being sent there, for six weeks we only made prizes of hundreds of the finny tribe by trawling off Quimper and L'Orient. This amusement, exercising guns, sails and lead, gave us full employment, and kept us out of mischief.

For nearly two months we had only seen four of our cruisers, and a few of the enemy's small craft going along shore, and although we frequently volunteered for boat service, our commander always closed his ears to our requests. He was no friend to boating, he said; it very seldom turned out successful, and it only answered, if it did at all, when courage was doubtful. 'And if you are not men of courage,' he used to add, 'you are not the men I took you for.' At length a cutter brought us orders to rejoin the Channel fleet under Lord Gardner, as the French fleet had increased to nineteen sail of the line, besides frigates. After joining, we were stationed off the Black Rocks, with four other ships, to watch Brest and the movements of the enemy's fleet. At this time we were seventeen sail of the line and three frigates, and were very sanguine that the ships at Brest would favour us with their company, as they had been practising their firing and sailing in Brest water. We strained our eyes and imaginations in vain. There they stuck, as the seamen used to say, like the *Merrydun*, of Dover, which took seven years in veering, and when she did so the fly of her ensign swept two flocks of sheep off Beachy Head, while her jib-boom knocked down the steeple of Calais church and killed the sexton. Cruising on this Siberian ground was horribly monotonous work. We sincerely wished the French fleet alongside of us, or in a warmer place. On one dark night we were caught in a heavy gale from the westward. We were under close-reefed main and foretop-sails and mizzen. The ship was settling down on Ushant rapidly, and we expected to strike every moment. The rebound of the water from the rocks caused the spray to fly half-way over the decks from to leeward. A rock called La Jument was on our lee bow. Luckily we saw the sea breaking over it. 'Port the helm!' called out one of the pilots, 'or the ship's lost. She must bear the main-sail, captain,' added he, 'or we shall not weather the island, and she will strike in less than half an hour.' The main-sail was cast loose, and after a severe contest, its unwilling tack and sheet were belayed. The ship was literally buried in the foam, and I expected to see the main-mast go by the board every instant. Orders had been given, in case of such an event, to have all the axes ready. Providentially the wind veered two points to the southward, which saved the ship and her crew. Had she struck, she must instantly have gone to pieces. The rocks were so perpendicular that in all probability the whole of us must have made food for fishes. In a quarter of an hour we were clear of the island. Had we been under sentence of death, and suddenly reprieved, the effect on our minds could not have been greater. Long, anxious faces coiled themselves up to half their length and became brighter. The captain, who had been pacing the quarter-deck in quick time, brought himself up all standing, and I could perceive his lips move, and, if I mistake not, he was offering up a mental prayer of thankfulness for our hair-breadth escape. At daylight the gale abated, when, on examining the masts, the maintop-mast was found sprung in the cap. The following evening we captured two French brigs from Martinique, laden with sugar and coffee, and the day after a Dutch ship from Smyrna bound to Amsterdam, laden with silks and cotton, in which I went as prize-master. On our arrival at Plymouth we were put into quarantine. The boat which came out to us kept on her oars. I could not forbear smiling when I requested our letters might be sent on shore by her to see the great and certainly necessary precautions taken by these cunning people. A long kind of sprit was held up, split at the end to receive the letters. When in the boat, one man clipped them with a pair of scissors, another fumigated them with brimstone, a third bedabbled them with dirty vinegar and threw them into a leathern bag, taking care not to touch them with his hands.

CHAPTER 15

A LINE OF BATTLE SHIP

The ship anchored at Cawsand Bay four days afterwards, when we joined her, leaving the prizes in charge of the agent. I found her with the yellow flag flying at the masthead. She had been put in quarantine on her arrival, which we paid off with the foretop-sail, as we sailed the day after for a six weeks' cruise in the chops of the Channel. At the end of that period we returned to our anchorage with another French brig laden with Colonial produce. Our gallant and would-be musical captain consulted us all respecting harmonious sounds, but, alas! we were weighed in the musical balance and found wanting. This, however, did not discourage him. Nine of the crew came forward with three of the marines, offering themselves as candidates for the band. The captain, after having consulted one of the sergeants of marines, who played the hautboy, whether anything might be made of the men who had come forward as musicians, it was determined *nem. con.* that a pease-barrel should be manufactured into a big drum, that two ramrods should be metamorphosed into triangles, that the two bassoons and the hautboy taken in the French frigate should be brought into action without loss of time, that the marine and ship's fifer, with the marine drummer, should be drilled with the others, under the direction of the sergeant, in the captain's cabin twice a day, and a horrible confusion of unmusical sounds they made for more than six weeks. The skipper was in his glory, and everybody else amazed. Some of my messmates prayed for them heartily, particularly the first lieutenant, who thought the captain musically mad. The mids declared they never would be respectable enough to be called a band, but would be bad enough to be called a banditti, as they looked more like brigands than musicians.

We had nearly completed our water and stores, when I was ordered to the dockyard with the launch for the remainder and two anchor-stocks. It was blowing fresh, and in consequence I desired the leaves of the anchor-stock to be triced up under the oars outside the boat, that in case of shipping a sea we might be able, if necessary, to cut them away. The last leaf was lowered down to the boat, when I felt a touch on my shoulder. I turned quickly round, when my nose, which is not very short, came in rude contact with a cocked hat, which it nearly knocked off the head of the wearer. It was the admiral, who was in stature a King John's man, four feet nothing. I immediately pulled off my hat and apologised. 'What are you doing, sir,' said he to me, 'with these anchor-stocks?' 'Tricing them up outside the boat, sir,' replied I. 'Why do you not boat them?' I explained my reasons for not doing so. After a short pause, he said, 'You are perfectly right. What ship do you belong to?' I informed him. He wished me good evening, and I repaired on board. The morning after we sailed, and in three days we joined the Channel fleet under Lord Gardner. For two long, lingering months we had our patience exercised, jogging backwards and forwards like a pig on a string. The *Prince* was our leader, and the ship astern of us the *Spartiate*. The former sailed like a haystack, the latter like a witch, and the sailors declared she was built of stolen wood, as she always sailed best at night. One squally night I was lieutenant of the middle watch, when the *Prince* split *her* maintop-sail, and we were in consequence obliged to show a light astern and shorten sail. The *Spartiate* shot up, and was nearly on board of us. The captain, hearing a bustle, was soon on deck. 'What are the fleet about?' asked he. 'What is the matter with that beastly *Prince*?' I informed him. 'And what the devil is the *Spartang* doing on our weather quarter?'

'Why,' replied I, 'if the *Prince* and the *Spartiate* could divide their sailing, we should do very well; but we are very critically placed, being constantly obliged to shorten sail for the former, for fear of pooping her, and in so doing we are in our turn in danger of being pooped by the latter.'

'Have you showed a light to the *Spartang*?' demanded he, for he always called her by that unheard-of name. I answered in the affirmative. 'D——n that *Prince*,' resumed he, '*she* ought to be ordered out of the line. When I go on board the admiral, I will report her.' The ships again fell into their stations, and the captain took his in his cot. It was now the depth of winter, and the weather very severe. I had caught cold which confined me to my cot, and when we arrived at Plymouth I had a violent rheumatic fever. I was carried on shore to sick quarters in blankets, and before I was sufficiently recovered the ship sailed.

When I was strong enough I requested permission from the admiral to go to London, which was granted. I had a run in the country for a few months, for I soon got tired of noisy, smoky London. Soon after this I was informed by the Admiralty that I was superseded in the last ship, and ordered to Portsmouth to join the *Tonnant*, an eighty-four. A few days after receiving my commission, I joined this glorious ship of ships. When

I took a perspective view of her gun-decks, I thought her an equal match for any ship afloat, and so she certainly was, and nobly proved it afterwards. Her gallant commander, Captain Troubridge, was from the Emerald Isle; had a slight touch of the brogue, and was replete with anecdote; he was good-humoured and a gentleman, and he never punished a man unless he richly deserved it. My messmates were all young men, and generally speaking well informed, with the exception of the master, who was a countryman of mine, and desperately fond of doggerel verse as well as cray-fish and conger eels.

We were again destined to make one of the Channel fleet, when to our great joy, after tacking and half-tacking for six weeks, we were ordered with some more ships of the line under Admiral Collingwood to proceed off Cadiz to watch the motions of the Spanish and French fleets, after the scratch they had with our fleet under Sir R F Calder. We occasionally ran into Gibraltar for refreshments and stores. On one of these occasions the Port-Admiral took it into his head to hoist his flag on board of one of the active ships, and ordered us with two others to make sail out of the harbour. As we were not acquainted with his object, we presumed he wanted to purify his constitution by a strong sea-breeze; if so, he was disappointed, as it fell calm two hours after we cleared Europa Point, and during the night we were under the shells and shot of Ceuta, which fortunately fell harmless. The day after we reached our former anchorage at Gibraltar, where we found Sir Richard Bickerton, who took us under his orders to cruise off Carthagena, where three Spanish line of battle ships were lying ready for sea.

On our way thither we anchored in Oran roads to procure bullocks for the squadron. As soon as the sails were furled a Turkish officer, dressed something like that figure of fun called Punch, came on board us, as we were the nearest ship, to inquire if the fort saluted us what number of guns would be fired in return. We referred him to the flag-ship; he took his departure with his interpreter who spoke broken English. About 1pm, whack came a large shot from the fort nearly into the bow, and presently several more. At first, as shot were fired so close to us, we could not exactly tell what was intended until the nineteenth shot was fired, when the battery was silent. The flag-ship returned seventeen guns. On inquiry we found that these barbarians always salute with shot, and endeavour to send them as near you as possible by way of compliment.

About 3pm three principal Turkish officers came on board, the youngest of whom was the commander or governor of the town. The purser, who had been eyeing him with a wicked look, said to us, 'I'll make that fellow drunk before he leaves the ship.' He had expressed a wish to see the ship, and I offered to take him round the decks. In the meanwhile the purser went to his cabin, mixed some strong punch, and made some sherbet. 'Now,' said he to me, 'when you show him the cockpit, hand him into my cabin.' The Pacha admired the ship and the guns, and said it was the largest vessel he had seen. He spoke a little broken English. At length we came to the purser's cabin which was neatly fitted up and well lighted. The Turk was requested to repose himself on the sofa, and to take some sherbet. 'First of all,' whispered the purser to me, 'we will try him with the punch.' A glass was accordingly handed to him, and we filled others for ourselves. It went down his throat like mother's milk. He declared it was the best sherbet he had ever drunk, and asked for another glass of it. Down that went without a pause. 'He'll do,' whispered the purser, 'he is a true Mussulman; he prefers stiff punch to cobbler's punch.' A tureen was now filled with yet stronger punch, of which he took three more tumblers, and down he fell. He was laid on the sofa until his friends were ready to leave the ship. When they came from the captain's cabin, where they had been taking refreshments, they inquired for the sub-governor. After some delay and more difficulty he made his appearance. His turban had fallen off, and his countenance was ghastly. He was so helpless that he was obliged to be lowered into the boat, to the astonishment and terror of all those who had brought him off, and to the amusement of all our officers and crew.

The following morning I received orders to go on shore with three boats, each containing two barrels of powder and a half barrel of musket balls as a present to the Bey. On our arrival alongside a kind of quay, hewn out of the solid rock, a number of Moors rushed into the boats and seized on the ammunition. I desired the boats' crews to take the stretchers and give them some gentle raps on their petit toes, which made them soon jump back again. I then ordered the boats to lie on their oars, and seeing a person who looked something in the shape of an Irishman, I asked him if he would go to the English Consul and inform him that I should not land anything until he made his appearance. 'Shure,' said he, 'I am the Consul's secretary; won't that do, so please ye?' 'No,' replied I, 'nothing less than the Consul.' 'He has not finished his dinner yet, sir,' was the answer. 'Now,' said I, 'Mr Consul's secretary, if you do not immediately go to the Consul and acquaint him that I am waiting for him, I will go on board, and you will all be hanged by the sentence of a court-martial.' 'Oh, sir, I shall be there in no time at all. Do not leave the harbour until you see me again.' 'Run,' returned I, 'for your life depends on your expedition.' The poor man, I believe, was as frightened as he appeared ignorant.

In about seven minutes down came a tall, large-boned Yankee-kind-of-person with the before-mentioned secretary. 'Will you, if you plaise, permit the boats to come on shore, sir,' he called out; 'I am His Majesty's Consul.' We again got alongside the jetty. 'Now, Mr Consul,' said I—— 'My name is Murphy, sir, if it's not bad manners.' 'Well, Mr Murphy, if any of those barbarians dare come into the boats, they will be thrown overboard. Our men will put the barrels on the rocks, and they may take them, but you will give me a receipt for them.' 'Shure that I'll do for you, sir, in a few minutes. Will you favour me with your company to my house?' 'By no means; my orders are not to set a foot on shore. But if you will purchase for me half a dozen of small bottles of otto of roses I will thank you. I cannot remain,' added I, 'more than a quarter of an hour longer.' Whilst we were waiting for His Majesty's Consul, who, I need not hint, was an Irishman, an animal made its appearance which the boat's crew declared was a woman. It was clad in a coarse, light brown wrapping gown almost in the shape of a sack with the mouth downwards, with two small holes in the upper part for the eyes. As soon as it came near the boats it was driven away by the Moors. At length Mr Murphy made his appearance with the requisite piece of paper and eight bottles of otto of roses, for which he did not forget to ask a good price. He informed me that bullocks would be sent off to the squadron next morning. We repaired on board, when my captain asked me if the Bey had sent me a sabre. 'No,' replied I, 'I have received nothing.' 'Then,' said he, 'he is worse than a Turk; he ought to have given you one.'

The day after we received twelve bullocks not much larger in size than an English calf, and I, with one of my messmates, went on shore outside the town. The soil we found very sandy. I took out my sketch book, and had drawn the outline of the batteries, when an armed Arab rode up to us at full gallop on a beautiful, small, dark chestnut horse. My messmate wore a highly polished steel-hilted hanger, the brightness of which, as it glittered in the sun's rays, attracted the Arab's attention. He spoke broken English, and asked to look at it. 'Yes,' said my companion, 'if you will let me look at yours.' He took it from his side without hesitation and presented it to him. The Arab admired the workmanship of the English sword, and then examined the blade. We had inspected his, and found it fine Damascus steel. 'Will you exchange,' said my messmate. He made a most contemptuous grimace at the question. 'I tell you what,' said he, 'English very good for handle, but Arab better for blade.' He then put spurs to his horse and galloped away, chuckling the whole time.

As we had not permission to enter the gates of the town we amused ourselves by examining the houses outside, which were low and white-washed. The windows were few, small and high, and some of these mean, wretched-looking hovels were surrounded by a mud and sand wall. We saw only Moors and a few Arabs. The country higher up appeared green and fresh, although much rock and sand abounded. The harbour, or rather bay, is small, and its depth of water from two to five fathoms. The principal battery is built on a solid tongue of rock which curves outward and forms a kind of harbour. I remarked the Spanish arms on the centre of it, and on inquiry I found it had been placed there by Charles the Fifth when he landed and took possession of the town.

On the morning of the third day we were under sail for Carthagena. On nearing the harbour, which is strongly fortified by an island at its mouth, we discovered two Spanish ships of the line at anchor, but so close under the island that it was impossible to make any impression on them. The next day they removed into the harbour and struck their top-masts. We cruised between Capes di Gata and Palos for a fortnight, occasionally looking into Carthagena to see if the Spaniards would take the hint. Finding all our wishes and hints fruitless, we left a frigate and a brig sloop to watch their motions and shaped our course for Gibraltar. Near the small island of Alberaw we fell in with two frigates convoying twenty sail of levanters, the commodore of which called me brother-in-law. As the wind was light I had permission to spend the day on board his frigate, where I partook of an Italian dinner, more shadow than substance, and after coffee I repaired on board my own ship, where I ordered something substantial to eat, as the Italian dinner had provoked a good appetite. We anchored at old Gib four days afterwards, and were ordered to refit with all expedition and join once more Admiral Collingwood off Cadiz, where the French and Spanish fleets still remained and were apparently ready for sea.

CHAPTER 16

BATTLE OF TRAFALGAR

In a week's time we formed one of the squadron, and shortly after were joined by fourteen sail of the line under Lord Nelson. The salutation was heartfelt and most gratifying. The dispositions of the fleet were soon made, and as they were as simple as possible, there could be no mistake. A cordon of frigates were ordered to repeat signals to us from the one nearest the shore, whilst we kept nearly out of sight of the land, and all our ships' sides were ordered to be painted yellow with black streaks, and the masts yellow.

We now mustered twenty-seven sail of the line, four frigates, and a schooner, and were waiting impatiently for the joyful signal from the frigates that the enemy were coming out of harbour. On the afternoon of the 20th of October, 1805, our longing eyes were blessed with the signal. We cleared for quarters and were in high spirits. At daylight we had the felicity to see them from the deck, and counted thirty-three sail of the line and three large frigates. They extended in line ahead.

We answered with alacrity the signal to make all sail for the enemy, preserving our order of sailing. The sails appeared to know their places and were spread like magic. The wind was very light, and it was nearly noon before we closed with the enemy. We remarked they had formed their ships alternately French and Spanish. All our ships that had bands were playing 'Rule Britannia,' 'Downfall of Paris,' etc. Our own struck up 'Britons, strike home.' We were so slow in moving through the water in consequence of the lightness of the wind that some of the enemy's ships gave us a royal salute before we could break their line, and we lost two of the band and had nine wounded before we opened our fire. The telegraph signal was flying from the masthead of the *Victory*, 'England expects every man to do his duty.' It was answered with three hearty cheers from each ship, which must have shaken the nerve of the enemy. We were saved the trouble of taking in our studding-sails, as our opponents had the civility to effect it by shot before we got into their line. At length we had the honour of nestling His Majesty's ship between a

French and a Spanish seventy-four, and so close that a biscuit might have been thrown on the decks of either of them. Our guns were all double-shotted. The order was given to fire; being so close every shot was poured into their hulls, down came the Frenchman's mizzen-mast, and after our second broadside the Spaniard's fore and cross-jack yards. A Spanish three-decker now crossed our bows and gave us a raking broadside which knocked away the fore and main top-masts, the main and foreyards with the jib-boom and sprit-sail yard, part of the head, and killed and wounded twenty-two of the men. One midshipman was cut literally in half. This was the more provoking as we could not return her the compliment, having full employment with those we first engaged.

We were in this situation about half-an-hour, when the Spaniard called out he had struck, but before we could take possession of him, a French ship of eighty guns with an admiral's flag came up, and poured a raking broadside into our stern which killed and wounded forty petty officers and men, nearly cut the rudder in two, and shattered the whole of the stern with the quarter galleries. She then in the most gallant manner locked her bow-sprit in our starboard main shrouds, and attempted to board us with the greater part of her officers and ship's company. She had rifle-men in her tops who did great execution. Our poop was soon cleared, and our gallant captain shot through the left thigh and obliged to be carried below. During this time we were not idle. We gave it to her most gloriously with the starboard lower and main-deckers, and turned the forecastle guns loaded with grape on the gentleman who wished to give us a fraternal hug. The marines kept up a warm and destructive fire on the boarders. Only one man made good his footing on our quarter-deck, when he was pinned through the calf of his right leg by one of the crew with his half-pike, whilst another was going to cut him down, which I prevented, and desired him to be taken to the cockpit. At this period the *Bellerophon*, seeing our critical position, gallantly steered between us and our first French antagonist and sheeted her home until she struck her colours. Our severe contest with the French admiral lasted more than half-an-hour, our sides grinding so much against each other that we were obliged to fire the lower deck guns without running them out.

At length both ships caught fire before the chest-trees, and our fire-men, with all the coolness and courage so inherent in British seamen, got the engine and played on both ships, and finally extinguished the flames, although two of them were severely wounded in doing so. At length we had the satisfaction of seeing her three lower masts go by the board, ripping the partners up in their fall, as they had been shot through below the deck, and carrying with them all their sharp-shooters to look sharper in the next world, for as all our boats were shot through we could not save one of them in this. The crew were then ordered with the second lieutenant to board her. They cheered and in a short time carried her. They found the gallant French Admiral Magon killed at the foot of the poop ladder, the captain dangerously wounded. Out of eight lieutenants five were killed, with three hundred petty officers and seamen, and about one hundred wounded. We left the second lieutenant and sixty men in charge of her, and took some of the prisoners on board when she swung clear of us. We had pummelled her so handsomely that fourteen of her lower deck guns were dismounted, and her larboard bow exhibited a mass of splinters.

After she cleared us another Spanish three-decker drifted nearly on board of us. We received her fire, which shot away the gaff. We returned her salute with interest, and her foremast went about four feet above her deck. We cheered and gave her another broadside, and down came her colours. We manned the jolly boat – the only boat that we thought would float – to take possession of her, but she had not proceeded more than a few yards when down she went, leaving the fourth lieutenant and her crew paddling like sea nondescripts. Having no boat that would float, four of the seamen jumped overboard to rescue those who could not swim, and they all regained the ship. Mr C, the lieutenant, was nearly drowned, and had it not been for a black man, who took him on his back, he must have sunk. (This man he never lost sight of and left him a handsome legacy when he died.) We were drifting like a pig upon a grating, and as helpless as a sucking shrimp, when the signal was made to repair damages. We soon cut away all that was useless, and in twenty minutes we were under topsails as courses, and top-gallant-sails as topsails.

The carpenters had cobbled up one of the cutters, in which I was sent on board the *Royal Sovereign* to report our condition and to request the assistance of one of the fleet to tow us, as in consequence of our rudder being so much shattered by shot it was rendered unserviceable. The *Defiance* was ordered to take us in tow; we shortly afterwards made the signal, that we were able to renew the action. The enemy's fleet were making for Cadiz. Nineteen sail of their line of battleships had surrendered, and one, the *Achille*, had blown up. The explosion she made was sublime and awful; a number of her crew were saved by the *Pickle* schooner. The wind still continued light, and the signal was flying to renew the attack. In about twenty minutes we were again in the rear of the enemy, who appeared to have had enough of it, as they had neared Cadiz, and all the prizes except four seventy-fours were making for the harbour. This was owing to their having so few of our men on board them, and to our not being able, in consequence of the loss of boats, to take out the prisoners. We gave them some parting salutes. There were so many of us in a crippled state it was thought prudent to haul to the westward, as the swell was throwing us towards the shore, and the sky had all the tokens of a gale of wind from the west-south-west. The signal was out to prepare to anchor if necessary. The *Royal Sovereign*, which had only her foremast standing, with four other ships of our fleet, had already anchored.

The *Santissima Trinidada*, one of the Spanish prizes, went down in consequence of having received so many shot between wind and water. Her crew were taken out by our frigates and she was scuttled. She was the largest ship and had four regular tiers of guns, mounting in the whole one hundred and thirty-six. About 7pm the wind began to freshen from the westward. The signal was made from the *Royal Sovereign* for all those ships that could carry sail to proceed to Gibraltar. About 9pm the wind increased to a heavy gale, and the ship which towed us was obliged to cast us off. We fortunately had been able to fix the quarter tackles to the ringbolts of the rudder before the gale came on. The night was passed in much painful anxiety, and we expected every time we wore to strike on the rocks of Cape Trafalgar. Providentially the wind drew more round to the north-east, and at daylight we weathered the Cape and about noon anchored at Gibraltar. We found the four prizes with several of our fleet lying there, and we were congratulated most cordially on our having escaped a lee shore, as they had given us up as lost.

I must retrograde a little here and relate a few occurrences which took place during the action, and of which I was an eye-witness. We had hoisted our colours before the action in four different places, at the ensign-staff, peak, and in the fore and main top-mast shrouds, that if one was shot away the others might be flying. A number of our fleet had done the same, and several of the enemy followed our example. The French admiral's ship who so gallantly attempted to board us had his flag hoisted in three places. One of our men, Fitzgerald, ran up his rigging and cut away one of them and placed it round his waist, and had nearly, after this daring exploit, reached his ship, when a rifleman shot him and he fell between the two ships and was no more seen. The principal signalman, whose name was White, and a captain of one of the guns on the poop, had his right great toe nearly severed from his foot. He deliberately took his knife and cut it away. He was desired to go below to the doctor. 'No, sir,' was his reply; 'I am not the fellow to go below for such a scratch as that. I wish to give the beggars,' meaning the enemy, 'a few more hard pills before I have done with them.' Saying this, he bound his foot up in his neck-handkerchief and served out double allowance until his carronade was dismounted by the carriage of it being shattered to pieces. He then hopped to another gun, where he amused himself at the Frenchman's expense until the action ceased.

We had fought on nearly empty stomachs. At the time we began the action it was dinner time, *ie* twelve o'clock; a small proportion of cheese had been given out and half allowance of grog. During the latter part of the action the captain, who was lying on a cot in the purser's cabin, sent for me. On entering the cockpit I found fourteen men waiting amputation of either an arm or a leg. A marine who had sailed with me in a former ship was standing up as I passed, with his left arm hanging down. 'What's the matter, Conelly?' said I to him. 'Not much,' replied he; 'I am only winged above my elbow, and I am waiting my turn to be lopped.' His arm was dreadfully broken by a grape-shot. I regret to mention that out of sixteen amputations only two survived. This was in consequence of the motion of the ship during the gale. Their stumps broke out afresh, and it was impossible to stop the hæmorrhage. One of them, whose name was Smith, after his leg was taken off, hearing the cheering on deck in consequence of another of the enemy striking her colours, cheered also. The exertion he made burst the vessels, and before they could be again taken up he died.

When I was sent on board Admiral Collingwood's ship during the action I observed a great anxiety in the officers' faces. It immediately occurred to me that Lord Nelson had fallen, and I put the question to one of the lieutenants, who told me he was mortally wounded and that he could not live long. Thus gloriously fell in the arms, and on the deck, of *Victory*, as brave, as intrepid, and as great a hero as ever existed, a seaman's friend and the father of the fleet. The love of his country was engraven on his heart. He was most zealous for her honour and welfare, and his discernment was clear and decisive. His death was deservedly and deeply felt by every man in the fleet. I must not omit that when the Commander of the French fleet, Admiral Villeneuve, was brought alongside us instead of the *Victory*, he was informed it was not Nelson's ship. 'My God,' said he, 'you are all Nelsons!'*

On mustering our ship's company after we were tolerably in order, we found we had twenty-six killed and fifty-eight wounded, the captain included, who, as soon as we arrived, went on shore. We sent our wounded men to the hospital, and began to refit. Our rudder was unshipped, or rather the wreck of it, to be spliced. On the fourth morn-

* See Appendix note C.

ing, at daylight, during a fog, we were not a little astonished at finding ourselves bombarded, and the shells and shot flying fast and thick amongst us. We had taken the precaution of keeping our guns towards the enemy shotted, but fortunately for us and for those people who were amusing themselves in the enemy's gun-boats, the fog was so dense that we neither could see them or they us. However, we fired as nearly as we could judge in the direction from whence their shells came, and I presume we must have done some execution among them. After our second broadside all was silent. We had only a few ropes shot away and one man wounded. The shells fell either short or over us on shore, where they did no injury. The shot were the most destructive. After this freak, which might have proved serious, we had additional guard boats during night.

The Governor, General Fox, sent an invitation to all the officers of the fleet requesting their company to a ball at the Government House. I understood it was well attended, and the ladies very amiable. I, having received a wound in the left hand, which was painful, did not attend. Before we sailed we had several dinner-parties and made excursions to St George's and other caves. One afternoon I had been rambling with another brother officer over the Rock, when, as we reached the O'Hara Tower, we were overtaken by a thunder-storm. As we stood in the tower, which, as Paddy would say, is no tower at all, we saw the thunder-clouds descend under us, and could distinctly see the lightning. It was to us a novel and awful scene. We soon removed from our position, as the small building under which we had taken shelter had been formerly struck by lightning, and we began to be apprehensive of its second visit. In descending we started two large baboons, who appeared as much surprised as we were. We soon lost sight of them among the rocks. It is strictly forbidden to use fire-arms or to destroy anything on the Rock. We also saw a few red-legged partridges, which were not very shy, and some large lizards.

The officers of the garrison gave a horse race on neutral ground, and invited the Governor of St Roch with his staff. He came with a numerous retinue. Flags of truce were stuck up beyond the Gibraltar limits, and we were at liberty to go nearly as far as the nearest Spanish fort. It was a singular coincidence to see us shaking hands and offering cigars to men whose duty it was an hour before to shoot us. Everything went off very pleasantly except with the poor, distressed horses, who had to run over deep sand. After the Spanish Governor and his officers had partaken of a plentiful collation under a large marquee, they took their departure, and we gave them three cheers. We at length received our rudder from the hands of the dockyard mateys. They had made a good job of it, and it answered admirably.

CHAPTER 17

OFF BREST

A few days after we sailed, with three other line of battle ships, under jury-masts, for old England. On our passage we spoke a frigate, who informed us that Sir Richard Strachan had taken the four sail of the line which had escaped from the French fleet. We were delighted as well as 'Dicky Strong', and gave three hearty cheers. On the eighth day we arrived at Spithead, and were cheered by all the ships lying there, which we returned. Some of the fleet had, we thought, made rather a show of their shot-holes, but our commodore declared that 'good wine needed no bush.' Our shot-holes, of which we had a good share, were painted over and not perceptible at any distance. The captain left us, and was heartily cheered as he left the ship. As soon as we were in the harbour I had permission from the Admiralty to return home for a month.

I found my sweetest half (for I had, without knowing why or wherefore, become a Benedict) in much anxiety, as our ship had been reported lost. She put into my arms a dear little black-eyed girl, who was born a week after the action. After spending three delightful weeks, the happiest of the happy, I tore myself away. On my rejoining the ship I found her in dock, and all the crew on board a hulk. I now became commanding officer, as the first lieutenant had leave of absence. I have here to remark that forty seamen and ten marines had leave to go to their families and friends for three weeks or a month, according to the distance, and out of six hundred men only one desertion occurred. I mention this circumstance to prove that seamen, when they become accustomed to a man-of-war, have no dislike to her discipline, provided they are properly encouraged when deserving, and the cat is only used when it is absolutely necessary, which was the case in our ship. Seamen are too valuable to be ill used.

Admiral Montague was the commander-in-chief at this port, and Sir Isaac Coffin, of inspecting memory, the rear-admiral. One morning one of the midshipmen, in stepping into the dockyard boat, had the misfortune to lose his dirk overboard. As it was blowing strong, he could not return to the hulk to borrow another. He consequently went to the yard without one. The rear-admiral, who was always in search of adventure, met him. 'Hulloa! officer,' said he; 'why are you without side arms?' The youngster related what had happened. 'Then, sir,' said he, 'you must buy another as fast as you can.' 'I have no money, sir,' replied the mid, 'and I know no one here.' 'Then I will put you in the way to get one. Come with me to my office.' The youngster followed him, and received the address of a sword cutler. 'And tell him,' said Sir Isaac, 'from me that you are to have a dirk. But,' added he, 'I had better write my name; he will then know I sent you.' Next morning the mid lost no time in repairing to the shop of the vendor of slaying instruments. He produced the rear-admiral's paper. The cutler at first hesitated. At length he said, 'Do you pay for it?' 'No,' answered the mid, 'not till I return from my next cruise.' 'Oh, never mind,' said the man of cut and thrust; 'Sir Isaac has signed the paper, and he will, of course, be responsible. What kind of dirk do you wish to have?' 'Oh, a good one,' returned the mid; 'one at about forty shillings.' It was given him; he gave his name and ship, and left the shop. In a few days after this an order came on board from the admiral to discharge a lieutenant and a midshipman into another ship bound to the West Indies. The sixth lieutenant and this youngster were selected. About four months afterwards the bill was sent to the rear-admiral for payment of the dirk. It was naturally refused. Some months passed, when the bill was again presented and refused. The poor mid was far away and not forthcoming, although he fully intended, had he not been so suddenly exiled, to pay it when he was able. The cutler now brought an action against the rear-admiral, and he was, as he had put his name to the paper, obliged to pay the account.

The shipwrights and carpenters having repaired the ship, she was hauled alongside the hulk, and in ten days was as majestic as ever. Another captain was appointed, and I was ordered to join the *Diamond* frigate, as first lieutenant, off Brest. I took an affectionate leave of my messmates, and procured a passage on board a passage-sloop going to Plymouth. We sailed in the evening, through the Needles passage, and when off the Shingles the head of the mast went in the hounds. After much exertion we got the main-sail out of the water, and the try-sail set. We reached, to my great joy, Portland Roads on the third day, where, as I found myself rather queerish on board the sloop, I salaamed the skipper of her, and mounted a horse, which they assured me was quiet enough to carry the parson. With this assurance, which was corroborated by three old men and two young women, I trusted myself once more on a horse's back. A brother officer, who was also going to join a ship at Plymouth, accompanied me. We dined at Weymouth, saw Gloucester Lodge, had a somersault, to the terror and astonishment of the lady housekeeper and servants, on all the Princesses' beds, viewed the closet of odd-and-end old china belonging to the amiable Princess Elizabeth, thought ourselves an inch taller when we sat ourselves down in the chair in which the good King dined at one o'clock, generally off a boiled leg of mutton and turnips, so we were informed, and in the evening hired a post-chaise and arrived at Dorchester, where we took the mail for Plymouth. On reaching the latter place we repaired to the admiral's office, where, as there was no present opportunity of joining my new ship, I remained five days, calling on my old acquaintances and talking of old times.

One day we made an excursion to Plympton, and entered a neat farmer's house. We inquired if we could be provided with some home-baked brown bread, and milk from the cow. The farmer's wife, who was a hale, buxom, youngish-looking woman, and had only nine children, brought out chairs and benches. We had some madeira with us, and we made delicious whip-syllabub. The nice, well-baked and wholesome brown loaves, with the milk and cream, were too good for city aldermen, but quite good enough for sailors. We did ample justice to the good wife's fare, of which she partook with her mother, who was sixty-five, and had eleven boys and nine girls all living. Nine of the former were on board different men-of-war, and the other two working with their father on the farm. 'And,' added the poor woman, with an anxious, smiling face, 'whenever we see a squadron of King's ships arrive we expect a son.' The girls, with the exception of three who were married, were out in respectable families. We made a trifling purse, which we gave to a fine boy about eleven years old for himself and brothers; recompensed our good hostess, shook hands, and departed in peace and good fellowship.

Two days later I went on board the *Alexandria* frigate for a passage to my proper ship, which we fell in with soon afterwards off the Black Rocks. I found her a fine, first-class frigate, but, alas! I also found she only sailed like the launch, stern foremost. The captain, a jolly, little, fresh-faced, rather corpulent man, welcomed me with a smile, and after a short conversation relating to the ship he inquired the news, on which I pre-sented him with the latest newspaper. The surgeon, a delicate, pale young man, came up to me and asked me to the gun-room. On entering it he introduced me to my future messmates. The second lieutenant was a fine-looking young man, highly connected, but unfortunately disgusted with the Service, and too fond of a very strong north-wester, which soon destroyed him, as he died a few months after I joined the frigate. The third lieutenant was a person of great consequence in his own opinion, and always imagined himself in the right. He was, nevertheless, an active officer and knew his duty. The master was a hardy north countryman, and knew what he was about. The marine officer was a well-informed, sensible man; the mids were a fine set of lads, ripe for mischief and alert on duty. The ship's company were, generally speaking, good and willing seamen, and I thought myself fortunate in being first lieutenant of such a ship and of having intellectual messmates.

We were placed as one of the look-out frigates to watch the enemy's vessels in Brest. The fleet was under the command of the brave and persevering Earl St Vincent, whose laws were those of the Medes and Persians in days of yore. Implicit obedience and non-resistance was his device, and woe to those who were disobedient. My messmates gave me the outline of the captain's character. They informed me he was more cut out for a country gentleman than the captain of a man-of-war, that he was very partial to a good dinner – 'Show me the man who is not,' interrupted I; – that he was highly nervous, and that he left everything to the first lieutenant, except the discipline of his cook. 'So be it,' cried I, 'I think we shall accord.' About ten days after being on board he sent for me into his cabin. 'Now,' said he to me, 'Mr Hoffman, we have had time enough to know each other. I approve of your method of carrying on the duty, and from henceforth I shall consider you as sailing, and myself as fighting, captain.' I thanked him for the confidence he reposed in me, and assured him that, being very partial to the profession, I never was happier than when in the path of duty. He then mentioned he was not fond of punishment with the cat. I informed him that, having been first lieutenant for nearly three years of a former ship, I would submit to his inspection a code of minor punishments which had proved beneficial to her discipline. 'Did you not use the cat at all?' demanded he. 'Never,' returned I, 'except for theft, drunkenness at sea and intentional disobedience of orders. On these occasions the punishment was severe, and they very seldom happened.'

When the wind was light, we generally anchored about two gun-shots from the shore, and in the evening the crew danced or got up a kind of farce, which was farcical enough. After seven long, lazy, tedious weeks, we were ordered to Plymouth to refit. We flew like a shovel-nosed barge against tide, and reached Hamoaze on the evening of the third day. Reader, I do not know whether you were ever at Plymouth. If you have not, go there. It is in a beautiful country, and very healthy. The people are very civil, and until the taxes and poor rates became so high, were very hospitable. Even in the poorest cottager's hut, if you happened to call at their dinner-hour, you were invited, with a hearty 'Do ye, God bless ye, sit down and take some-at. There be more than we can eat.' We frequently made social picnic parties to the small farmhouses. I have heard sailors declare they would rather be hanged in their native country than die a natural death in any other. It is not very agreeable to be hanged even in Paradise, but I certainly prefer residing in the neighbourhood of Plymouth to any other part of England. The month we were in harbour vanished like a dream. We cast off the moorings, and soon after anchored at Spithead.

The following week we were again on the Siberian or Black Rock station. One night, in consequence of a light westerly wind with a heavy swell and a counter current, we had drifted so near the south-west end of Ushant that we were obliged to let go an anchor in rocky ground. For more than six hours it was a question whether the cable would part or hold on: had the latter occurred, the frigate must have gone on shore. After hoping, wishing and expecting a breeze from the eastward, it made its appearance by cat's-paws. We weighed, and found the cackling and one strand of the cable cut through. As the wind freshened we worked up to our old station off Point St Matthew, and anchored. The following morning we reconnoitred Brest, could make out fourteen of the enemy's ships of the line with their top-gallant yards crossed, and five others refitting. The same day a cutter joined us with our letters and two bullocks. After cruising between Ushant and the Saints, the small rocky island Beriguet and Douarnenez Bay, until we were tired of seeing them, we, at the expiration of two months, were again ordered to Plymouth to refit, but not before the considerate old Earl had taken from us thirty of our best seamen, which so much pleased our noble captain that he declared if he was ordered to rejoin the Channel fleet he would give up the frigate. After having refitted, to our great mortification we were again under orders for the detestable station off Brest. The captain wrote to be superseded, and as there was no lack of sharp half-pay skippers looking-out, his request was immediately complied with.

His successor was a shambling, red-nosed, not sailor-like looking man, who had persuaded a counterpart of himself, the village barber, to accompany him as his steward. Sure such a pair was never seen before! The hands were turned up and his commission read. 'Well, my men,' said he, addressing the crew, 'I understand you know how to do your duty, therefore my advice to you is to do it. That's all,' said he to me; 'pipe down if you please, sir,' and after adding, 'We shall sail to-morrow morning, and I shall be on board in the evening,' he ordered a cutter to be manned, and went on shore. At the time appointed we were under weigh, and three days afterwards off the Black Rocks, which made us look black enough. The enemy's fleet were much in the same state, with little prospect of their coming out. Easterly winds were prevalent, and we were generally at anchor, one half of the ship's company doing nothing, and the other helping them. I soon found that our noble commander was fond of the game of chess and a stiff glass of grog, and I frequently found him *en chemise* with those companions at daylight on one of the cabin lockers. He was an unmarried man, but a great admirer of the fair sex of all descriptions, and was sometimes heard to say he was astonished at their want of taste in not admiring him. He was not altogether an unread man, but his manners were like his dress, slovenly, and too often coarse. He had been, when he was a lieutenant, in command of a cutter, and afterwards of a lugger. There, the mids declared, he ought to have remained, as he was out of his element on the quarter-deck of a fine frigate. They were not singular in their opinion. He was, without exception, the most slovenly officer I ever had the misfortune to sail with. I am probably rather severe. His only redeeming quality was certainly good nature. He, unfortunately for himself and in some measure for the Service, courted a kind of left-handed popularity amongst the seamen, and neglected the officers. The consequence was, that in less than two months the discipline of the ship became so relaxed that the crew, from being one of the smartest in the fleet, was now the slackest. After a disagreeable cruise of nine weeks, in which time we had carried away the main and foretopmasts, we were ordered to Portsmouth. After refitting we joined another frigate to cruise off Havre de Grace, where the enemy had two frigates and a corvette nearly ready for sea. We were shortly after joined by a sloop of war. At the full and change of the moon we always anchored inside the Cape, in order to watch the enemy's motions more effectively, and, when under weigh, we sometimes trawled and dredged, and frequently caught sufficient fish for the whole crew, as well as a quantity of oysters.

On one unlucky evening we ran on board the sloop of war, carried away the mainmast, and destroyed a part of her upper works. Fortunately for the officer of the watch the captain was on deck, and had been giving orders respecting the sails, which took the responsibility from the shoulders of the former. The sloop was so ill-treated by us that she was, without delay, obliged to proceed to Portsmouth. A few days after this accident we were ordered to the same port. On our arrival a court of inquiry sat to investigate the reason why the mainmast of one of His Majesty's cruisers should be so unceremoniously knocked away by the jib-boom of another. The answers not being quite satisfactory our captain was reprimanded and the other admonished. We sailed shortly after, and resumed our station. Of all duties imposed on an active mind blockading vessels in an enemy's port, from whence there is not much probability of their sailing, is the most tiresome. The mids declared that had patient Job been on board the ten weeks we were off Havre he would have lost his patience in the fifth week and thrown up his commission. After a lazy cruise of nearly eleven weeks the frigate once more sat like a duck at Spithead.

CHAPTER 18

'ORDERED FOREIGN'

After a refit and taking on board six months' provisions and stores, as we were ordered to fit foreign, our signal was made to proceed to sea under sealed orders, taking with us a sloop of war. On the tenth day we anchored in Funchal Roads, Madeira, with our consort. The day following was the natal day of our gracious Queen, on which occasion we both fired a royal salute and dressed the ships with flags. The captain, with as many of the officers as could be spared, was invited to dine with the consul at Funchal. At four o'clock the captain, two of my messmates and myself, left the ship, and in half an hour afterwards we reached the consul's house, where we met an agreeable party, consisting of four English ladies and eight gentlemen. It was the month of June, and the weather was very warm, but it did not prevent us from seeing the town and visiting some of the nunneries. The former was scarcely worth our trouble, and the latter gave us, from the nuns' appearance, no very high opinion of female beauty. We visited some of the vineyards. The vines, trained over arched trellis work, extend to some distance, and when in full leaf afford a delightful shade. The grapes are generally remarkably large and of a delicious flavour. The morning before sailing I found the best bower cable was two-thirds cut through by some small, sharp instrument on the turn round the bit-head. The hands were turned up and singly interrogated. Nobody knew anything about it. All appeared anxious to find out the culprit, but in vain. Had the cable parted in the night we should not have had room to have let go the small bower, and must have gone on the rocks.

In the afternoon we sailed, ran along the Canary Islands, and in five days afterwards anchored off the island of Goree. This small, tolerably well-fortified island is a few miles from Cape de Verde. It possesses no harbour, but the anchorage off the town is good. It produces nothing but a few cotton bushes. The inhabitants are very poor. They manufacture cotton cloths, in which they clothe themselves. They are a mixture of black, brown and white. Their features are more of the Arabian than the

African cast. They speak corrupt English, French and Portuguese. They are very proud and equally independent. The better class live in small houses made of mud and clay, the inferiors in cone-shaped buildings something like Indian kraals, formed neatly of bamboo and surrounded by a bamboo wall. The Governor, Colonel Lloyd, gave us an invitation to dinner and a ball. I was one of the party. The former consisted of buffalo soup, fish, and Muscovy ducks, the latter of a number of brown ladies dressed like bales of cotton. Dancing with them might be compared to a cooper working round a cask. Some few had tolerably regular features, and I noticed the captain making love like a Greenland bear to the girl I danced with.

The second morning after our arrival I was sent with two cutters to haul the seine off the mainland about three miles to the westward of Cape de Verde. As soon as we had made the first haul, in which we had taken a quantity of herrings, about twenty of the inhabitants of that part of the coast rushed towards the fish with the intention of seizing them. I desired the marines we had with us to present their muskets in order to frighten them. It answered perfectly, and they retired. I then desired two of the seamen to take a quantity of the fish and lay them down at some short distance, and I beckoned to the natives to come and take them, which they did, tumbling over each other in the scramble. After having taken a quantity of herrings in three hauls, besides several larger fish, I proceeded with one of the marines and the coxswain to the town.

I found it a miserable place, much like Goree, but three times the size, and surrounded by a high fence of thick bamboo matting, supported by long stakes. All I could purchase were two old Muscovy ducks, some pumpkins, and a few cocoanuts. One of the ducks got adrift, and a long, lean, hungry girl caught it and ran off with it into the brushwood, where we lost sight of her. The people of Goree informed us they were terrible thieves, and we proved it. The following day I again paid a visit to these Patagonian people, for the greater part of the men at Cape de Verde were more than six feet in stature and very slight. They all carried long lances, principally because of the numerous pattigoes, or hyenas, in their neighbourhood. The purser, who was with me, purchased with some rum which the coxswain of the boat brought with him two sacks of beans and some oranges. I mentioned the loss of my duck the day before to a man who understood English and spoke it indifferently. As I stood alongside of him, both the purser and myself, who were five feet seven, appeared like pigmies. He was at least seven feet two inches, and had an amazing long lance in his hand. He laughed loud and long at my recital. 'Ah, Buckra,' at last he chuckled out, 'you takee care anoder time, eh! and you no lettee de duck run abay; if you do, anoder piccaninny girl hab it again, eh?'

'Confound this fellow!' said the purser; 'I believe he is a worse rogue than the girl. Have you had enough of his palaver?' 'Almost too much,' answered I. 'Let us pull foot.' We returned to the boat, and after an hour's row got on board. The following day I dined with Commissary Hamilton, who showed me a letter from the interesting Mr Mungo Park, who was surgeon of the regiment he belonged to. Mr Hamilton told me he had set out with forty in his party, but that in consequence of sickness it was reduced to twenty-five; but notwithstanding these drawbacks Park wrote in good spirits, and was determined to persevere in his journey to Timbuctoo.

Before we sailed I made another excursion on the mainland, and fell in with fourteen Arabian travelling merchants. They were seated on the ground like London tailors, surrounded by their bales of goods, principally rough cotton, with six camels and two tame ostriches. The former were lying down, the latter walking about and searching for food among the short, rank grass and stones. Some of the latter I observed they swallowed. I purchased from the merchants some ostrich eggs. They asked me to give them rum. One of them, who spoke a little English, and was interpreter for the others, told me they intended coming on board to see the ship, and to shake hands with the captain. I informed him he would feel himself highly flattered by such Arabian condescension, but that they must make haste, as the ship would sail in a day or two. They all begged to shake hands with us, for the marine officer accompanied me. On returning to the boat we found two of the natives, who appeared at a distance more like maypoles than men, endeavouring to hold a conversation with the boat's crew. The coxswain told me they had fallen in love with the boat-hook, and offered in exchange one of their lances. When we appeared their thoughts were turned from the boat-hook to the marine officer's sword, and they requested him, by signs, to make an exchange. Another native had joined the other two, armed with a musket. I made signs to him to let me look at it, but he would not trust it out of his hands. I remarked it was an old English worn-out gun without a hammer to the lock. Perceiving that they were beginning to be troublesome, we jumped into the boat and threw them some biscuits, which they devoured with the appetite of wolves.

We had not been on board an hour when we were honoured with a visit from four of the Arabians, who, without ceremony, went up to the captain and shook him by the hand, and asked him for the purser. The latter very opportunely made his appearance, when the captain pointed him out to the Arab who spoke broken English. He soon left the latter, and accosted the former with unblushing effrontery, and asked him for a cask of flour. 'And for what?' demanded the purser. 'Because I your good friend,' was the answer. 'You are an impudent, beggarly rascal,' said our hasty-tempered purveyor of provisions to him. 'What can I see in your precious ugly black face that will induce me to give you anything but a good kicking?' 'Patience and policy, messmate,' I said. 'Where is your philosophy? Let your steward give them a few biscuits and a dram, and get rid of them.' To this proposal, after a grumble, he assented, and they departed.

The following morning we weighed, and made all sail for Cape Coast Roads. On our passage we experienced heavy squalls of wind and rain, which frequently obliged us to clew all up. We anchored at Sierra Leone on the fourth day, and found the colony healthy. After remaining two days to complete our water, we left it, and proceeded to our destination. We anchored off Cape Coast a few days afterwards, at a respectable distance, as the surf breaks two miles from the shore. The ship's boats on this part of the coast are useless. Were they to attempt to land they would soon be swamped and knocked to pieces, and the crews drowned. Native canoes of from eight to twenty paddles are only used, and it requires great caution and dexterity by the black boatmen to prevent their being upset. I once came off in a large canoe with twenty paddles. On the third rolling surf she was half filled, and I was washed out of the chair among the paddlers. As soon as the sails were furled, a large canoe came off from the Governor with an invitation for the captain to dine with him. I remarked that the greater part of the coal-coloured crew of the canoe had the wool on their heads tied into about thirty tails an inch in length. A painter might have manufactured a tolerable Gorgonian head from among them.

On the following day we were visited by several flat-nosed, thick-lipped, black-skinned ladies, who came off with the express purpose of being married to some of the man-of-war buckras. They soon found husbands. In the afternoon a canoe came alongside with a tall grasshopper of a woman as ugly as sin and as black as the ace of spades, with a little girl about seven years old a shade, if possible, blacker, and as great a beauty as herself. One of the canoe men came on the quarter-deck with them. He made a leg and pulled one of the many tails of his wool, and addressed me as follows: 'Massa officer, Massa Buckra Captain hab sent him wife off and him piccaninny.' Saying this he gave me a note, which was addressed to his steward, the barber, who came and told me, to my amazement, that the animal on two ill-formed legs was to have the use of the captain's cabin. Thinks I to myself, 'Wonders will never cease. There is no accounting for taste. Some people are over nice, some not nice enough.' About two hours after our gallant captain came on board, I presume love-sick, for he either looked love or shame-stricken. Probably I was mistaken, as I concluded he had discarded the latter when he entered the Service as an unmanly appendage.

Whilst here I went on shore with some of my messmates, and dined with the mess at the Castle off goat, boiled, broiled, roasted, stewed, and devilled, and some fish. In short they have nothing else except some half-starved fowls and Muscovy ducks; sometimes, but not very often, buffalo beef, which is so tough that after you have swallowed it – for you cannot chew it – you are liable to indigestion for two months or so; so naturally they prefer young goat. The Castle, which stands on an eminence, is strong on the sea face, but I presume it would not hold out long on the land side against a regular siege, but as I am no engineer, I will leave it, as Moore's Almanac says of the hieroglyphic, to the learned and the curious. The town consists of small, low huts, the greater part of which are built of stakes and mud, whitewashed over, and thatched with palm leaves. I saw a spot of parched, arid ground which was designated a botanical garden. If it did not contain many exotics, it did a most savage tiger, which was enclosed in an iron cage.

We had been cruising along the coast, and sometimes anchoring for about five weeks, when the captain of the sloop of war was promoted from this fleeting world to a better. I was, in consequence, appointed as her captain, being in my ninth year as lieutenant when I obtained my promotion. I parted company with the frigate shortly afterwards, and anchored off Accrah. A canoe soon came off with an invitation from the Governor requesting my company to dinner. I accepted it and went on shore, where I was received by a young man who was more merchant than soldier, but who had command of the fort which commanded the roadstead and the town. He informed me that a little distance from the town was a large lagoon or lake in which were frequently found four or more large tame alligators. 'For,' added he, 'although the natives often suffer from their depredations, and once one of their children was devoured by one of these reptiles, they hold them sacred, and they are "fetiched" or made holy.' 'I should much like to see one,' said I. 'I will,' answered he, 'send for one of the Cabaceers, or head men of the town, and we shall soon know if there are any in the neighbourhood.' A quarter of an hour had elapsed when in came a grave-looking black man dressed in blue serge, with a gold-headed long cane in his hand, the badge of his office. He informed the Governor there was a large alligator at the bottom of the lake, and that if he would provide him with a white fowl and a bottle of rum, his people might possibly lure him out. About an hour expired when we heard a bustle not far distant, and a man came to apprise us that the alligator was in the town, that a marabout, or priest, was ready to fetich it, and only waited for us. We had not proceeded more than twelve yards from the fort when we saw the reptile, which was about eighteen feet long, in full trot after a man who held the unfortunate fowl destined to be the victim. As soon as we approached he turned short round. The reptile, with his upper jaw nearly thrown on the back of his head, was some time in turning, owing to its length and the shortness of its legs, and was again in chase of the man who held the fowl. The marabout now came after it, and when close to its tail, threw the rum over it, mumbling some strange sounds. It was then considered sacred, and death would have been the punishment of those who hurt it. Before it came to the margin of the lagoon, the man with the poor fowl, which was more than half-dead with fright, slackened his pace, and threw it into the alligator's mouth. The reptile then made for the water, sank to the bottom, and ate the miserable bird. We returned to dinner, which consisted of a hearty welcome, some excellent fish, fowl soup, boiled fowl with harm, and a roasted saddle of kid, with yams and plantains, pine-apples and oranges, madeira and sherry. In the evening I took leave of my hospitable host and repaired on board, and the following morning put to sea.

After cruising for six weeks in chase of the wind – for we saw nothing during that period except two slave ships from Liverpool, from whom we procured a few indifferent potatoes – we again anchored off Cape Coast. I went on shore and paid my respects to the Governor, General Tourenne, in a new character. I had once dined with him when lieutenant of the frigate; he did not recollect me, but requested me whenever I was disposed to take up my residence at the Castle, and to consider it my home during the time I remained on the station. 'The Ashantee, or Assentee nation have,' continued he, 'been very troublesome of late and have declared war against the Fantee nation, who are under our protection, as it is through them all the commerce along the coast takes place, and of this, the Ashantees, who are the inland nation, wish to partake. Your being in the roads will in some measure check them.' I promised to visit the roads as often as my other duties would permit me, and if necessary assist with the marines.

CHAPTER 19

WEST COAST ADVENTURES

After remaining a few days, during which time nothing transpired that required our presence, we again weighed and sailed along the coast towards the Bight of Benin. We experienced frequent calms with much squally weather, attended with vivid lightning and heavy rain. Finding a current setting round the bight to the eastward, we were obliged to carry a press of sail to act against it, and were nearly three weeks working up from Cape St Paul's to Dix Cove, where we anchored. On this part of the coast, particularly Dix Cove, you may land without the assistance of a canoe, as the surf is not so rolling or so high. There is a small English settlement here, which I visited, and dined with the principal settler. The town is small and not worth a description. We procured a quantity of oranges and cocoanuts, and I had the opportunity of witnessing the native dancing. A tom-tom, or rough kind of long drum, is beaten by two men, to the noise of which (for it was anything but music) they keep time. The dancers, particularly the women, appeared by their gestures and movements to be in a state of delirium; they certainly were much excited, and kept up such a continued howl that I soon took my departure.

As I turned round I came in contact with a most pitiable object – a sickly, dead-white coloured native. I had heard of such beings, but had never seen one. He was about five feet five inches high, and very thin; his features were rather more prominent than those of a negro, his eyes were very small, very weak, and of a reddish hue. He appeared by his manner to be an idiot. He held out his hands to me in a supplicating manner. I gave him a small piece of money; he looked earnestly in my face, and mixed with the crowd. On returning to the town I passed three females with different coloured ochres smeared over their bodies. On inquiry, I found they were subject to fever and ague, and the application of different earths was their best mode of treating this complaint. Three weeks afterwards we again visited Cape Coast Roads, where we found the frigate, who had lost the marine officer and several of the seamen. Whenever the surgeon reported five men on the sick list in harbour I immediately put to sea, and to amuse the crew we got up some pantomimes. They were ridiculous enough, but they answered the purpose and kept all hands in good humour. The consequence was that we did not lose one man during the four months we were on the coast.

I received orders from the captain of the frigate to repair to Sierra Leone and proceed to the West Indies with the slave ships as soon as they were ready. We had now been more than two months on this station without capturing anything, and we were much pleased with the order to change. On taking leave of the Governor, he told me he had had a palaver with the King of the Ashantees, whom he described as a fine, high-spirited young man. 'I have been trying,' said he, 'to prevail on him to make peace with the Fantees. The King's answer to my request was brief and positive. "What," asked he, "is your most sacred oath?" "We swear by our God," I replied. "Then," said the king of the savages, "I swear by an Englishman's God that instead of making peace with the Fantee nation I will exterminate the whole race." "Not those under the protection of the British flag?" said I. "Yes," returned he, "all, and without exception." "Then if you do persist in so fatal a purpose, you must take the consequences, for I also swear that if you or any of your people come in a hostile manner within reach of our guns, I will shoot every one of you." He gave me a look of fierce defiance, and informed me by the interpreter that the palaver was over. On which I took my leave, not highly pleased. You are going to leave us, I understand,' said he. 'I much regret it, for we have just made your acquaintance, and I should like to have continued it.' I acknowledged the compliment, which I believe was sincere. 'To-morrow,' continued he, 'I am invited to dine at the Danish settlement. The Governor is a very good kind of man, well-informed, and hospitable. Would you like to accompany me? He speaks English, and I am sure would feel flattered by your visit.'

I consented, and at four o'clock in the afternoon on the following day I was at the Castle, where eight stout black men, with palanquins, were ready to carry us. I found this mode of travelling very easy and agreeable. The hammock in which I reclined was made of a long grass, stained with several colours; two of the bearers carried it on their shoulders by a pole, the other two sang songs, kept off the mosquitoes and sunflies by whisking about a branch of a cocoanut tree over the hammock, and occasionally relieved the others. On our journey we paid a short visit and took Schnapps with the Governor of a Dutch settlement, who saluted us with his four guns (all he had), and in so doing knocked down some of the parapet of his fort, which dismounted half of them. My bearers were so frightened by the report that they let me fall. As their fears soon subsided, and I was not hurt, we continued our journey. About three-quarters of an hour brought us within sight of Cronenburg Castle, the Danish settlement, when we were met by a set of wild black men, who called themselves men of war. They had a leathern case containing a musket cartridge hanging from the cartilage of their noses. This gave them the appearance of having large moustachios, and if they did not look very warlike, they looked ridiculously savage. They kept constantly charging and firing muskets, without any order, in honour of our visit.

We at length entered the great gate, and were ushered, by two black lacqueys in livery, into a large hall, which, for Africa, was tolerably furnished. The Danish Governor, who was dressed in a blue embroidered coat, soon made his appearance. He was a portly person, with much good humour in his countenance. At six we sat down to dinner, which was abundant, and, for the first time, I ate some kous-kous, or palm nut soup. I thought it excellent, and the pepper pot was magnificent – so a Frenchman would have said had he been one of the party. My old acquaintance, goat's flesh, did not make its appearance, but instead we had not badly-flavoured mutton – which, to tell you a secret, was not very tender. We remained until half-past nine o'clock, when we took our departure. The men of war with their cartridge moustachios saluted us by firing their muskets, the wadding of which struck me and my palanquin, for which I did not thank them, as a bit of the wadding burnt my cheek.

On reaching the Castle at Cape Coast I was so wearied that I was almost too lazy to undress. I slept soundly, and ate a late breakfast, took a final leave of the good General (who made me a present of a fine pointer), repaired on board the frigate, whose captain was tormented with the blue devils; he requested me to remain until the following day, when, as he had chased them away by a few glasses of his favourite beverage – good stiff grog – and there was no further hope of posting myself into the frigate, I ordered the anchor to be tripped, and we soon made the sparkling, transparent wave curl like an old maid's wig before us.

We were three tedious weeks before we reached Sierra Leone, owing to what sailors term 'Irish hurricanes' – when the wind is perpendicular, or, in plain English, no wind at all. On landing, I met the Governor, Mr Ludlow, who had kindly come to welcome me, and begged that I would consider the Fort my home. I made suitable acknowledgments, and accompanied him to his house, which was convenient, tolerably cool, and comfortable. He showed me a clean, cool room, which he was pleased to call my sleeping room. I found him an amiable and good person, and was happy and proud of his acquaintance. He told me he intended to make an excursion into the interior, in order to discover the source of a water-fall, and invited me to be one of the party, to which, as I was naturally fond of voyages of discovery, I willingly consented.

The day after, at daybreak, we started, the Governor and myself in palanquins with awnings and mosquito nets. We were thirty-five in party, including twenty-four black pioneers, the captain of whom was an intelligent white man. We cut a path through an immense large forest, which boasted some noble-looking cotton, manchinel and iron trees, and a red tree something resembling the bastard mahogany. Although we had penetrated and ascended more than half-way up one of the Mountains of Lions, we discovered nothing living but a variety of beautifully-plumaged birds, which, unused to the intrusion of other bipeds, uttered most discordant screams. After a fatiguing march, in which we were directed by a pocket compass, we descried a small rivulet. We followed its course for some time, and at length arrived at the base of a stupendous rock from which it issued. We, by calculation, were distant at this time from the town nineteen miles, nearly seven of which we had cut through the forest. We all took refreshment and drank His Majesty's health, first in wine and then in a crystal draught from the spring. In returning we kept on the bank of the rivulet until it swelled into a small river. The ground then became thickly beset with jungle and swampy.

By five o'clock in the afternoon we arrived at the fall, which, by measurement, was one hundred and seven feet perpendicular, and about forty-two wide without a break – it was a beautiful sight. We dined on a large rock about a quarter of a mile from its base, and even at that distance our clothes were damp from its spray. We discovered a large rock of granite from which issued a small stream of water that became tributary to that of the fall. We also saw two brown monkeys, one of which was shot. Some of the blacks brought it with them; it was of the small kind, and they told me it was good eating.

We arrived at the Fort at three o'clock the next morning, when I was suddenly attacked with a severe headache and a violent fit of the bile. As this was nothing new to me, I kept myself quiet, and Nature was my best physician. The slave convoy for the West Indies, I found, consisted of three ships and a brig, with about eleven hundred slaves. As the rice season was backward, I was petitioned by the merchants to postpone the convoy a fortnight, to which I consented, and made a short cruise off the Los Islands, where I anchored and made an excursion up the Rio Pongo. I passed a small English settlement near its mouth, not fortified, at which I landed, and was informed that a slave ship belonging to Bristol was in a state of mutiny, and that her surgeon was confined in irons. As she was lying about twenty miles farther up the river, and we had to pull that distance under a burning sun, I thought it no joke. However, as there was no alternative, we made up our minds to bear it, and reached her after a fatiguing four hours' pull. I found her a rakish-looking vessel with her boarding netting triced up. On gaining her deck I inquired for her captain. 'He is on shore,' was the answer. 'Who are you?' said I to the spokesman. 'The chief mate,' returned he. 'Turn your hands up and let me see what sort of stuff you are made of. You look very privateerish outside.' Nine men made their appearance, some of whom looked sickly. 'These are not all your crew; where are the remainder?' 'On shore, sir?' 'Where is the surgeon?' 'On shore also.' 'Show me the ship's papers.' 'The captain has them.' 'Now,' said I, 'I tell you what, Master Mate, I am going on shore to have some conversation with the African Prince Lawrence, and if your captain and surgeon are not with me at the chieftain's house in half an hour after I land, I will put an officer and men on board your ship, and if everything I have heard against his conduct is not cleared up to my satisfaction, I will carry her to Jamaica.'

The river at this beautiful place, for the country appeared green and fresh and ornamented with a profusion of lofty palm and cocoanut trees, was much wider than at its mouth. On landing, a number of the natives had assembled on the shore to view us as sea-monsters or curiosities, as they had never seen two men-of-war's boats at their settlement before. The prince's son, who was among them, came up to me. He was dressed in a white linen jacket and trousers, with a white English hat. He spoke tolerable English. He requested me to go to his father's house, which was a long, low, white-washed building, with a four-pounder sticking out of a kind of window at one end of it, and before it was a mud battery of four more four-pounders in bad repair. On being introduced to him I found he also spoke English. He asked me the occasion of my visit. I acquainted him, when he, without ceremony, summoned one of the cabaceers, or principal men, and desired him to find the captain of the slave-ship and bring him with him. 'I dine at three o'clock,' said he; 'I hope you will favour me with your company.' I accepted the invitation. This prince's appearance was like that of an European, his features were regular and pleasing. He informed me his father was an Arabian chief, but that he was born on the spot where he now resided, and that he had married one of the native king's daughters. He had two sons; the eldest was with him, and the other in England for his education. 'I am very partial to the English,' added he, 'and should like to go to England, but that is impossible.' Our conversation was interrupted by the entrance of the native magistrate with the master of the slave-ship, a sharp-looking, rather slight man. He pulled off his hat. 'I understand, sir, that you wish to speak with me.' 'I most assuredly do,' answered I. 'Have you brought the ship's papers and the surgeon with you?' 'I have the first about me,' saying this he took them from his coat-pocket and gave them to me. 'As for the surgeon,' said he, 'he has behaved infamously and ungratefully. I paid his lodgings at Bristol, and if he had not come with me he must have starved or have been put in prison.' 'This,' answered I, 'is your concern and not mine. I want to know where he is.' 'He is in a house about a quarter of a mile off, where I intend keeping him until I am ready for sea, for he has also made a mutiny in the ship and the greater part of the men have gone on shore without leave.' 'I have only one order to give,' said I, 'and that is that you show my lieutenant and two marines, whom I will send with you, where you have confined the surgeon.' He reluctantly consented, and in about an hour the lieutenant and his party returned with an emaciated, tall young man. He had been confined in irons and fed on bread and water, with sometimes a few vegetables.

As it was too long a story for me to investigate, I left it to be discussed by the proper authorities on the ship's arrival at Jamaica. I had the men who had left the ship brought before me. They refused to join her again until I told them that if they did not I would impress the whole of them. Five of the best of them immediately stepped forward and begged to enter. As there were fourteen others I accepted them. The others returned to the ship on the captain promising to use them well and to overlook all past grievances. The papers were regular, which I returned, admonishing him at the same time to be more considerate in his conduct to his men. A dinner was sent to the boats' crews by the prince, and I desired the midshipmen to entertain the surgeon, who had expressed a wish to join our ship.

After all this much ado about something, I was ready for my dinner, and in a quarter of an hour it was announced by the blowing of a conch. In passing through a large hall I found myself surrounded by coal-coloured gentlemen of all grades, one of whom wished to look at my dirk. He examined it very closely; it appeared to take his fancy as it was silver gilt, but as I did not take the hint, and was very hungry, I took it from him and hastened into the dining-room. The dinner was laid out on a large table on trestles; all the dishes were covered with cones made of cane and stained different colours. The table was also covered with light cane mats; altogether it had a very pretty effect. The eatables consisted of fowls stewed to death, ducks and buffalo, and an abundance of rice, which was served up with every dish. My favourite dish, pepper-pot, was much in request, and I could, by a sly peep, see some of the Massa Blackies use their fingers instead of their spoons. Roasted plantain was eaten instead of bread; palm-wine and grog were the principal beverages, although the prince, the lieutenant and myself drank two bottles of madeira which I had brought in the boat. The princess was amiability itself; she was very black, very fat and very good-natured. After dinner we walked round the mansion. In one of the yards the young prince showed us a black ostrich, which was considered a rarity. It stood with its neck erect, and was about eleven feet high to the crown of its head. Its eyes were fierce and resembled rubies.

At six o'clock I took my leave of the chieftain and his wife. On entering the boat, I found a milch cow and calf, two dozen ducks, and a dozen fowls, besides bows and quivers filled with arrows, a variety of fruits, and some tiger skins. He had also, at parting, presented me with a gold ring weighing four ounces. I was overpowered with his disinterested kindness, and sent him some rum and gunpowder. Before I left the place I obtained from the master of the slave-ship an order, payable at Jamaica, for the surgeon's salary and wages of the seamen who had entered. We got on board the same evening. The next morning I visited the largest of the Los or Loes Islands, which, I presume, in days of yore had been created by a volcanic eruption. I struck off some of the rock which contained iron, and had a ringing sound, and on rubbing it together it smelt of sulphur. There were a few small houses on the island inhabited by fishermen, who appeared as poor as Job's stable-boy.

CHAPTER 20

WITH SLAVE CONVOY

Finding little and seeing less, I repaired on board and made sail for Sierra Leone, where we anchored next morning. I went on shore and dined with the Governor, and the day following received an invitation to a dinner from the principal merchants, which I accepted, and was introduced to the native king who had sold the settlement to the English. He was dressed in an embroidered blue silk coat, white satin waistcoat and inexpressibles, with a gold-laced cocked hat and a pair of heavy ammunition shoes. He wore no stockings, he was old and ugly, and his shins were sharp and curved. I gave him an invitation to dine on board, which he declined. Before we sailed, I joined a picnic party to Bence Island, which is situated about fourteen miles up the river from Free Town. We dined there very pleasantly, and one of the merchants made me a present of a collection of insects and handsome shells, in return for which I sent him some views. The 21st of October falling on the day before our departure, I asked the Governor, the officers of the regiment, and the merchants to dine on board. We dressed the ship and decorated the quarter-deck. At five o'clock we sat down to a dinner, consisting of all the delicacies of Sierra Leone and the ship's provision. Port and madeira circulated freely, and the company began to get in high spirits; and as there were two white ladies, wives of the two military commanding officers, who accompanied their husbands, a dance was proposed on the quarter-deck. The only musicians we could muster were the marine drummer, ship's fifer, and my steward, who performed on the clarionet. I opened the ball with the Honourable Mrs Forbes, and was followed by most of the others, until it became too ridiculous, as few knew anything about dancing. Before confusion became rife I proposed singing. My steward sung in the style of Incledon, and he was much applauded; and one of the marines, after the manner of Braham – he also had his share of applause and encores. Punch was now the order of the night, and, after laying in a good stock, they all ordered their canoes and paddled on shore, huzzaing the whole time. The Governor had taken his departure in one of the ship's boats some time before, to avoid the uproar. I shall not mention the toasts that were given; as we were all loyal and true, they were the quintessence of loyalty. The morning before sailing I breakfasted at the Fort. The convoy, consisting of five sail, were ready. I bid an affectionate farewell to the Governor, who had been uniformly kind, and I was soon on board, where I found a note from the Honourable Captain Forbes, and one from the Governor. The first was to beg I would accept some excellent bacon, a beautiful live fawn, and some cane mats. The last was accompanied by a fine crown bird, which stood five feet high, two dozen fowls, and some Muscovy ducks. My feelings were quite overcome by so much genuine kindness, and I shall ever retain it in grateful recollection, and I have real pleasure in recording it in this narrative.

I must not omit to inform my readers that during the time I was at Bence Island, which was the great mart for slave dealing, forty of those unfortunate beings arrived, most of them half famished. The principal merchant, who was a mulatto, told me that the greater part of them had been pledged for rice, which is the principal food in Africa, that they had not been redeemed at the time appointed, and in consequence had become the property of those who supplied the food. The remainder were those taken prisoners in the skirmishes occasioned by their trespassing on each other's ground, particularly on the rice patches when the grain was nearly ripe. A black woman offered me her son, a boy about eleven years of age, for a cob – about four-and-sixpence. I gave her the money, and advised her to keep her son. Poor thing! she stared with astonishment, and instantly gave me one of her earrings, which was made of small shells. It was like the widow's mite, all she had to bestow. We were soon under sail, and next morning Africa was as a dream; it was no longer seen.

During the passage in fine weather I myself or some of the officers visited the Guinea men, and found them orderly and clean, and the slaves healthy. On the seventh week we arrived at Barbadoes, saw Lady Rodney, Sally Neblet, and several more of the true Barbadian born, drawling, dignity ladies, who entreated in no very dignified manner to 'hab de honour for wash for massa captain'. I gave the preference to the relict of Lord Rodney, as she was the oldest acquaintance, and remembered me when I was 'a lilly piccaninny midshipman'. I paid my respects to the Admiral, Sir Alex. Cochrane, who asked me to dinner, where I met the Governor and some more bigwigs. The Admiral's secretary, Maxwell, who appeared to have a snug berth in the country, requested me to dine with him the day after, and he sent a kittereen, or one-horse gig, for me. I met at dinner some brother officers and a few military men. Our entertainment did credit to the donor, who appeared a hospitable, frank kind of man. In the evening I went on board, and next morning received a chest of money for the troops at Tobago. At noon we cheered the flagship and sailed. On the evening of the following day we anchored at Tobago, got rid of the soldiers' money, and sailed next morning for Trinidad, which we made the same evening, but owing to the strong current opposing us through the Boca Chien, or, as it is otherwise called, the Great Dragon's Mouth, we did not gain the anchorage before noon on the following day.

On opening a sealed order I had received from the Commander-in-Chief at Barbadoes I found I was to take on board some casks of lime juice for the men of the hospitals of Jamaica. Thinks I to myself, this is what Mr Hume would have, in the Commons House, called jobbery, and a poor kind of job it turned out; for, on inspecting the lime juice at Port Royal, some of it was condemned as unfit for use. The two days I remained at Trinidad I dined with the Governor, Sir Thos. Heslip, who was urbanity itself. I visited the pitch lake at this place, which is a most extraordinary phenomenon. I remarked several large chasms in it, where small fish were enjoying themselves. I was told by the officer who accompanied me that the pitch could not be applied to any use. Whilst we were looking at it one of the smaller chasms, or rents, closed with a bubbling noise, and the water above it appeared as if boiling. At daylight on the third day I sailed with the convoy for Jamaica, and anchored at Port Royal. The day after I waited on the Admiral at the Pen, where I dined, and met a number of my brother officers, whose conversation after dinner was principally respecting their ships. As the ship I commanded was healthy I was, if possible, determined to keep her so, and I requested permission to sail on a long cruise as soon as we were refitted. The Pen, or the Government House, where the Admiral resides, is about three short miles from Greenwich. It is enclosed in a park, and the views from it are extensive and beautiful. Some of my former parti-coloured beauties of Port Royal had gone on the other tack – that is, they had taken up their everlasting abode among the land crabs on the Palisades, and as I partook of those crustaceous fish I very possibly might have eaten some part of them. If I did, I thought them very good.

The yellow fever was making rapid strides on board the squadron. It fortunately did not reach us, and we sailed on the tenth day after our arrival. My cruising ground was between the north side of Jamaica and Cuba. I frequently sighted the Moro Castle at the entrance of the river where I was formerly taken prisoner and sent to the town of St Jago. The good Spanish Governor's kindness held a lively recollection in my memory, but the captain of an American vessel who had sailed from thence the day before I fell in with him, informed me that he was numbered with the dead. Peace to his 'manes'. We had been out a fortnight when one afternoon we fell in with two large Spanish schooner privateers. They were to windward, and standing for St Jago. 'Now,' thought I, 'if I can get you once under our guns, I will pay off old scores.' The sea breeze was fresh, and we were closing fast. They at first, I believe, took us for an American, as I had hoisted the Yankee colours. When they came nearly within gun-shot they, unfortunately for us, saw their mistake, and hauled in for the shore. I tacked, and had got within gun-shot of them, when the lower fort of the Moro opened its fire on us, one of the shot passing through the main top-sail. They also fired, and their shot went over us. Finding the breeze lulling, and that we had no hope of capturing them, I gave them our passing broadsides, and as one of them yawed, I had reason to believe some of our shot took effect. The battery gave us a parting salute without doing us injury, when, as the evening was closing, and the enemy's vessels had run into the mouth of the river, I was obliged to haul off.

After blockading the mouth of the river for ten days without the slightest prospect of success, I anchored at Montego Bay, and procured fresh beef for the crew. During the two days I remained at anchor I was invited, with some of my officers, to the ball given by the inhabitants. It was well attended, and I was agreeably surprised to meet so many of my fair countrywomen, some of whom were handsome and still in their teens. I soon became acquainted with several respectable families, and if my heart had not been in safe keeping in beloved England by a still more beloved being, I fear I should have lost it. Montego Bay is well fortified, and the town and its background, consisting of several ranges of hills and mountains, form a rich and pleasing picture. On the morning of the third day we sailed, and were soon on our former cruising ground. Off Ochre Bay we started a small Spanish privateer, which ran into a creek. I sent the boats armed in pursuit of her, and after a smart contest of a quarter of an hour, in which the gunner and one of the men were wounded, they brought her out. The crew had landed and taken her gun – a six-pounder – with them, which did the mischief to our boats. The gun they threw into deep water, after having spiked it. She was a small schooner, about seventy-five tons. I kept her as a tender, put an eighteen-pound carronade, a master's mate, and twenty men on board her, and a few days afterwards she captured a very pretty schooner coming round Cape Mayzi.

My time being expired, I bore up for Jamaica with my two prizes, and arrived at Port Royal on the second day. My health, which had been delicate since leaving Africa, began to decline, and I was tormented with a rash, particularly in my face, which affected my eyesight. I had, at different periods, been twelve years on the West India station, and I thought I had had a sufficient share of a torrid zone. The Admiral, hearing of my indisposition, invited me for change of air to the Pen. This kindness, however, did but little good to my health. One morning, as I was strolling in the Park, calling the crown bird I had given to the Admiral, and feeding him and some Curaçoa birds which were his companions, I was accosted by the captain of a sloop of war who was ordered to take a convoy of mahogany ships from Honduras to England, and in the course of conversation he mentioned that he understood I intended to give up my ship and invalid. 'Whoever informed you that I intended to invalid,' I replied, 'must have laboured under a gross mistake. I would rather go to "Kingdom come" quietly than run from my post.' 'Well,' said he, 'be it so, but if the Admiral were to consent to your exchanging with me, as I am almost a Johnny Newcome in this part of the world, and you are an old standard, would this accord with your way of thinking?' 'As I am so unwell,' returned I, 'it certainly is a great temptation, but we must both have the Admiral's opinion and consent, and I will give you an answer in two days, provided I do not get better, and Fishly, the builder, shall give me his opinion respecting your sloop, whether Government, on my arrival in England, will consider her an effective ship.'

He met me at the builder's at Port Royal the following day, when the latter assured me the ship's repairs would be comparatively trifling, and that he was certain, as those class of vessels were much wanted in the Channel, she would be kept in commission. Three days afterwards we effected the exchange, and I sailed to cruise again off Cuba for six weeks. Working up against a fiery sea breeze tries the minds of those on board as well as the rigging, masts and yards of His Majesty's ships. A few topmasts sprung and yards carried away are trifles, and you may think yourself fortunate if it does not happen to a lower mast. We looked into Tiberoon, crossed over to Cape St Nicholas Mole, beat up between the island of Tortuga and the larger island, overhauled the Grange and Cape François, took a small row-boat with six swivels and fourteen sharp-looking, smutty-coloured gentlemen, destroyed her, and bore up for the north side of Cuba, where we captured a small Balaker schooner, who informed us that a Spanish corvette of eighteen guns was lying at Barracow. I immediately proceeded off that port, and finding the information correct, sent her a challenge, and that I should remain three days waiting for her. I might as well have sent my defiance to the Eddystone lighthouse. She sent word that I might remain three years if I chose. The harbour was difficult to enter, and well fortified, otherwise her three years would not have been three hours before we were alongside of her. I remained a week watching her movements, which, by-the-bye, were no movements at all except that she had struck her top-masts and hauled further inshore. Finding hope, respecting her, hopeless, and our cruise at its last gasp, I stood close in and fired a gun unshotted by way of showing our contempt, which probably the Spaniards laughed at, and made sail once more for Jamaica.

CHAPTER 21

HOME WITH MAHOGANY

The sloop of war I now commanded was a fine sixteen-gun brig carrying twenty-four-pound-carronades, with a crew of one hundred and twenty as fine men as any in the fleet. They had been some time together, and only wished for an opportunity of making the splinters fly out of a Frenchman's side, and hauling down his tricoloured piece of bunting. I found on my reaching Port Royal that Admiral Rowley had arrived to supersede Admiral Dacres. In the afternoon I dined with both Admirals, and met the Duke of Manchester, who was a fine-looking man, but unfortunately had a nervous affection of the head. He asked me several questions respecting the different islands, and appeared amused by my description of them. After we had refitted we sailed for Honduras, the Admiral first taking from me the master, without appointing another, for which I did not thank him. We made the Swan Islands, which are small, uninhabited, and surrounded by a reef of coral, and on the morning of the third day anchored off the town at the mouth of the Belize river. Colonel Drummond, who was the commanding officer, received us very civilly, and requested I would dine with him as often as I could. A deputation of the merchants waited on me to say the convoy would be ready in a fortnight. I dined frequently at the military mess, and found the officers generally gentlemanly. I gave two parties on board, but as I had no music there was no dancing. We revelled in Calepache and Calapee, and I think some of the city aldermen would have envied us the mouthfuls of green fat we swallowed. I made an excursion up the river with Colonel Drummond in a scow, a flat boat so called, or rather float, and slept at a pavilion he had on the bank of it. I shall never forget my nocturnal visitors, the bullfrogs, who, *sans façon*, jumped about the room as if dancing a quadrille, not to my amusement but their own, making a most unmusical noise to the tune of something like, 'Pay your debts, pay your debts, pay your debts.' After the third croak they paused, probably to give time for everybody to become honest. I made daily excursions to the neighbouring quays, and picked up a quantity of beautiful shells.

Dining one day with Colonel Drummond, I remarked that the black servant who stood near me had a piebald neck, and mentioned it as something singular. 'Why,' said the Colonel, "thereby hangs a very curious tale, and not a pleasant one to him, poor fellow. He is a native of Panama, and formerly was employed to float rafts of mahogany down the Belize river. He is an expert canoe-man and something of a carpenter, and as he was a free man I took him into my household. At my request he related to me the cause of those white marks on his neck. It was thus. As he and another black man were floating down the river on a large raft of mahogany, it being Sunday he wished to bathe, and jumped into the river for that purpose. As he was swimming after the raft, which was close to the mangroves, and had nearly reached it, a large alligator seized him by the neck. He roared most piteously; the animal, either alarmed at the noise he made, or wishing to have a more convenient grip, threw him up, and in so doing he fortunately fell on the raft. His companion bound up his wounds, which were deep, and soon after he arrived at Belize he was sent to the hospital, when, on his recovery, he became my servant. 'It was a most providential escape,' exclaimed I. 'Indeed it was,' replied the Colonel, 'and so he thinks himself.' On reaching the ship in the evening I found a beautiful mahogany canoe alongside, and on entering my cabin the steward brought me a glass globe containing two Panama tortoises, which, when full-grown, are richly marked and not larger than a crown piece. The native name of these pretty animals is *chinqua*. They were a present from Captain Bromley. At the time appointed, seven vessels, deeply laden with mahogany, were ready for sea. I spent the last day on shore, dined at the military mess, bade adieu to all my red-coat friends, and the following morning got under weigh with my haystack convoy for England.

We doubled Cape Antonio on the third day, and when off the Havannah we perceived a frigate standing out of the harbour. We concluded she was Spanish. I consulted the officers respecting the probability of taking her by laying her alongside and boarding her. They thought it might be effected. I turned the hands up and acquainted them of my intention. Three hearty cheers was the response. We prepared for action, and stood towards her. We were three gunshots from her when it fell calm, as well as dusk, and about an hour afterwards a large boat came near us. We presumed she was a Spanish gunboat, and had taken us for a merchant vessel. I let her come alongside, having the marines ready to give them a reception when they boarded, and to quietly disarm and hand them down the hatchway. The first man who came up was a lieutenant of our service. 'Hulloa, sir, how is this, and where have you come from?' said

I. 'From the *Melpomene*,' replied he, 'the frigate you see off the Havannah.' 'This is a terrible disappointment,' resumed I. 'We had made up our minds to board and, if possible, carry that frigate, supposing her Spanish.' 'Why, sir,' said he, 'we yesterday carried the disagreeable news to the Governor of Cuba of a Spanish peace, and seeing you with a convoy, Captain Parker despatched me with some letters for England, if you will have the goodness to take charge of them.' 'Willingly,' replied I, 'and pray acquaint him with our mortification.'

He shortly after left us, and we proceeded through the Gulf with the convoy. Nothing of any importance transpired during our passage of nine long, tedious weeks, when we anchored in the Downs, where I got rid of all our snail-sailing mahogany haystacks. The three days we lay in the Downs I took up my quarters at the 'Hoop and Griffin.' Bread and butter, with delicious oysters, were my orders of the day, but, alas, my former pretty maid was no longer there. She was married, had children, and I sincerely hope was happy. On the same floor, the father-in-law to the First Lord of the Admiralty, with his daughter and niece, had taken up their abode for a few days on their return journey to London from a tour in Wales. Before I was acquainted with this information, seeing a carriage at the door and an old gentleman with two ladies alight from it, I asked the waiter who they were. He answered he did not know, but that they had arrived yesterday and that the gentleman appeared much out of spirits, and one of the ladies very much out of health. The purser had been dining with me, and we were enjoying our wine, when I said to the waiter, in a half-joking manner, 'Give my compliments to the old gentleman, and request him to hand himself in, that we may have a look at him.' He fulfilled his commission, although I did not intend he should do so, to the letter, and in walked a stately, gentlemanly-looking man, about seventy. He gave us a look that appeared to say, 'Surely this is some mistake, I know you not.' On perceiving his embarrassment I advanced towards him, and begged, although there was some little mistake, that if he were not engaged, he would do me the favour to take a glass of wine. 'I see,' said he, 'you are officers of the navy,' and without further hesitation, sat down and became quite cheerful. In the course of conversation he informed me that he had tried the air of Wales for the benefit of his daughter, who was married to a captain in the navy, and that his other daughter was married to Lord Mulgrave, First Lord of the Admiralty. I told him we had come from the West Indies and were going to sail for Sheerness in the morning; that if he thought his daughter would like to go so far on her journey by sea, instead of by land, my cabin was entirely at his service. He thanked me cordially, but declined it. After finishing a brace of decanters of wine he took his leave, first giving me his address in London. A month afterwards I heard of his death. The following morning we sailed, and arrived at Sheerness next day, when I received orders to pay off the ship, in consequence of her being iron-fastened and wanting so much repair. She was afterwards sold out of the Service. I need not say I was much disappointed, and thought the builder at Port Royal something of an old woman, and only fit for superannuation. I found one of my old captains commissioner at this place, to whom I gave a turtle, a pig, and a bag of bread dust, for he thought one without the other useless, and for which he did not even invite me to his house. 'Oh, what is friendship but a name that lulls the fool to sleep,' etc. On the sixth day the ship was put out of commission and myself out of full pay. I took a postchaise with my light luggage, and I arrived in the evening at my dear home, kissed my wife and all the women I could meet with that were worth the trouble, sat myself down in a snug elbow-chair near a comfortable English fire, told a long, tough yarn about mountains of sugar and rivers of rum, bottle-nosed porpoises, sharks, grampuses, and flying-fish, until I fell sound asleep, but, however, not so sound to prevent my hearing my best end of the ship whispering to someone to put more coals on the fire, and roast a chicken for my supper, and then she added, with her dear, musical, soft voice, 'Dear fellow! How sound he sleeps. I hope he will awake quite refreshed, and eat his supper with a good appetite. How rejoiced I am he is once more at home.' I could have jumped up and hugged her, but I thought it better to enjoy my sleep. If this narrative meets the eye of a bachelor sailor I could wish him to splice himself to such another clean-looking frigate as my wife, but mind, not without he has a purse well filled with the right sort, and as long at least as the maintop bowline, or two cables spliced on end. Love is very pretty, very sentimental, and sometimes very romantic, but love without rhino is bewildering misery.

When I awoke next morning I scarcely could believe my senses, it appeared too much happiness. The *élite* of the village favoured me with calls and congratulations, as well as invitations to tea and *petit soupers*, with a seasoning of scandal. I in return entertained them occasionally with a few King's yarns, which, my gentle reader, are not tarred, and are what the seamen vulgarly call rogue's yarns, so called because one or more are twisted in large ropes and cables made in the King's dockyards, to distinguish them from those made in the merchants' yards, and should they be embezzled or clandestinely sold, the rogue's or white yarn is evidence against the possessor. I had been some months on shore when I began to get tired of looking at green fields and grass combers, and longed to be once more on the salt seas. My family had increased to seven boys and girls, and I thought it criminal to be longer idle, and, after many applications, Mr Yorke, the First Lord of the Admiralty, favoured me with an appointment to command a sloop of war on the Downs station.

I joined her in the cold, uncomfortable month of December. The weather was remarkably severe, and it was five days before I could get a launch to put me on board her. At length I made my footing on the quarter-deck. The first lieutenant received me and informed me the captain was unwell in the cabin, but that he wished to see me. I descended into a complete den, filled with smoke and dirt. The first object I perceived looming through the dense vapour was the captain's nose, which was a dingy red. His linen was the colour of chocolate, his beard had, I presumed, a month's growth. I informed him of my errand, to which he answered with something like a growl. As it was impossible to remain in the cabin without a chance of being suffocated, I begged him, if he possibly could, to accompany me to the quarter-deck. He followed me with a slow step. I expressed my wish to have my commission read. He then gave orders to the first lieutenant to turn the hands up. After this ceremony I took the command, made a short speech to the crew, in which I assured them they should have every indulgence the Service afforded. I then turned to my predecessor, and asked him when he wished to leave the ship. He informed me that to-morrow would suit him. I gave the necessary orders and went on shore. The admiral, Sir G Campbell, received me very kindly, and invited me to dinner, where I met Lady C, the admiral's wife, a ladylike, pleasant person. The dinner party consisted of brother officers. The admiral was a quiet, gentlemanly, pleasing man, and a distinguished and good officer. As I sat next him he was kind enough to inform me that the captain of the sloop I superseded was considered out of his mind, that the officers had represented to him that the discipline on board her was worse than on a privateer, and that he would neither punish for insubordination nor have the decks washed. 'In consequence of which,' continued the Admiral, 'I was obliged to order a Court of Inquiry. The report was to his disadvantage; he was advised to go on shore, to which, after some hesitation, he consented, and another captain was applied for. You have superseded him, and I make no doubt you will soon make her once more a man-of-war.' I thanked him for his kind communication, and assured him that zeal on my part should not be wanting to make her equal to one of his best cruisers. On rejoining the ship, as I had been the first lieutenant for five years in former ships, I told the officers I wished to make my own observation on the men's conduct, and I would endeavour to effect a reform when I found it necessary. The officers, with the exception of the master, who was a rough, practical seaman, were gentlemanly, well-informed men, and I was not surprised at their wishing to get rid of their insane chief, although, in any other case, it might have proved to them a difficult and probably a dangerous experiment. A few days afterwards I called on him. I found him in small lodgings in an obscure part of the town. I was accompanied by Captain J, an old messmate of his in former times. He neither knew us nor asked us to take a seat. He had a large loaf under his left arm, and in his right hand a dinner knife. He appeared to wear the same chocolate-coloured chemise and beard, his stockings were down over his shoes, and his clothes all over flue. We wished him health and happiness, to which he returned no answer, but began cutting his loaf. The people of the house told us he would neither wash himself nor take his clothes off when going to bed, but that he was perfectly quiet. I understood, before I sailed, that his sister had come from the north of England to stay with him, and that she had been of great use to him.

CHAPTER 22

OFF BOULOGNE

On the ninth day after joining, we sailed to cruise off Boulogne. The vessel I now commanded was a brig sloop of fourteen 24-pounders, the ship's company by no means a bad set, and in the course of the cruise I had the satisfaction of seeing them alert, clean and obedient. This was in a great measure owing to the officers, who, when supported, were firm, discriminating and encouraging. The consequence was that during the time I commanded her there was only one desertion in eighteen months, and the cat did not see daylight once in three months. I found off Boulogne another cruiser watching the French privateers and Bonaparte's boast – the flotilla. The captain of her was a Job's comforter. He told me he was both sick and sorry to be on such a wear-and-tear, monotonous, do-nothing station, that he had been out two months without effecting anything, that he had frequently had the enemy's privateers under his guns, but that the run was so short, they were always sure of escaping.

'One morning,' said he, 'about five months ago, I had got within musket-shot of one of those vagabonds, and had been sure of him, when a shell fired from Cape Grisnez fell directly down the main hatchway, bedded in one of the water-casks, and shortly after exploded, without, fortunately, doing more mischief than destroying a few more casks and splintering the beams and deck without wounding a man. I was in consequence reluctantly obliged to give up the chase, but not before I had taken ample revenge. In tacking I gave her all the larboard broadside, and not a vestige of her was to be seen: but,' continued he, 'I hear of their taking prizes; but where the devil do they carry them to?' 'Not into Boulogne or Calais,' replied I. 'Havre and Cherbourg are the ports to sell them in.' 'Then why,' said he, 'do they keep so many of us on this station and so few to the westward?' 'I presume it is,' I replied, 'because this being the narrowest part of the Channel, there is more risk of our vessels being captured, and you know all the old women, with the Mayor and Aldermen, would petition the Admiralty to have the fleet back again to watch that frightful bugbear the half-rotten flotilla, which sometimes prevents them from taking their night's rest. And it is very probable that, was this station neglected, our vessels would be cut out from the Downs.' 'I never dreamed of that,' answered he. 'It's all right, and if I can only take six of their privateers, or about twenty of their flotilla, I will not say a word more.'

I remained out nearly three months, watching the flotilla and the privateers. We sometimes anchored just beyond range of their shells, and frequently when the wind was light hauled the trawl, and were richly rewarded by a quantity of fine fish. I was at length relieved by another cruiser, and again anchored in the Downs. We were a fortnight refitting, during which time I dined several times at the admiral's table, where I had the pleasure of meeting Sir R Strachan, Sir P Durham, and several other distinguished officers. One day, after dinner, the characters of several eccentric officers were the subject of conversation.

'I make no doubt,' said a veteran captain, 'that most of the present company recollect a man by the name of Billy Culmer, a distant relation of Lord Hood's. He was a short time one of my lieutenants, and was between thirty and forty years of age before he obtained his commission. The next time I dined with Lord Hood, who was then one of the Admirals in the Channel Fleet, I was determined to request his lordship to give me a brief outline of his history, which was nearly this. Shall I proceed, Lady Campbell?' 'Oh, by all means, Captain M.'

'"The Culmers were distantly related to me by marriage," said his lordship. 'Billy, as he was always called, was sent to me when I hoisted my pendant as master and commander. He unfortunately had lost an eye when a boy in one of his freaks, for they could do nothing with him at home. When he came on board I was not prepossessed in his favour; his manners were rough and bearish, although he had some redeeming qualities, for he was straightforward and frank. After being with me about two years, he said he was tired of being a midshipman, and requested me to obtain his discharge into the merchant service. I remonstrated with him to no purpose. To prevent his deserting, which he declared he would do, I procured his discharge, and he entered on board a West India ship going to Jamaica. I had lost sight of this extraordinary being for more than eight years,' continued his lordship, 'when, as I was standing on the platform at Portsmouth, waiting for a boat from the frigate I commanded, I was much surprised to see Billy Culmer, in a dirty sailor's dress, a few yards from me. He perceived me, and pulled off his hat. 'Hulloa!' said I, 'Billy; where have you come from? I understood you were dead.' 'Not so hard up as that, sir,' replied he. 'I am d – d.' 'Explain yourself,' said I. 'Why,' said he, 'I am d – d in the King's service, for I shall never be able to enter it again, in consequence of my folly in requesting you to get me discharged.' 'I probably may have interest enough, Billy, to get you once more on the quarter-deck if you will promise me faithfully to remain steady.' 'I promise you solemnly I will,' replied he. 'Then meet me at the admiral's office to-morrow at ten o'clock,' returned I. 'And I suppose, from your appearance, you are pretty well aground. Here is something that will keep your body and soul together.' He made a leg and took his departure.' But I am afraid, Lady Campbell, you have had enough of this rigmarole story, for it is rather a long one, and to those who know nothing of the man it may not be an interesting one.' 'Why, Captain M,' said Lady Campbell, 'as the weather is disagreeable, and we do not intend to take a drive this evening, we may as well hear about Billy Culmer as anybody else. Do you not think so, Admiral?' The admiral, who appeared more inclined for a nap than to listen to a long-spun yarn, I verily believe, wished the narrator and the subject of his narration at the masthead together. However, he nodded assent, and the story went on.

'"On speaking to the admiral, Billy was again under my command," resumed his lordship, 'and was appointed mate of the hold. When I was promoted to my flag, Billy and I parted company, for he had followed me steadily from the frigate to a ship of the line. As soon as he had served his six years, I sent for him and told him he must go to London to pass his examination. 'You must excuse me, my lord,' was his answer; 'I would rather remain the oldest midshipman than the youngest lieutenant,' and he persisted in this whim for more than three years. At the end of that period the ship he belonged to arrived at Spithead, and he came on board me to pay his respects. 'Well,' said I, 'Culmer, will you now pass your examination, or are you determined to die the oldest midshipman in the service?' 'I have been thinking of it,' was his reply, 'but I have no money to carry me to London.' 'That,' said I, 'I will give you. And if you can mount a horse, I will procure that also.' In a few days Billy started for London, where he arrived a week after, having sold my horse on the road, without informing me of his having done so. When he made his appearance before the Commissioners at Somerset Place, they were all younger than himself, and one of them had been a mid in the same ship where he was mate. This last addressed him, and in a half comic, half serious manner, said: 'Well, Mr Culmer, I make no doubt you are well prepared for your examination.' 'And who the devil put you there,' answered Billy sharply, 'to pass one who taught you to be something of a sailor? Do you remember the *colting* I gave you when you were a youngster in my charge? But I never could beat much seamanship into you. So you are to examine me, are you?' The two other commissioners, who knew the whimsical character of the person before them, called him to order, and requested he would answer some questions, as he could not obtain his certificate without doing so. 'Begin,' said Billy, turning his quid and hitching up his trousers. 'You are running into Plymouth Sound in a heavy gale from the S.E.; how would you proceed in coming to an anchor? Your topgallant masts are supposed to be on deck.' 'I would first furl all and run under the storm forestay sail, unfid the topmasts going in, and have a long range of both bower cables on deck, and the sheet anchor ready. On coming to the proper anchorage I would let go the best bower and lower the topmasts as she tended head to wind; veer away half a cable and let go the small bower; veer away on both cables until the best bower splice came to the hatchway. I should then half a whole cable on one and half a cable on the other.'

'"The gale increases, and there is a heavy scud, and you find both anchors are coming home. What then?'

'"Then I would veer to one and a half on the best and a whole on the other.'

'"In snubbing the best bower, it parts in the splice. What then?'

'"What then?' exclaimed Billy sharply, for he began to be tired of being interrogated respecting a part of seamanship he thought he knew better than themselves. 'Why,' replied he, taking a fresh quid of tobacco, 'I would let go the sheet anchor.'

'"But,' interrupted the elder Commissioner, 'there is not, in consequence of having dragged the bower anchors, room to veer more than a few fathoms before you tail on the Hoe; consequently your sheet anchor, being only under foot, will be of little or no use, and the strain being on the small bower, it soon after parts.'

'"What humbug!' cried Billy, who could not contain himself longer. 'I tell you, gentlemen, what I would do. I would let her go on shore and be d——d, and wish you were all on board her.'

'"Sit down, Mr Culmer,' said the second Commissioner, 'and calm yourself. We shall leave you a short time. Probably we may ask you a few more questions.'

'"Hem!' muttered Billy, and he scratched his head. After an interval of half an hour, the Commissioner who had been his former messmate, entered with his certificate.

'"I have much pleasure,' said he, 'in having the power to present you your passing certificate, and I hope your speedy promotion will follow. Do you stay long in London?'

'"Only to have a cruise in Wapping and to see St Paul's and the Monument,' returned Billy, 'and then I shall make all sail for Portsmouth.'

""Have you any shot in your locker?' asked Captain T. 'As much as will serve this turn,' replied Billy, 'for Lord Hood has sent me an order for ten pounds on his banker.' 'Good afternoon, Culmer,' said the former. 'I wish you your health.' 'Thank you,' replied Billy; 'the same to you; but give me more sea-room next time you examine me, and do not let me tail on the Hoe.'" Billy, through the interest of Lord Hood, was quickly installed lieutenant, but died shortly afterwards.'

'Well,' said the admiral's lady, 'I think, Captain M, had I known this Billy Culmer, as you call him, I certainly should have made a pet of him.'

'I am afraid, my dear,' answered the Admiral, who appeared relieved now the story was at an end, 'you would have found him very pettish.' The admiral's play on the word produced a smile.

A young captain who sat near Lady Campbell asked her if she had ever heard of a captain who was, in consequence of his extravagant behaviour, called 'Mad Montague?' 'Pray, my dear,' cried the Admiral, who appeared terrified at the idea of another story, 'let us have our coffee.'

The hint was sufficient, we sipped our beverage and *chasse*, and departed in peace.

Being ready for sea we left the Downs, and in a few hours were off our old cruising ground to watch the terrible flotilla and the privateers, which were principally lugger-rigged and carried long guns of different calibres, with from fifty to seventy-five men. Some few had ten or fourteen guns, besides swivels. The vessels forming the flotilla consisted of praams, ship-rigged, and brigs carrying one or two eighteen or twenty-four pounders, and the largest a thirty-two pounder (with sixty or ninety men), all of them flat-bottomed. They sometimes, when the wind blew fresh from the westward, ran down in squadrons close in shore, under the protection of their batteries, to Calais. One Sunday I chased twenty-seven and made the shot tell among some of them, until the pilots warned me that if I stood further in they would give up charge of the ship. I chased them, with the exception of one, who ran aground near Calais, into that port. In hauling off after giving them a few more shot, their battery favoured us with one which struck us between wind and water. As the shells were now falling plentifully around us, I thought it prudent to make more sail, as one of the shells had gone through the foretop-sail. Our force generally consisted of three sloops of war to watch Boulogne, the senior officer being the commodore, but in spite of all our vigilance the privateers crept along shore under cover of the night without being seen, and they sometimes tantalized us by anchoring outside, but so close in and under their batteries that it was impossible to get at them in that position. We, one morning at daybreak, captured a row-boat with twenty-two men, armed with swivels and muskets. We had disguised the ship so much that she took us for a merchantman, and before she discovered her mistake was within pistol-shot. Three months had now expired, which had been passed much in the same manner as the last cruise, when a cutter came out to order us into the Downs.

CHAPTER 23

THE SAME WEARY ROUND

On our arrival, in consequence of the vessel wanting material repairs, we were desired to repair to Sheerness. The commander-in-chief at this ill-flavoured town was a King John's man, four feet something without his shoes, and so devoted to the reading of the Scriptures that he sometimes carried that sacred book under his arm. Some ill-natured people said he understood little of its doctrines, as he was too cross and unsociable to be a good Christian. Be that as it may he gave me leave, whilst the ship was refitting, to go home for four days. Where is the man who does not, after he has been absent from his family for nearly ten months, yearn to be with a fond wife and half a house full of dear children once more. During the short period I was at home, I thought myself in the seventh heaven. Alas, the time flew away on rapid wings. How soon our joy is changed to sorrow. I tore myself from the house that contained my dearest treasures, and was soon again among tar jackets and tar barrels. The admiral appeared satisfied with my punctuality, but he did not invite me to dinner, and as he did not I repaired to the principal inn with a few brother officers, and ordered some fish and a boiled leg of mutton and mashed turnips. 'It is very extraordinary, gentlemen,' replied the head waiter when we mentioned the articles we wished for dinner. 'There are thirteen different naval parties in the house, and they have all ordered the same. But,' added he, 'I am not at all surprised, for our mutton is excellent.' The following morning the signal was made for all captains to repair to the dockyard to receive the Duke of Clarence. At one o'clock he arrived in the commissioner's yacht from Chatham. I had the honour of being presented to him first, as I happened to be nearest. He asked me a few questions of no importance, and then passed on to another officer. He inspected the yard and the troops, we all following him. As he was afterwards to breakfast, or rather lunch, with Commissioner Lobb, the latter was considerate enough to invite us all to meet him, and a curious kind of meeting it was. The distinguished and illustrious admiral was very chatty, and appeared from the manner of his eating to be sharp set. The little

Admiral of the Port did not, for some reason, attend. His friends said he ought to have given the refreshment instead of the commissioner, but it was not his fashion. I was not sorry when the Duke took his departure, as his presence brought everything to a standstill.

In a week's time we were ready for sea, and I left Sheerness, the little hospitable admiral, and all its contents without shedding one tear. Off Margate the pilot had the kindness to bump us on shore, but as the tide was making, the vessel was soon afloat without receiving any injury. His wife had predicted this in her preceding night's dream, and he, silly man, had not sense enough to give up his turn to another pilot. On arriving in the Downs, I was ordered next day to repair to my old tiresome cruising ground, where, during a period of three long, lingering months, we cruised, anchored, fished, and frequently on Sundays engaged the old women's terror, the flotilla. We also took a *chasse marée* laden with plaster of Paris. As I imagined I should gratify the honest people at Dover, particularly the female part, who might be twisting their papillotes and talking scandal for want of other amusement, by sending in a vessel with the English flag flying above the French, I was determined to do so, although I knew she would scarcely pay her condemnation. A few days afterwards I received a note from the prize agent to request I would not send in any more of the same description, as there was a balance of six pounds against us for Proctor's fees, etc. Thinks I to myself, how odd. So, as the sailor says, after venturing life and limb in capturing an enemy's vessel, I am to pay for taking her. D——n me, Jack, that's too bad. I'll write to Joseph Hume to bring it before the House of Commons. I know he is a great reformer and a sailor's friend, although he terms them a dead weight.

We were at the end of our cruise relieved, and anchored again in the Downs, where I was informed Sir G Campbell had been relieved by Sir Thos. Foley, his counterpart in worth and gallantry.

I waited on the gallant admiral, left my card on Lady Lucy, and was invited to dinner. The admiral, as he is well known, and considered one of our most distinguished officers, I need not describe. His lady was a lively, hospitable, agreeable person, and I often reflect on the many pleasant hours I passed at the admiral's house. I understand she is now a saint and is very charitable. Generally speaking, I do not admire saints. They are too pure to mix with this sinful world, and are not fond of sailors. A fortnight passed away when we once more sighted our anchors, and the day after that eye-sore Boulogne. Our occupation was much the same as the last cruise, except that I was ordered shortly after I sailed to take charge of a large convoy outward bound, and to proceed with them as far as Portsmouth. On my arrival there I went on shore and waited on the admiral, Sir R Curtis, whom I found walking, what he termed his long-shore quarter-deck, the platform. He was a little, shrewd man, and knew a handspike from a capstan bar. I informed him from whence I came, and that I had fulfilled my orders respecting the convoy. I then presented him the necessary papers belonging to my own ship. 'Come with me to my office,' was the order. In going there we had to pass part of the market, where the admiral was well-known. He conversed in passing with several pretty market girls, and chucked them under the chin. 'Ho, ho!' thought I. On breaking the seal of the envelope of the papers I had given him, he said, 'I find all perfectly in order. How long have you been a commander?' I informed him. 'Your seniors,' returned he, 'may blush and take your correctness for a pattern.' I made my bow. 'You will sail to-morrow for your station,' continued he. 'Foley is a good fellow, and I will not detain you longer than that time, so that you may take prizes for him. There will be a knife and fork at my table at five o'clock, where, if you are not engaged, I hope to see you.' He then withdrew. If I had not known this gallant officer's character as a courtier, I should have been highly flattered by his compliments. Had anyone else stood in my shoes, his language would most likely have been the same. However, it put me in good humour, for who is there that does not like to be commended and sometimes flattered? At the admiral's table I met his amiable daughter, who did not appear in health, and some old brother officers.

At daylight I robbed Spithead of some of its mud, and was soon in sight of detested Boulogne, and of its, if possible, more hated flotilla; and I almost believe that if our men could have caught some of its crew they would have eaten them alive. This cruise we assisted, as the French say, in taking one of their privateers, the prize-money of which gave soap to the ship's company for the next cruise; what other good we did I say not. At the expiration of another three months, His Majesty's sloop's anchors once more bit the mud in the Downs. On my going on shore to the admiral's office, I was informed that I was to repair to Plymouth and there refit. I was, as Sir R Strachan said in his despatch, 'delighted.' I hoped we should be ordered to the Mediterranean. I dined with the admiral, and the day after we tore the anchors from their unwilling bed and made all sail. As I passed the coast near Boulogne I made my bow and wished it good-bye, I hoped for ever. On the fourth day we graced Plymouth Sound. I made my bow to the commander-in-chief, Sir R Calder, who asked me, with some surprise, where I came from, and what I did at Plymouth. I produced my order, etc. 'This is a mistake of some of the offices; I have no orders respecting you. However, as you are here, I suppose we must make good your defects, and, notwithstanding that you have taken us by surprise, I hope I shall have the pleasure of seeing you at six o'clock to dinner.'

I repaired on board with a pilot and brought the vessel into Hamoaze. At the appointed time I waited on the admiral. The dinner I thought passed off heavily. There were no ladies to embellish the table, and after coffee I went on board. Next morning I waited on the commissioner, Fanshaw, who received me very graciously, as I was known to several of his family. As the vessel was to be docked and fresh coppered, we were hulked, and I took lodgings on shore, where the commissioner did me the honour of calling on me and requested me to dine with him the following day. The dinner party consisted of another brother officer, his own family, who were very amiable, and myself. During the fortnight I remained here, as I was well acquainted with several families, I contrived to pass my time very agreeably.

I expected every hour orders to fit foreign, but, oh! reader, judge of my mortification when the admiral informed me I was to go back from whence I came in a few days, and take with me a heavy-laden convoy. My mind had been filled with Italian skies and burnished golden sunsets, ladies with tender black eyes, Sicilian coral necklaces, tunny-fish and tusks. I was to give up all these and to return to that never-to-be-forgotten, good-for-nothing rotten flotilla, to see Dover pier, the lighthouse, and the steeple of Boulogne, to cross and re-cross from one to the other to provoke an appetite. If I had had interest enough I would have changed the Board of Admiralty for having sent me to Plymouth on a fool's errand. My thoughts were bitter and seven fathoms deep. Again I cruised, like an armadillo on a grassplat, there and back again. After our usual time we again disturbed the mud, and most likely a number of fish, by letting go our anchors in the Downs, I little thought for the last time. How blind is man to future events, and fortunate it is he is so!

On the ninth day His Majesty's brig was again dividing the water and making it fly to the right and left in delicate wavy curls. We wished Boulogne, Bonaparte, and his flotilla burnt to a cinder during this cruise; we were generally at anchor off that detested place, and took nothing, for there was nothing to take. On Sunday we were usually firing at the flotilla as they anchored outside the pier, but so close to it that I fear our shot made little impression. At this time they were erecting a column on the heights, on which, we understood from the fishing-boats, an equestrian statue of that great dethroner, Bonaparte, was to be placed. A large division of the army of England, as they chose to call themselves, were encamped round it. We occasionally anchored at Dungeness for a few hours to procure fresh beef and vegetables. Our cruise was nearly terminated when the sloop of war, whose captain was senior to myself, made my signal. On repairing on board her, he informed me that a division of the flotilla was to run along shore for Cherbourg that night, and that it was necessary to keep the vessels as close in shore as possible, in order to intercept them.

I again joined my ship and remained on deck until midnight in the hope of encountering these bugbears, and making them pay dearly for all the trouble they had given us; but, alas! how futile is the expectation of man! I had gone to my cabin and thrown myself on the sofa, and fallen into a canine slumber – that is, one eye shut and the other open – when I heard a confused kind of rumbling noise, and soon afterwards the officer of the watch tumbled down the hatchway and called out to me that the ship was aground on the French coast, but that the fog, which had come on about an hour after I quitted the deck, was so dense that the land could not be seen. I had only taken off my coat and shoes. I was immediately on deck, where I saw, to my sorrow and amazement, my commanding officer hard and fast about half pistol-shot from us. I asked the pilots, whose carelessness had done us this favour, what time of tide it was. 'The infant ebb of the spring,' was the comfortable answer. 'I wish you were both hanged,' I replied. 'So be it,' responded the officers. During this period we were not idle; the boats were got out as well as an anchor astern, and the sails hove aback, the water started, the pumps set going, guns thrown overboard over the bows as well as shot, but all our efforts proved fruitless – you might as well have tried to start the Monument; and, to conclude this distressing and disastrous scene, a heavy battery began pouring its shot into the vessel I commanded, she being the nearest, and the fort not more than an eighth of a mile from us on the edge of a cliff. A boat came from the sloop to request that I would make preparations to blow up my vessel and quit her with the crew. 'Sooner said than done,' replied I to the officer sent; 'my boats will not carry the whole of us, and however I may wish to go to heaven in a hurry, probably those who are obliged to remain may not be willing to bear me company.' As the vessel began to heel over towards the battery, I ordered the boats to be manned, and all left the ship except nineteen men and myself, who had the felicity to be fired at like rabbits, as the enemy had now brought some field-pieces to bear on us. Our rigging was soon shot away and our sails cut into ribbons. At length away went the lower masts a little above the deck, while about two hundred men were pegging away at us with muskets. To make our happiness supreme, the sloop of war which had been set on fire and abandoned, blew up, and set us partially in a blaze, and while we were endeavouring to extinguish it the enemy took the cowardly advantage of wounding the purser, gunner, and two seamen, as well as myself, though only slightly. We had now fallen so much on the side that we stood with our feet on the combings of the hatchways, with our backs against the deck. What a charming sight, as my Lady Dangerfield might have said, to see four heavy guns from the battery, three field-pieces, and about two hundred soldiers firing at a nearly deserted vessel, and endeavouring to pick off and send to 'Kingdom come' the unfortunate few of her crew who remained. The captain of the other sloop, finding I was not in the boats, pulled back in a gallant manner under a most galling fire to entreat me to come into his boat. This I declined, as I could not in justice leave those who were obliged to remain behind. Finding he could not prevail on me to leave, he joined the other boats and proceeded to England, where, happily, they all arrived in the evening. We had now been aground about four hours, and the enemy had amused himself by firing at us for about two hours and a half.*

* See Appendix note D.

CHAPTER 24

TAKEN PRISONER

When the tide had receded sufficiently for the enemy to board us without wetting their delicate feet, about one hundred and fifty disgraced our decks. About thirty of these civil gentlemen, principally officers, paid a visit to my cabin without asking permission. The wine, of which I had ten dozen on board, was their first object, which I make no doubt they found suited their palate, as they drank it with much zest. My clothes, spyglasses, knives and forks, as well as the crockeryware, were seized on in turn; and it appeared by their smirking looks and lively conversation that all they had achieved was perfectly to their satisfaction, and that instead of plundering a few ship-wrecked suffers they had only been asked to a *fête* given by me. The commanding officer of these brave and honest men desired us to go on shore, where we were met by another officer, who ordered us to the guard-house near the battery, and an hour afterwards we marched for Boulogne, which was four miles distant, escorted by about forty of our tormentors. On our arrival we had the unexpected happiness of being lodged in the common gaol, cooped up in a dirty tiled room of twelve feet by eight, with a small well-grated window. 'Well,' said I to the doctor, who had remained behind to dress the wounded, 'what will the marines say to this? The sailors will never believe it.' Whilst we were prosing with our elbows on our knees and our chins on our thumbs, looking very dolefully at each other, the ill-looking man who had locked us up made his appearance with a servant in a rich livery, who asked in French for the commandant. I stood up and said I was that person, on which he presented me with the following note:

'Le Général Comte Lemaroix, Aide de Camp de sa Majesté l'Empereur et Roi, Commandant en Chef le Camp de Boulogne, etc, prie Monsieur Hoffeman, officer, de lui faire l'honneur de venir dîner avec lui aujourd'hui, lundi, à 4 heures.

'*R.S.V.P.*'

'Now,' said I, 'doctor,' addressing my surgeon, 'you are my senior in age and I think in experience; be my mentor on this occasion. In the first place, I have no inclination to go, for I am too sulky; in the second, I am wet and dirty.' 'Oh, do go, sir!' they all exclaimed. 'It may better our situation, and we may have our parole.' 'On your account I will accept the invitation,' said I. As I had no writing implements I sent a verbal answer in the affirmative, and made myself as much an Adonis as I was able. At the appointed hour the same servant and two gendarmes made their appearance, and from the gaol to the general's house I appeared, to judge by the people staring at me, to be the lion of the day. On my arrival I was ushered into the general's presence. The Comte Lemaroix, who was about forty years of age, was of a pleasing manner and countenance. He informed me he was sorry for my misfortune, but it was the fortune of war. I apologised for my dress, which was as wretched as my thoughts. At this time a young man in the French naval uniform came to me and asked me how I was. I remembered him as one of the officers sent to capture us. He spoke indifferent English, and as my knowledge of the French language was slight, I was glad to pair off with him. At the dinner-table were ten officers and one lady. I was seated on the left side of the Comte. I cut a sorry figure among so many smart and star-coated men. The dinner was plentiful and good, and everybody chatty and in good humour, in which I could not help, notwithstanding my situation, taking a part. After we had taken our coffee I naturally concluded I should be on parole. When I took my leave the captain in the navy and another officer said they would walk with me as it was dusk, and I presumed we were going to an inn – but, oh, horror of horrors! I was conducted to the prison from whence I came. They there wished me good-night, and I wished them at the devil. Next morning, after a restless night on a bed of straw, we were awakened by the grim, hard-featured gaoler who had been kind enough to lock us up. He asked the doctor if we wished to have breakfast, and if we could pay for it; he answered in the affirmative. This turnkey gentleman informed us that our first admiral, Mons. Poncevan, had been killed by an assassin. This report puzzled all our wise heads. An hour afterwards our *café-au-lait* entered, and with it the principal gaoler, or, as he was called, Mons. le Gouverneur. He was a stout, square-built man, and gave us an inquisitive look. The doctor, who was an Irishman and our interpreter, asked him the news, and if he were ever at Cork. 'No,' answered he, 'I never was in America! but,' said he, 'I understand that your Prime Minister, Mr Piercevell, has been shot by an assassin.' He meant Mr Percival. We were sorry to hear such bad news, as Mr Percival was certainly a loss to his country and his large family. However, it did not destroy our appetite for breakfast. The considerate governor only charged us as much more for it as we should have paid at the best coffee-house in the town.

After two days of durance vile I was visited by three very wise-looking men, who, I understood, were some sort of lawyers. One of them produced a printed paper, and asked me if I were acquainted with its contents. I answered, 'No.' 'Do you know for what purpose they were intended, for we have more than thirty of them which were found on board your ship?' I answered as before. 'This appears very extraordinary that you, as captain of the ship where they were found, should not know they were on board her.' 'It may be so,' I answered with indifference. 'You may think it a trifle,' said one of them 'but it may, without it is satisfactorily explained, prove in the end very serious to you.' 'Indeed,' returned I, 'that will be still more extraordinary. Probably it may be the means of a change of residence, for I cannot be worse off than where I am at present.' 'Monsieur chooses to be pleasant, but he must give us some account of these papers before we leave him.' One of them then translated their contents. As I had never heard of them before I was rather struck with their purport, which was to create a counter-revolution, and cause that English-loving man, Bonaparte, to be dethroned. 'Doctor,' said I, 'do you know anything about these terrible papers?' 'Very little,' replied he. 'They were, I believe, in circulation about two years ago, in Mr Pitt's time, and they were called his projects, for he loved Napoleon with all his heart.' 'Pray,' said I, turning to the commissioner who had the longest and most snuffy nose, and who had translated the paper, 'in what part of the vessel were these projects found?' 'In the second cabin,' was his answer. He meant the gun-room, where the officers slept and messed. 'What is their date?' '1808.' 'Come,' resumed I, 'I think you will not shoot me this time. I did not join the ship until 1810, when they were never given into my charge. Now, gentlemen, you may either remain or depart; no more answers or explanation will I give.' They grouped into the corner of the room, and after taking a pinch of snuff with a few shrugs of their shoulders and some whispering, took their leave.

Soon after the turnkey appeared with another worthy person as interpreter, and to whom I was to pay three francs a day and give him a dinner. I remonstrated, and said the doctor was my interpreter. 'Bah, bah!' said the fellow, and marched out of the room, the door of which he locked. This person, whom the turnkey had so unceremoniously introduced, had, it appeared, been sent for by the *gouverneur*, as he chose to understand we wished to have 'un maître de la langue Française,' who could act as interpreter when required. The poor man, who appeared as if he had fallen from a balloon, apologised for the intrusion, which he said did not lie with him, he had been sent for and came, but that when the turnkey unlocked the door he would withdraw. 'No,' said I, 'as you are here and you speak good English,' which he did, 'I will, if you have a grammar, take a lesson in French, and you may come every day during our stay in this abominable place, which I suppose will not be long.' He pulled a grammar from his pocket, and I began with the verbs. 'I intend sending a letter to the Comte Lemaroix. Will you,' said I to him, 'take it for me?' 'Willingly,' replied he. I drew it up, and he translated it. It was to request that myself and officers might have our parole, but as day after day rolled on I do not think he received it, as my request was not complied with.

I was again examined by a military court respecting those fearful papers, but they, as well as myself, were not satisfied, I for being sent for on so useless an errand, and losing my French lesson, and they because they could not discover whether I was a spy, or prove that I had circulated those papers among the fishing boats. After this tedious and ridiculous examination the President, who appeared half sailor and half soldier, asked me in so mild a manner as if sugar-candy would not have dissolved in his mouth, 'Pray, sir, will you acquaint me how many cruisers you have in the Channel?' 'Your question, Mr President, is a delicate one,' replied I, 'and the only way you can gain that information is to send all your frigates that have been lying at anchor so long in your different harbours to ascertain the fact.' I thought my answer made him look cross, two others look sulky, and the remainder smile. 'I think we may discharge the prisoner,' said he, turning to the other wise men; 'we can elucidate nothing.' 'No,' said I to myself, 'you will get nothing out of me.' On the tenth day after the shipwreck we were ordered to march, and had the honour of having two livery servants, in the shape of gendarmes on horseback, to attend us. I begged to have a carriage, but I was refused, although I offered to pay liberally for one.

We reached Montreuil-sur-Mer in the evening, where we marched into the common gaol. I was much fatigued, as I had never walked so far in my life; my feet were becoming blistered, and I was very hungry. 'Do,' said I, 'doctor, let us have something to eat, for we have fasted since breakfast. Have they any eggs?' The *gouverneur du château* appeared, and informed us he had plenty of eggs, and could give us a *fricassée de mouton* and *pommes de terre au maître d'hôtel*, 'but,' added the doctor, 'those d——d fellows the gendarmes must dine with us.' This I did not like, and requested him to speak to the gaoler, which he did; but the former declared it was customary, when they escorted prisoners they always eat with them. We were obliged to conform to the nuisance. After dinner, or rather supper, or, more correctly speaking, the two in one, I fell asleep in my chair until a dirty-looking girl shook me by the arm to say that my bed was ready. I gave her a look that had she been milk it would have turned her into vinegar. I followed her, however, into a room about twelve feet by seven, where there were two crib bed-places like those on board the packets. They were, considering the place, tolerably decent, and I turned in half-rigged. At half after two in the morning our two horse attendants had the civility to wake us out of tired Nature's sweet reposer, balmy sleep. I looked daggers, and they looked determined on their plan of making us march at three o'clock. The dirty, but civil damsel, brought me a basin of water. I shook my feathers and refreshed myself. She then appeared with some porringers filled with what she called *café-au-lait* – ie, milk bedevilled, and some tolerable bread and salt butter. However, as we presumed we had another long march to encounter, we made no hesitation in accepting it, and for which and the supper I had to pay most extravagantly. We began our agreeable walk before daybreak, accompanied by our two attendant cavaliers. As I walked rather lame one of them offered me his horse, which I thought civil. I declined it, as I preferred walking with my officers, although in pain.

About three in the afternoon we reached Hesdin, our destination for that night, having marched nineteen miles, and were ushered into the gaol. 'May the devil run a-hunting with these rascally vagabonds!' said the doctor. 'Amen,' responded the rest. We were put into a dirty brick-floored room with a grated window, in which there were three beds. 'Now,' said I to the doctor, 'let us hunt for something to eat, for notwithstanding all my miseries I am very hungry.' The *gouverneur du château* made his appearance; he was a brigadier of gendarmes. 'What do you wish?' said he. 'What have you to eat?' asked the man of physic. 'Eggs, a fowl, and some excellent ham.' 'Let us have them,' cried I, 'as soon as possible.' Whilst these good things were getting ready I bathed my feet in warm water, they were much swollen, and the blisters on them had broken. I afterwards rubbed them with brandy. The dinner was put on table, and the gendarmes took their seats *sans façons*. After I had taken my second tumbler of wine I began to revive. The dinner was not bad, and by the time it was finished we were in good humour. 'Now,' said I, 'doctor,' for he was my factotum, 'tell our attendants if they will not allow me to have some kind of carriage I will not step a foot further. My feet are so bad I cannot walk, and they must carry me.' The Brigadier was sent for, and after a consultation of a few minutes I was told I might have one if I paid for it, but it could be only a covered cart. 'Very well,' said I, 'any port in a storm.' We were now informed it was time to go to rest. This was no punishment; and notwithstanding being bug- and flea-bitten, I slept well and forgot all my sorrows. At six I was roused by the men at arms, had a tolerable good breakfast, and stepped into my travelling machine with two of my officers, the top of the cart being so low we were obliged to lie down, and if it had not been for its abominable jolting we should have found ourselves snug enough.

CHAPTER 25

AT CAMBRAY

We reached Arras in the afternoon. On entering the town we were followed by a crowd of idlers, who I rather think took us for a caravan of wild beasts. Among this choice assemblage I perceived a sailor who looked like an Englishman. 'What are you doing here?' I called out at a venture. 'I am Lieutenant Horton's servant,' answered he. 'Pray,' said I, 'who is he?' 'He is the lieutenant of the sailors at this depôt.'

'Then,' said I, 'take this to him,' giving him a piece of paper with my name on it. 'Aye, aye, sir,' said he, and ran off to execute his errand. We were, as before, ushered into the common gaol with due ceremony, where we were received by another Brigadier, who had the honour of being *gouverneur*. The gaol was considerably larger than those we had lodged in on the road, and the people were civil. We ordered dinner, which I had to pay for without doing it justice, in consequence of the appearance of Lieutenant Horton with a French commissary, to inform myself and officers we were on parole, and the former, like a generous sailor, begged us all to dine with him at his house. We made ourselves as smart as circumstances would allow, and accompanied him to a snug little house where he lived. He introduced us to his wife, who was a very kind person and paid us every attention, and I shall ever retain a feeling of gratitude for their hospitality. In the evening we were joined by the English surgeon of the depôt, who engaged us to dine with him the following day. A servant was sent to the American hotel to bespeak rooms for us, and the day after I engaged a carriage to take us to Verdun, for which I was to pay eight napoleons, and find the coachman. In the evening, or rather night, we took possession of our new quarters, which from what I had lately been accustomed to, appeared a paradise, although the doctor and purser declared they were half bled to death by bugs and fleas. We breakfasted like gentlemen, and afterwards strolled about the town, to the amusement of the inhabitants, who, as we passed them, made great eyes at us. I shall not trouble my readers with a description of Arras, as they may satisfy their curiosity, if they wish it, by consulting a Gazeteer. At five o'clock the lieutenant called on me, and we all repaired to the surgeon's house. He gave us a good dinner, and was very attentive. At ten o'clock they accompanied us to the inn, where they took their final leave, as we were to start in our new vehicle at five in the morning.

At the appointed time behold us seated in our coach chattering like magpies, and going at the rapid speed of about five miles an hour. At Cambray we dined and slept. We visited the cathedral, which, thanks to those honest, religious men, the Republicans, was in total ruins. All the Virgins and saints were decapitated and the quiet repose of the dead disturbed by their pure, delicate hands. 'Erin's curse be upon them!' exclaimed my man of medicine. 'The devil has them by this time,' said the purser. 'What a set of impious scoundrels,' ejaculated the midshipman. 'I am afraid,' added I, 'France has in a great measure brought all her misfortunes on herself. It the King and the nobles had stood firm to their guns and given a more liberal constitution, millions of lives might have been saved, and we should not have had the supreme happiness of being attended by the gendarmes or of taking up our abode in their filthy, loathsome gaols, besides a thousand other circumstances, of which, as you have been partakers, I need not mention, as they are too agreeable to bear in memory.' We reached a small place called Cateau Cambresis, where we dined at a fourth-rate inn, formerly the country palace of the good Archbishop Fénélon. At dinner, which, like the *auberge*, was also of the fourth class, I had a silver fork with the armorial bearings of an archbishop. I remarked the fact to my *maître d'hotel*, the doctor. 'I have a spoon with the same,' replied he. 'This, you are aware, was Fénélon's favourite country palace, and as a quantity of family plate was buried during the Revolution, these very likely belonged to him.' When the woman who attended us at dinner came in again, the doctor interrogated her respecting them. She informed him they had been found among some old rubbish in the yard. I asked her if she would sell them; she answered in the affirmative, and demanded thirty francs. I gave her twenty-four, and took possession of my prizes.

In a remote part of the building I found some Englishmen at work manufacturing what the French were then little acquainted with, dimity. They told me they had permission to sleep out of the prison, and that the French allowed them a franc a day and some wine. I asked them if they were working on their own account; they answered, no, but on that of the French Government. 'Bonaparte has his wits about him,' said I to myself, 'and appears wide awake.'

We reached Verdun on the sixth day. I waited on Captain Otter of the navy and the senior officer, who introduced me to the commandant, the

Baron de Beauchêne, who, by his rubicund face, appeared to be fond of good living. My name was registered at the police office, where I was desired to sport my graceful figure the first day of every month. Several officers did me the honour of a visit, but as my news was like salted cod – rather stale – they were not much edified. The day following I dined with Captain and Mrs Otter, who were good, kind of homespun people. I met at their table the worthy chaplain, Gordon. Some of his friends said he was too mundane, and bowed to the pleasures of the world most unclerically. I found him an agreeable, gentlemanly person in society, and a plain-sailing parson in the pulpit. There were two officers here who were most amusing, Captains Miller and Lyall, and when dining with them, which I frequently did, I do not know which I enjoyed most, their dinner or their dry jokes. I also became acquainted with Captain Blennerhassett, and sometimes took a cold dinner at a small house he rented on the banks of the Meuse. We dubbed it Frogmore Hall, in consequence of a vast quantity of those creatures infesting it. Lord Blaney, who once wrote a book, principally on the best mode of cooking, figured away here. He was a good-natured but not a very wise man. He could not bear the midshipmen, because, he said, they cheated him out of his best cigars and made him give them a dinner when he did not wish for their company. This was, strange to say, sometimes the case.

There were about twelve hundred prisoners at this depôt, principally officers of the army and navy, and a few masters of merchant ships, as well as some people detained in a most unjust manner by a decree of Bonaparte when the war broke out. About two miles from the town was a racecourse, made by the officers and kept up by subscription, where, I was informed, there was as much jockeyship practised as at Newmarket. It made a variety, and the ladies say variety is charming. After residing in this town, where every description of vice was practised, about a month, I remarked that the mids, of whom there were about one hundred and twenty, were idle, dissipated, and running into debt. The greater part of them were fine lads. I proposed to Captain Otter the establishment of a school for them, and said that if the requisite masters could be procured I would superintend it. He entered into my views most willingly and wrote to the Admiralty respecting them, informing their lordships the expenses for a hundred midshipmen would not be more than eighty pounds a year. Not receiving an answer, he established it at his own risk; whether he was ever remunerated is a problem I am not enabled to solve. Six lieutenants volunteered to assist me, and attended the school hours in turn.* Everything went on exceedingly well for twelve months, when unfortu-

* See Appendix notes E and F.

nately the Baron de Beauchêne died, and was succeeded by a man who ordered the school to be broken up. This was as unexpected as unmerited. Captain Otter and myself remonstrated, but in vain. The youngsters were sent to the right-about; but I am happy to say that the greater part of them had the good sense to form themselves into classes at their own lodgings, where the same masters attended them. Finding my services of no further use, I sighed for country air and a change of scene. The town manners shocked my delicacy, and I much feared I should lose my innocence. The copy I frequently wrote when at school stared me in the face – that 'Evil communications corrupt good manners.' I therefore determined before I became contaminated to change my quarters. I waited on the commandant and obtained leave to live at a small village two miles from the town. My new residence was a small *château*, the proprietress of which was the widow of a colonel of cuirassiers in the old time. I took possession of a good-sized bedroom and drawing-room, for which I paid, with my board, seventy napoleons a year. The establishment consisted of a house-keeper, more like a man than a woman, one maid servant, and two men. The widow was an agreeable person, nearly in her seventieth year, but very healthy and active. At the back of the *château* was a delightful garden, with a brook running through it, in which were some trout, carp and tench. Adjoining it were vineyards belonging to the house. I could now, in the literal sense of the word, in which one of our poets intended it, 'From the loopholes of my retreat peep at such a world' without partaking of its folly.

My time was occupied with a French master, and in drawing, and reading French authors, and if my mind had not been tortured by my being a captive, and not knowing how long I was likely to remain so, I should have been comparatively happy. Our letters, when we did receive them, were always broken open and read to the commandant by one of the gendarmes who could blunder out a little English. If they contained anything against the French Government, or treated on politics, they never reached us. By these honourable means all our domestic concerns became known to the mighty chief, the ignorant, left-handed, blundering translator, and a host of others. In short, our letters, after having run the gauntlet through a number of dirty hands, with still more dirty minds, were scarcely worth receiving.

One morning, as I was sitting at breakfast in not a very cheerful mood, a woman, of not very prepossessing appearance, entered. She came, she said, to make a complaint against three wicked mids. They had taken the figure of Bonaparte from the mantelpiece and knocked his head off; for so doing she threatened to complain to the commandant if they did not pay her a five-franc piece. I told her I would send for the decapitating youngsters, and, if I found her complaint to be well-grounded, they should remunerate her by giving her another Emperor, or paying her for the old one. She departed, but not in peace, as I could hear her grumbling as she went along the vestibule. At noon next day these Emperor-destroying lads came to my lodgings to answer the complaint.

'We lodge in this woman's house,' said one of them, 'and one morning we thought we would amuse ourselves by bringing Bonaparte fairly to a court martial. Our charges against him were tyranny and oppression, imprisonment against our consent, and not granting an exchange of prisoners. We found him guilty on all the charges, and as he could make no defence, we sentenced him first to be shot, but we thought that too honourable for him; then to be hanged, and lastly, to have his mischief-making head chopped off by a case-knife, which sentence was carried into execution; but as we do not wish the woman to quarrel with us, we have no objection to pay her two francs, which we think is too much by thirty-nine sous.'

'You value Emperors, gentlemen,' said I, 'at a very cheap rate.' 'Yes,' replied they, 'such an Emperor as Bonaparte, who we think is a most unrelenting tyrant.' 'Hush!' cried I, 'walls sometimes have ears. Go and make your peace with your landlady, offer her the two francs, and if she will not accept it send her to me, for, to tell you the truth, were she to go with her complaint to the commandant, you most likely would be shut up in the old convent and kept there for a month.' I gave them a glass of wine, in which they drank the downfall of Bonaparte and departed. I understood afterwards this knotty point was settled amicably; the woman, not wishing to lose her lodgers, accepted the money. As the lying 'Moniteur' was the only paper we could read, we of course were always deceived, and supposed from its contents that France was carrying everything before her. More than eighteen months had now passed away, like a disturbed dream, since I became a prisoner, when the order came, like a flash of lightning, from the police to desire all the English prisoners to be ready to quit Verdun in forty-eight hours and proceed to Blois. To those who had the misfortune to be married to French women and had children it was a thunder-stroke. The weather had set in with great severity, it being the month of December. Another brother officer and his nephew joined me in purchasing a covered cart and two cart horses; and a captain of a merchant vessel, said to be a descendant of the immortal Bruce, volunteered to be our coachman, provided we lodged and fed him on the road, to which we, without hesitation, agreed.

CHAPTER 26

END OF CAPTIVITY

At the time appointed we had our machine ready. The gendarmes were literally driving some of the officers out of the town. To save them the trouble of doing us the same favour we departed early. On the first stage from Verdun, in descending a steep, long hill, a hailstorm overtook us, and as the hailstones fell they froze. The horses could not keep their feet, nor could our sailor coachman keep his seat. The animals slid down part of the way very comfortably. At length, after much struggling, they once more gained a footing, and in so doing, the fore wheels came in contact with their hinder feet, which unfortunately frightened and set them off at full speed. I got hold of the reins with the coachman, and endeavoured to pull them into a ditch to the left – on the right was a precipice – the reins broke, and we had no longer command over them. We were in this state of anxiety for a few minutes, when the fore wheels detached themselves from the carriage, and over it went on its larboard broadside. I was, with the coachman, thrown head foremost into the ditch, which, being half filled with snow, broke the violence of our launch. I soon floundered out of it, without being much hurt. My falling companion, being a much stouter man than myself did not fare so well, as his right shoulder received a severe contusion. The noble man-of-war captain inside had his face much cut with the bottles of wine that were in the pockets of the vehicle, and he would have made an excellent phantasmagoria. His nephew had one of his legs very much injured. Here we were in a most pitiable condition, not knowing what to do, as we could not move our travelling machine without assistance. As we were scratching our wise heads, and looking at each other with forlorn faces, a party of French soldiers approached, and for a five-franc piece they assisted us in righting the carriage and catching the horses, which had been stopped at the bottom of the hill. On an examination of our cart we found that, fortunately for us, the traverse pin of the fore-wheels had jumped out, which freed them and the horses, and occasioned our turning turtle. Had not this taken place, we most likely should have gone over the precipice. We, after some sailor-like contrivances, got under weigh. As we were grown wiser by this mishap, we took care to lock the hinder wheels when going down hill in future. We reached Clermont in the dusk of the evening, and glad I was to turn into a bed replete with hoppers, crawlers, and wisdom, for it was very hard. Being much fatigued, I slept soundly, notwithstanding my numerous biting companions.

After a most suffering, cold, and uncomfortable journey of six days we reached Blois. A number of our soldiers and sailors perished with cold on the road. We assisted some few of them with money and something to eat. Poor fellows! some were so worn out that they threw themselves down on the stubble in the fields, where the severe frost soon put an end to their sufferings. The day we quitted Verdun the retreating French army from Moscow, with numerous waggons full of their frostbitten and wounded men, entered it. That and the allied army advancing on the French borders were the cause of our being sent away with so much speed. When this division of the enemy's army marched through Verdun for the purpose of conquering Russia, it was the general remark amongst the English that the appearance of the men and their appointments could not be better in any country; but to see them return in the extreme of wretchedness and suffering was truly pitiable. Oh, Bonaparte! I charge thee fling away ambition; it is, unfortunately for the world, thy besetting sin. It cannot continue for ever, and you will be brought up with a severe round turn before you are many years older – such is my prophecy.

We had not been settled at Blois a month before we had orders to quit it and to proceed to Gueret on the river Creuse. We understood the allied army having entered France was the cause of our removal.

As I had never heard of Gueret before, I requested my landlord to give me some information respecting it. 'Why,' said he, with a most awful shrug of his shoulders, 'it is where Louis the Fourteenth banished his *petite noblesse*, and is now filled with lawyers, who, as the town is small and the inhabitants are not numerous, go to law with each other to keep themselves, I suppose, in practice. Oh, you will find the roads rough and much out of order; we call it *"un chemin perdu,"* and as the town is insignificant, and produces nothing, we call it *"un endroit inconnu."* I do not think,' added he, 'there are more than *cinquante cheminées à feu* in the whole town.'

This information did not raise my spirits. However, there was no alternative, and it was of little use to be downhearted. The weather continued very severe, and we had again to encounter frost, snow, and intense cold. We prayed for the humane Emperor of France, and wished him elevated on Haman's gibbet. Our journey was most horrible and fatiguing; the roads in some places were literally lost, and we were obliged to drive over ploughed fields in order to avoid the deep ruts. I thought we should have had all our bones dislocated. The five days we were on this wretched road will never be effaced from my memory. We slept where we could. Inns there were very few, and those few the abodes of poverty, filth, and rags. The small farms sometimes took us in, where, whilst eating the coarse brown bread and tough fowls they put before us, and for which they made us pay most extravagantly, the pigs and poultry kept us company during our repast.

One night, at one of these abominable places, I was obliged to lie on a table, as they had not a bed to give me. I was awakened early by a most horrible smell. I thought I should be suffocated. I procured a light and inspected the room. On opening an old press I found several half-putrid cheeses, full of jumping gentlemen, and probably ladies, for there was a large assembly of them. I made my escape from this savoury, not sweet-smelling den, and threw myself into what they called a chair, which, from its form and ease must have been fabricated before the time of Adam. I found I had seated myself before a kind of crib, something like a corn-bin, in which was lying, fast asleep and snoring, the landlady, who was a coarse, dingy beauty of about forty. 'Lead me not into temptation and deliver me from evil,' ejaculated I to myself. At this time a huge cock that had been roosting in some part of the kitchen gave a loud crow. She started up and called out 'Oh, mon Dieu, je ne puis pas dormir à cause de cette bête là!' I pretended to be asleep, although I made a loop-hole with my left eye. A short time afterwards she was snoring as loud as before.

When daylight began to break I went out into the yard, and was saluted by the barking of a very large dog, who was chained to a small shed. This roused all the inmates of the house. We had some milk and eggs, and once more assumed our most agreeable journey. On entering Gueret, I verily believe all the men, women, children and dogs came to meet us. I do not know what they thought of us. We appeared, I thought, like a set of wild men in search of a more civilised country than that whence they came. It was soon understood we wanted lodgings, and the importunity of the females was most embarrassing. I took up my abode over a small grocer's shop. The only room I could obtain, which contained a small bed, a minikin table, and two common chairs, cost me fifty francs a month, (about two pounds sterling), and I was considered fortunate in having such good lodgings. I sometimes dined at the principal inn, where I met the *élite* of the town, such as bankers and half broken-down noblemen who had been pigeoned by their dearly-beloved Napoleon. One day at dinner I overheard a conversation between two of these last, one of whom wished, if he could find two officers among us who preferred living in the country, to have them as lodgers. I seized the opportunity of introducing myself to them when we rose from table. An officer in one of our regiments offered himself as the other inmate.

We were mutually satisfied with each other, and two days afterwards I obtained leave from the French commandant to remove to Masignon, about four leagues from Gueret. On reaching the village I was directed to a large *château* with two embattled towers. I was much pleased with its romantic appearance, but more so with its amiable inmates, which consisted of the Dowager Countess de Barton, the count, her son, and the two young countesses, her daughters, the eldest in her twenty-fourth and the youngest in her twenty-second year.

There were seven saddle horses and a carriage, all of which were at our service, and I had a chamberlain to attend on me. The domain was very extensive. We had the privilege of shooting and fishing, and I found myself as comfortable as I could possibly wish, and I much regretted I was deprived of the happiness of seeing my wife and dear children in such distinguished and amiable society.

One evening as we were all sitting in the large drawing room, it suddenly appeared to be going on one side, and immediately after we were much alarmed by a roaring noise like the flame in a chimney when on fire. I attempted to move and nearly fell.

This was occasioned by the shock of an earthquake. During the anxious suspense we were in, the servants had rushed into the room with horror in their countenances, exclaiming, 'Oh, mesdames, le château va tomber, et nous serons écrasées!'

'Peace,' said the elder countess; 'remain where you are.' By the time she had spoken the trembling ceased, nor had we another shock. After a short interval we resumed our conversation as it nothing had occurred.

This part of France is much infested with wolves, and I frequently in the night heard them near the house, but I only saw one of them in the day. I fired at him, but as he was at some distance, he escaped without injury.

I had resided with this amiable family nearly a month, when one of the servants who had been to Gueret entered nearly out of breath to say that, 'La belle France était prise!' At the same time he handed a small printed paper to the mother countess.

She smiled at the idea of the servant's report, and turning to me she said, 'I am rejoiced to be the first to announce to you that you are no longer in captivity. The allied armies have taken Paris and Bonaparte has abdicated. This is the "Gazette", I am happy to see once more decorated with the *Fleur de Lys*.'

I kissed her hand for the intelligence, and assured her although the joyful news was everything I wished, I should much regret quitting her family, where, during my short stay, I could not have experienced more affection and kindness from my own relations than she had shown to me.

On the second day after this delightful intelligence, I took an affectionate leave of the ladies. The count was absent.

At Gueret I joined the same party who had been my companions in misery and fatigue. Our nags had been well taken care of, and the nine hundred and ninety-ninth cousin of the brave, but unfortunate, Bruce deserved praise.

I will not describe our tiresome and wretched journey of nine days. At length we reached Fontainebleau, where we remained two days to rest ourselves as well as the horses. In passing through its forest, which is very fine, we were almost poisoned by the stench occasioned by dead men and horses. We saw the palace, and the ink on the table where Bonaparte had signed his abdication was so fresh that it came off by rubbing it a little with the finger.

Two days after we entered Paris, which we found in possession of the allied armies, and it was with the greatest difficulty that we procured lodgings even in the Faubourg St Antoine. They were at the top of the house, only five stories and an entresol to mount! and alarmingly dear as well as dirty and small. We sold our stud and carriage for a little more than we gave for them.

During the three days we remained in Paris, I visited the Louvre and its stolen goods. It was a brilliant treat; never was any palace so decorated with such gems of art, nor, I hope, under the same circumstances, ever will be again. On the day Louis le Désiré entered, I paid a napoleon for half a window in the Rue St Denis to view the procession.

Nearly opposite the window the King halted to receive the address from the Moulins and Poissardes, some of whom appeared to me drunk. A child dressed like a cupid, with a chaplet of flowers in its hand, was handed to the Duchess d'Angoulême, who sat on the left hand of the King. I remarked she was much confused and scarcely knew what to do with the child, who was about five years of age, and who put the chaplet on her head. At length she kissed it and returned it to its mother.

The window of the houses were dressed with pieces of tapestry and white flags, which appeared to my view nothing more than sheets and table-cloths. The Garde Nationale lined the streets, and by the acclamations of, 'Vive Louis le Dixhuit, Louis le Désiré, les Bourbons!' and other cries, all foreigners who had never visited France or conversed with its natives, would have exclaimed, 'Look at these loyal people; how they love the Bourbon dynasty!'

The mounted National Guard who came after the royal carriage out-Heroded Herod by their deafening cries of loyalty. Who would have imagined these gentlemen would have played the harlequin and receive their dethroned Emperor as they did when he entered Paris again? 'Put not your trust in men, particularly Frenchmen in 1814, O ye house of Bourbon, for they made ye march out of France without beat of drum.'

I was much amused with the conduct of the Imperial Guard who followed the national heroes. The Poissardes cried out, 'Vive le Garde Impériale!' All they uttered was 'Vive les Poissardes!' They looked as black as thunder.

I understood there was a cause of dissatisfaction among them in consequence of a mark of distinction having been given to the shop-keeping soldiers and not any to them. This was the Comte d'Artois' clever policy; at least, so I was informed by my companion who had taken the other half of the window where we stood. My thoughts were seven fathoms deep.

CHAPTER 27

HONOURABLY ACQUITTED

The morning before my departure I waited on Lord Aberdeen, requesting a passport to England; he referred me to Prince Metternich. I reached his hotel, and had to wade through a host of long-whiskered, long-piped gentlemen, who were smoking with all their might and main, and spitting in all directions.

As I advanced, a genteel-looking young man, who was dressed in an aide-de-camp's uniform, came to me and asked in French the purport of my visit. I informed him. He left me, and soon returned and requested I would walk into another room, where I found the German Prince, who received me very cavalierly, and asked me what I did in Paris when there were transports waiting at Bordeaux to carry over the English.

'I thank your Highness for the information, but I do not wish to go by that route. My intention is to return to England by Havre, and I shall feel obliged by your granting me a passport to that effect.'

'You should go to Lord Aberdeen for one.'

'I have already seen him, and he directed me to you, as you were in command of the capital,' I replied.

He muttered something which I could not, nor did I wish to, understand. After a pause he asked me my rank. I informed him, when he directed his secretary to make out my passport, and here ended much ado about nothing.

We started next morning, slept at Rouen, revisited its ancient cathedral, which had been struck by lightning, breakfasted, and arrived at Havre, where we remained two days, waiting for a vessel to take us across the Channel. I viewed this town with much interest, as it had saluted the vessels I had belonged to with several hundred shot.

We arrived at Spithead in the evening, but too late to go on shore. There were nine of us – men, women, and squalling children – and we had the comfort of lying on the cabin deck, there being no sleeping berths, as the vessel was only about fifty tons, and not fitted up for passengers.

When I landed next morning I appeared to tread on air, but I could not help laughing out aloud at the, I thought, ridiculous and anything but picturesque dresses of the women. Their coal-scuttle bonnets and their long waists diverted me, although I was sorry to observe in my healthy and fair country-women such an ignorance of good taste. I took a hasty mutton chop at the 'Fountain,' and started for London by the first stage coach.

On my arrival at dear home I found all I loved in good health. My excellent wife and affectionate boys and girls clung round me, and I was as happy as an innocent sucking pig, or, if my reader thinks the simile not in place, as happy as a city alderman at a turtle feast.

A few days after my appearance at the Admiralty I was ordered to proceed to Portsmouth, to undergo my trial for the loss of the ship, which, as a son of the Emerald Isle would say, was no loss at all, as she was retaken afterwards.

My sentence was as honourable to the officers of the court martial as it was to myself. I received my sword from the President, Admiral Sir George Martin, with a high encomium.

The days of my youth have floated by like a dream, and after having been forty-five years in the Navy my remuneration is a hundred and eighty pounds a year, without any prospect of its being increased. If the generality of parents would take my advice they never would send one of their boys into the service without sufficient interest and some fortune. If they do, their child, if he behaves well, may die in his old age, possibly as a lieutenant, with scarcely an income to support himself; and if he should under these circumstances have the misfortune to have married and have children, God, I hope, will help him, for I very much fear no one else will!

Here ends my eventful but matter-of-fact history, which, if it has afforded my reader any amusement, my pains are well repaid.

APPENDIX

Note A

If the French accounts are to be credited General Rochambeau had a garrison of only 600 men, 400 of whom were militia (*cf.* 'Victoires et Conquêtes,' tome iii., p. 249). At any rate, when Fort Bourbon surrendered the garrison was found to be only 200, including the wounded (*cf.* James, vol. i., p. 219).

Note B

James, in his account of this brilliant feat (vol. ii., p. 360 *et seq.*), gives several interesting details of the affair. 'Every man was to be dressed in blue, and no white of any kind to be seen. The password was "Britannia" and the answer "Ireland."' The boarding party proceeded in six boats, each being instructed to effect an entrance on a particular part of the *Hermione*. 'From the moment of quitting the *Surprise* till the *Hermione* was boarded Captain Hamilton never lost sight of her for a moment. He stood up in the pinnace with his night-glass, by the aid of which he steered a direct course towards the frigate.' When still a mile from the *Hermione* the boats were discovered by two Spanish gunboats. Some of Hamilton's boats disobeyed orders by attacking these gunboats instead of concentrating their attention on the *Hermione*, and thus nearly spoilt the attack.

James adds that: 'In effecting this surprising capture the British sustained so comparatively slight a loss as 12 wounded, including Captain Hamilton. Of their 365 in crew the Spaniards had 119 killed and 97 wounded, most of them dangerously.'

Note C

Copy of letter written by Lieutenant Hoffman to his wife immediately after the action of Trafalgar: –

'TONNANT, *Oct. 27th, 1805*. Off Cadiz.

'MY BELOVED SARAH, – It has pleased Providence once more to bless our favoured isle with astonishing success. On the 21st of the month the combined enemy's fleet, consisting of thirty-four sail of the line, four frigates, and two brigs, were seen by us. At five minutes after twelve afternoon we broke their line and engaged them. Captain Tyler gallantly placed the *Tonnant*, and I hope we as gallantly defended her. We have lost twenty-six brave fellows and fifty wounded in our ship only. We have captured sixteen sail of the line, French and Spanish, and sunk one of the line and one blew up. We are now going for Gibraltar to refit, as we are decently maul'd. We were twenty-six of the line, three frigates, a cutter and a schooner. I am very sorry to relate Lord Nelson has gloriously fallen, covered with heroic wounds. Captain Tyler is wounded rather dangerously, but I hope he will soon recover. The French Admiral Magon, in the *Algerzaries* (*sic*), of equal force, laid us alongside, and attempted boarding, but found it ineffectual. At the same time we were engaged by three other sail of the line. After engaging this fine fellow for about an hour he struck his flag, and we took possession of her (*sic*); in short, with this noble ship's company we humbled three of nearly equal force. This battle, my beloved, plainly shows it is not always to the strong. An Almighty Hand fought it for us. To Him we trust in this and every future event. May He protect my Sarah.'

Note D

Captain Hoffman's report to the Admiralty of the loss of the *Apelles*: –

'Verdun, France, *May 28th*, 1812.

'Sir, – Captain Boxer, of H.M.S. *Skylark*, and my senior officer, having communicated to me on the evening of the 2nd of May he had received information of a large division of the flotilla being in readiness to escape from Boulogne to Cherberg that night, he thought it necessary that his sloop the *Skylark* and the *Apelles*, under my command, should be kept as close in shore as possible between Boulogne and Etaples in order to intercept them. But it is with feelings of regret I have to acquaint you, for the information of the Lords of the Admiralty, that on Sunday, a.m. the 3rd of May, H.M.S. *Apelles* ran aground about eighteen miles to the westward of Boulogne, as also did H.M.S. *Skylark*. The wind at this time was moderate at N.E. with a dense fog.

'The sloop, on a wind, heads E.S.E., going about five knots an hour, the land not perceived. Shortly after it became clear enough to discern that we were about a musket shot from a battery elevated above our mastheads, which, on perceiving our situation, opened a most destructive fire on the *Apelles*, she being the nearest vessel. During this time the boats were got out, and an anchor carried astern to heave the sloop off. Guns, shot, and heavy stores, etc., were thrown overboard, from before the chest tree the water started and pumped out, in order to lighten the vessel, but without effect, as, unfortunately, the sloops had run on shore on the infant ebb spring tide, and it receded much faster than it was possible to lighten them. About half-past five the *Apelles* fell over on her starboard side, with her decks entirely exposed to the battery, field pieces, and musketry from the beach and sandhills. At six she became a complete wreck, the shot from the enemy having cut away nearly all the standing rigging, as well as the sails to ribands. In this state Captain Boxer sent his first lieutenant on board the *Apelles* to request I would set fire to her and abandon her without loss of time, as he thought it was impracticable to get either of the vessels off. I then called a council of the officers and pilots, who were unanimous in the positive necessity of quitting the vessels. The pilots further added that as the tide was so rapidly ebbing, the vessels would soon be left dry on the beach, and if the crews were not sent immediately away there would be no possibility of escape. I then ordered the boats to be manned, and shortly afterwards they left the *Apelles* with the greater part of the officers, leaving on board the following in consequence of their not being able to contain more, some of them (boats) having been struck by shot:

'F. HOFFMAN, *Commander*.
'Mr MANNING, *Surgeon*.
'Mr HANNEY, *Purser*.
'Mr TAYLOR, *Gunner*.
'Mr JOHNSTON, *Mid*.
'WM WHITTAKER, *Clerk*.

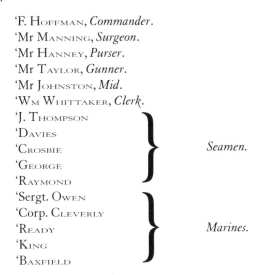

'J. THOMPSON
'DAVIES
'CROSBIE   }   *Seamen.*
'GEORGE
'RAYMOND
'Sergt. OWEN
'Corp. CLEVERLY
'READY   }   *Marines.*
'KING
'BAXFIELD

'On the boats of the *Apelles* joining those of the *Skylark* Captain Boxer, finding I remained behind, he, in a most gallant manner, pulled towards the *Apelles* with his deeply laden boat under a heavy discharge of shot and musketry from the enemy to entreat me to go with him. This I refused, but begged him to make the best of his way with the boats to

England, for as he had not room in the boats for those remaining as well as myself I could not, as a point of humanity, as well as duty, think of quitting the *Apelles* whilst a man was compelled to remain behind. Finding he could not prevail he gave up the point. He joined the other boats, and was soon out of sight. I need not express my feelings to their Lordships, or to you, Sir, on this trying occasion; I cannot describe them. Shortly after the boats had left the sloops both masts of the *Apelles* fell by the board, having been nearly severed in two by the shot of the enemy. At this time the *Skylark*, having grounded within hail of us, was enveloped in flame and partially exploded, some of her shot striking the *Apelles*. I now ordered a white flag to be shown by holding it up. This at length appeared to silence the enemy, who had been incessantly firing at us from the time we grounded until about seven o'clock. About twenty minutes afterwards the *Apelles*, being partly dry, was boarded by about 200 men, principally soldiers, who compelled us to leave the sloop, and almost immediately afterwards followed us, as the *Skylark* exploded with an appalling report, setting fire to the *Apelles*. Owing to her being previously dismasted consisted her safety. The enemy soon after the explosion returned to the *Apelles*, and extinguished the fire on board her. Only a vestige of the sternpost of *Skylark* now remained, half buried in the sand.

'Through this severe trial of more than three hours, whilst the shot were going through the sides of the *Apelles*, and destroying her masts and rigging, every officer and man behaved with that coolness inherent in British seamen, and which I trust will speak favourably of their conduct to their Lordships.

'I have now to remark that although we were under the painful necessity of lowering His Majesty's colours, which was not done until the last extremity, the enemy did not desist from firing into us for an hour afterwards. Seeing the crippled and distressed state we were in, his motive was certainly not that of humanity. I have to add that Mr Hanney, the purser, was wounded in the head, and Mr Taylor, the gunner, in the shoulder and left hand, but neither dangerously. I am now happy to add their wounds are nearly healed.

'The signal books and instructions of every description were burnt in the galley fire by the Purser and myself when we saw there was no possibility of our escape.

			'I have the honour to remain, Sir,
					'Your obedient servant,
	(Signed)				'F. HOFFMAN,
				'Late Commander of H.M.S. *Apelles*.

'W<small>M</small> C<small>ROKER</small>, Esq., &c., &c., &c.,
 Admiralty.'

N<small>OTE</small> E

Letter from Captain Otter respecting the establishment of a school for midshipmen at Verdun.

'V<small>ERDUN</small>, *Oct. 26th*, 1812.

'D<small>EAR</small> S<small>IR</small>, – As I am very anxious that the establishment of a school should be supported with our utmost endeavours, it is with the greatest satisfaction I perceive you enter into the plans, and undertake the conducting of it, with all the energy I could wish. I have already spoken to Lieutenants Lambert, Brown, Thackstone, Carslake, Robins, Boyack, Bogle, and Kennicote, who have volunteered to assist you, and I have no doubt but that they will always be ready to follow such instruction as you may think proper to give them.

'It is my wish that all the young gentlemen of the age of eighteen and under attend the school, and that it may be open to those above that age who will submit to the rules, and who wish to benefit by the attending masters.

'As the intention of the school is solely for the improvement of the young gentlemen of the Navy, it is presumed they will be sufficiently sensible of the advantages they may derive from it, and by their regular attendance and strict attention when in school, both show their desire of improvement, and their respect to the gentlemen who have so kindly volunteered to attend during the school hours.

'Wishing you every success in this your laudable undertaking,
  'I remain, dear Sir,
   'Yours truly,
    'C. O<small>TTER</small>,
'Senior full-pay Captain of the Naval Department.'

N<small>OTE</small> F

Testimonial from Captain Otter.

'B<small>IDEFORD</small>, D<small>EVON</small>, *Aug. 1st*, 1827.

'M<small>Y</small> D<small>EAR</small> S<small>IR</small>, – I have sincere pleasure in acknowledging the great assistance you afforded me by your voluntarily taking the trouble of superintending, and also the able manner you conducted the school established by me, as senior naval officer of the depôt of Verdun.

'I have likewise great satisfaction in testifying to your good conduct as an officer and gentleman during the time you were a prisoner in France.

"I remain, dear Sir,

'Yours very truly,

'C. OTTER.

'F. HOFFMAN, Esq., Commander R.N.'

INDEX

Also available in the 'Sailors' Tales' series

THE NARRATIVE OF WILLIAM SPAVENS
A CHATHAM PENSIONER, BY HIMSELF
A Unique Lower Deck View of the 18th Century Navy
This remarkable first-hand account of life at sea by an ordinary seaman
of Anson's time is one of the most fascinating, and rarest,
autobiographies to emerge from the Age of Sail
216 × 138mm, 192pp, paperback
ISBN 1 86176 083 3 £9.95

NELSONIAN REMINISCENCES
A Dramatic Eye-Witness Account of the War at Sea 1795–1810
Lieutenant G S Parsons RN
Lieutenant Parsons served throughout the Napoleonic Wars, but the
highlight of his career was his time under Nelson's command in
the Mediterranean, during the great naval hero's controversial
time at Naples, with Emma Hamilton.
216 × 138mm, 200pp, paperback
ISBN 1 86176 084 1 £9.95

REMINISCENCES OF A NAVAL OFFICER
A Quarter-Deck View of the War against Napoleon
Captain A Crawford RN
Between 1800 and 1815, Abraham Crawford saw service on blockade duty
in the Channel, at Admiral Duckworth's forcing of the Dardanelles, and in
support of the army ashore in eastern Spain.
216 × 138mm, 320pp, paperback
ISBN 1 86176 109 0 £12.95

For a full illustrated catalogue of all Chatham Publishing books, please contact:
The Marketing Department, Chatham Publishing,
61 Frith Street, London W1V 5TA
Tel: 0171–434–4242. Fax: 0171–434–4415